JACQUES COPEAU

JACQUES COPEAU

Biography of a Theater

MAURICE KURTZ

Southern Illinois University Press
Carbondale and Edwardsville

Frontispiece: Jacques Copeau in 1946 at age 67. (Author's collection)

Library of Congress Cataloging-in-Publication Data
Kurtz, Maurice, 1913–
    Jacques Copeau : biography of a theater / Maurice Kurtz.
        p.   cm.
Includes bibliographical references and index.

    1. Copeau, Jacques, 1879–1949. 2. Théâtre du Vieux-Colombier.
I. Title.
PN2638.C74K84 1999   98-33222
792'.023'092—dc21   CIP
ISBN 0-8093-2257-9 (cloth : alk. paper)

The paper used in this publication meets the minimum requirements of
American National Standard for Information Sciences—Permanence of
Paper for Printed Library Materials, ANSI Z39.48-1984. ♾

To my wife, Lélie Kurtz

Contents

List of Illustrations ix

Preface xi

Acknowledgments xv

A Letter from Jacques Copeau xvii

1. The Birth of a Theater 1

2. The First Season's Struggle (1913–1914) 19

3. Three Years of Silent Life (1914–1917) 32

4. New York (1917–1919) 50

5. Reaching the Parisian Heights (1919–1921) 62

6. The Ways and Means of Copeau's Art 79

7. Bitter Fruits of Fame (1921–1923) 95

8. The Last Season (1923–1924) 107

9. Ideals Multiplied (1924–1949) 121

10. Conclusions 147

   Postscript (1949–1999) 154

Notes 163

Bibliography 171

Index 175

Illustrations

Following page 78

Emblem of the two doves
Poster for the opening of the Vieux-Colombier Theater
Members of the Vieux-Colombier company
Scene from the *The Brothers Karamazov*
Copeau as Ivan in *The Brothers Karamazov*
Costume sketches for *Twelfth Night*
Poster for the Vieux-Colombier's first season in America
Copeau in *Les Fourberies de Scapin*
Copeau in *Washington*
Theater school in the courtyard of the Vieux-Colombier
The old-fashioned Athénée Saint-Germain Theater in 1913
Drawing of the remodeled Vieux-Colombier Theater
Louis Jouvet with maquette for the New York stage
New York set for *The Doctor in Spite of Himself*
The Vieux-Colombier Theater in 1919
Drawing of the 1920 Vieux-Colombier stage
Costume sketch for a clown in *The Winter's Tale*
Costume sketch for Autolycus in *The Winter's Tale*
Costume sketch for the High Priest in *Saül*
Cast members of *The Brothers Karamazov*
Copeau in 1927

Preface

JACQUES COPEAU AND ANDRÉ ANTOINE, two leading theater innovators of our century, were born a generation apart, came on the scene in their maturity, rebelled against the staginess of their day, and proceeded to assert two different visions of dramatic art.

Antoine, whom Copeau called "our ancestor," was an amateur actor employed by the gas company. In 1887 he set up his Théâtre Libre (Free Stage) off a steep side street in Montmartre, in a tiny workplace for writers, actors, and painters who agreed to unite talent and ambition under Antoine as their coordinator and stage director. For him the curtain was the Fourth Wall. Once it was raised, the audience was plunged into a new style of naturalism—a dark, stark realism that soon would influence Stanislavsky, then Belasco, whose mediocre show-biz version came to dominate Broadway.

Antoine's rejection of the "well made" boulevard commercial product brought on literary and art trends, which had their day and faded into past fame. His career ended in 1913, a victim of ruinously realistic extravaganzas of Molière and Shakespeare. That same year Jacques Copeau, writer, editor, and indignant drama critic, launched his Théâtre du Vieux-Colombier "to prepare a shelter for future talent . . . on a bare stage." By May 1914, Paris and Europe acclaimed the freshness and poetry he had restored to Shakespeare and Molière. Contrast and coincidence could not be more vivid.

Copeau undertook his "renovation of dramatic art" in reaction to Antoine and against the helter-skelter star system of the day. He was determined to sweep Theater clean of overacting, overdressing, and flashy house trappings; of anything artificial that sought to impress, depress, or flatter audiences willing to pay for this "service." To do so he created a fixed, architectural acting space where dramatic literature and theater technique could live in harmony and thrive in freedom of thought and movement.

To this day, the Vieux-Colombier incarnates the ideal of Copeau's stubborn struggle to remain strong in the face of indifference, independent in the face of success, proud in the face of defeat. It is the story of group spirit in its purest, most eloquent form, the spirit of personal sacrifice of all for the dignity of their art.

I have tried to recreate that spirit, which inspired artists in and out of France with enough faith and enthusiasm to transform experiment into tradition. The life of Jacques Copeau's Théâtre du Vieux-Colombier embodies the qualities and challenges of an art crusade destined to become the heritage of civilization.

Material for *Jacques Copeau: Biography of a Theater* was found in publications at Columbia University, the Library of Congress, and the New York Public Library. The Bibliothèque Nationale de France (Département des Arts du Spectacle) contains a wealth of memorabilia, articles, and illustrative documentation on every phase of Jacques Copeau's activities and writings; Charles Dullin, for example, is well represented in the National Library; so are Louis Jouvet and Copeau's devoted, talented actress Valentine Tessier, who had previously opened for me their unpublished correspondence with him. I translated this and all other French source material into English.

Waldo Frank's essay "The Art of the Vieux-Colombier" dealt with a single pre–World War I season. Private talks with him brought me up to date.

A major unforeseen event during research gave me unique insight into the daily work and production excitement of a professional experimental theater. For about three years, I was an assiduous student-assistant to Erwin Piscator, the distinguished German director of the Dramatic Workshop and five-hundred-seat Studio Theater in the New School for Social Research on West 12th Street in New York City. My teachers at the workshop were Stella Adler for acting, John Gassner for playwriting, Piscator for directing. Students included Tennessee Williams and Marlon Brando. No library or university in the early forties could offer similar "doctoral" training, except perhaps Yale.

In exchange for that privilege, I adapted plays from German and French into English, including a stage version of *War and Peace*. My translation of Romain Rolland's *Robespierre* brought me into close contact with Fernand Léger, who was to prepare the sets, while Darius Milhaud was to compose the music. David Dubinsky, head of the powerful Women's Wear Union, was to back this antifascist play for Broadway. (I say "was" because Pétain's Vichy ambassador in Washington, Henry Haye, threatened that if the play was produced, the Nazis in reprisal might imprison Romain Rolland, then living in Occupied France. The production had to be dropped.)

I was constantly with Piscator during rehearsal, to weigh script and acting problems, to step in for an absent player, often to exchange ideas with refugee artists from Germany, France, Austria, Belgium, Hungary, Czechoslovakia. Playwright-novelist Jules Romains, the first director in 1920 of the Vieux-Colombier Theater School in Paris, was also in exile. He introduced me to Piscator because, he assured me, the Dramatic Workshop followed the precepts of Copeau. Romains and Maurice Maeterlinck, a refugee for the second time in his case, submitted new plays for possible production. Fluency in French and a degree from the Sorbonne designated me as reader, reviewer, dramaturge, and also, alas, trembling young intermediary to "judge" their scripts and report back Piscator's polite rejection.

Soon after my army service in World War II, Julian Huxley, director of UNESCO, heard of my work at the international theater hub in the New School and invited me to join his organization in London, then Paris, to "dream up," as he put it, a program for worldwide contacts in the performing arts. The project I submitted was inspired, in great part, by my New School experience and won the active support, within UNESCO, of Julian Huxley and Leon Blum, Archibald MacLeish and Stephen Spender, and especially the unstinting personal participation of creative artists, among them J. B. Priestley, Tyrone Guthrie, Jean-Louis Barrault, Lillian Hellman, and other leading theater people from fifteen countries. Their collaboration with UNESCO led to the founding of a non-governmental organization, the International Theater Institute (I.T.I.), which in 1999 has national and regional cooperating centers in some ninety countries, with headquarters in Paris, at UNESCO.

The only guide, if that is the word, for my Copeau project was Professor Waxman's book on Antoine and the Théâtre Libre (1926), which focused on the literary side, analyzing in detail the plays that gave Antoine the importance he deserved. My objective was to study the Vieux-Colombier in the whole as a breakthrough in dramatic art. I attempted no artificial separation, however, allowing myself to be led by the facts which identify Copeau's contribution as theatrical more than literary. A Nietzschean thought comes to mind: "He who has a *why* to live can bear with almost any *how*."

Jacques Copeau revealed *how* his constant search for authentic, imaginative, credible writing and staging, not to speak of acting, brought about endless discoveries, and *why* this offered more impact and greater satisfaction for new and old audiences alike.

Acknowledgments

WHATEVER MERIT THIS BOOK MAY have can be attributed in no small measure to those who have given time and self to help me set forth as accurately and effectively as possible the life of a unique team in theater arts, including friends and fans.

To begin with, my deep thanks and gratitude go to Jacques Copeau himself, *le Patron* (the Chief) as he was called, for his assistance, corrections and suggestions, and for his letter of approval.

I am indebted to several of his close associates: Jules Romains, Georges Duhamel, Jean Schlumberger, Gaston Gallimard; to actresses Valentine Tessier and Blanche Albane (Madame Georges Duhamel), and to *la chère* Suzanne Bing, actress and zealous teacher who actually lived in the apartment house over the theater.

The younger generation of Vieux-Colombier disciples clarified many an obscure point: André Obey, a playwright directly inspired by Copeau, as he made clear to me when I spoke with him at length in his office as head of the Comédie-Française; director Michel Saint-Denis and Marie-Hélène Dasté ("Maiène"), actress and costume designer, respectively Copeau's nephew and daughter.

I am pleased and gratified to include in this group many members of the early Theater Guild company, Copeau's direct successor in 1919 after he returned to Paris following two seasons in New York. The Guild invited him back in 1926 to stage the English adaptation of his version of *The Brothers Karamazov*. Fifteen years after that production, their welcome to me was overwhelming. I was received in homes and dressing rooms, restaurants and offices. All gave me detailed accounts of what they had heard and learned from their French director: Alfred Lunt, Dudley Digges, Morris Carnovsky, Lee Simonson, Philip Moeller, Theresa Helburn, Lawrence Langner, Maurice Wertheim (the Guild's financial manager and stage-struck stockbroker), Harold Clurman, Copeau's interpreter and assistant.

Columbia University professors of French offered me invaluable advice on planning and drafting, in particular Justin O'Brien and two annual visiting scholars of great distinction, Paul Hazard of the Collège de France and the French Academy, and Henri Peyre of Yale University. M. Peyre showed tremendous understanding by proposing to his fractious student the appropriate subject as a doctoral thesis, which enriched a passionate lifelong experience in theater.

This experience was shared throughout by my wife, Lélie. In every phase of research and editing, she applied her love of gardening to words, to plant, trim, and weed. Without her the manuscript would no doubt be "on the road" far from publication. For her help in the pursuit of elusive ideals—elements of truth and *le mot juste*—I ask her to accept the dedication of this book.

Opinions and comments from many others will be found in these pages. My sincere thanks go to them.

For assistance in preparing this book, I am indebted to George Badame and Dominican Friar Claude Richard in Toronto, Canada, to Carolyn Jones Silver in Charlottesville, Virginia, for weaving corrections and additions into a final presentation, and to Charles MacNealy who took over transatlantic faxing and e-mail for script changes from our end in Paris, France.

A Letter from Jacques Copeau

Burgundy, February 9, 1946

Dear Monsieur Kurtz

I knew nothing about you or your manuscript, I was beginning to forget my very self, when you came along with your musette bag slung over your back, to seek me out in my solitude and place this bouquet of memories at the threshold of my sixty-seventh year.

In spite of your youth, I am not afraid of calling "memories" this mass of documents in which your ability and your fervor were able to retain so much freshness and life.

Without causing me boredom or sadness, without affecting the ritual either of an academic discourse or of a funeral eulogy, you have accomplished the prodigious feat of relating to me my whole lifetime, of which certain moments were on the verge of vanishing from my memory. Thanks to you, my friends in America will know that I am not dead and that my progeny is doing well. I thank you for bringing them this double message.

And I thank you above all for having been true in your observations, true to someone you did not know. Having had to recount a rather large part of history, which your intelligence and your culture helped you to understand, but of which you had not been a witness, you were able to reconstruct from a distance the meaning of my efforts. Nowhere have you falsified the nature of my work. There exists henceforth a sum of information to which people can refer with confidence. And I, myself, when I shall want to recall "my life in art," am assured of finding some of my principal props in your "biography" of the Vieux-Colombier. Thus you can say that you, too, collaborated with the Vieux-Colombier.

With that small Vieux-Colombier which was quite frail when it landed for the first time in the United States. But it was to find there so much friendship, so much devotion. I can never recall without emotion, without tender emotion, that period when we worked so hard.

Your name is added, dear Monsieur Kurtz, to all those names towards which the Vieux-Colombier has contracted a debt of gratitude. All those who welcomed us, encouraged, defended, advised, consoled us when it was necessary, at a time when we probably had no other merit than that of being pioneers. We were young, we were strong. We had just plowed for a whole season through old, weary ground. We were offered new fields to spread our work. What feeling but gratitude could we have?

If in addition, the examples of our art that we were able to produce in New York and in a few other cities have made an impression on actors, audiences, directors and art patrons, if they have had some influence and so prepared the way for the great Constantin Stanislavsky, we are today happy and very proud.

Please accept, dear Monsieur Kurtz, along with the assurance of my gratitude, that of my most sincere personal esteem.

Jacques Copeau

JACQUES COPEAU

1

The Birth of a Theater

"AN APPEAL TO YOUTH AND the Literary Public!" Then, the orange and blue poster continued:

Grand Opening
Théâtre du Vieux-Colombier
October 22, 1913
Une femme tuée par la douceur
(A Woman Killed With Kindness)
by
Thomas Heywood
(Adapted by Jacques Copeau)
also
L'Amour médecin
by
Molière

A few critics ventured across the Seine into the Latin Quarter expecting to find just another art theater with some original notions to exhibit. Instead, they found a neat little playhouse, devoid of anything "arty," snugly installed and looking for all the world as if it meant to stay for a long time.[1] The critical heads of *le tout-Paris* nodded approval at the charming, unexpected welcome they received from the small Molière bust in a lobby skillfully decorated in black and yellow. As they stepped inside, they saw that the gaudy gilt of the former Théâtre de l'Athénée-Saint-Germain was gone and in its place were plain buff-colored panels. The proscenium was a flattened black frame from which hung a solid green curtain of billiard table material. The house-lights were subdued and transformed the theater into a place of meditation and repose. When the first-night audience glanced at their programs, they perceived two doves, copied from the pavement of San Miniato in Florence, encased in a medallion. One seemed to be asking the other Mallarmé's question, also printed on the program: "Do you go to the theater? No, almost never. Oh well, neither do I."

As the curtain gracefully parted from the center on the first act of the Heywood play, there appeared a second frame of rectangular drapes in yellowish gray. The play's Elizabethan interior was designed by Francis Jourdain; it contained two high-backed chairs and a gate-legged table. Valentine Rau created costumes that suggested the period without attracting undue attention.

The audience was in a receptive mood when the first actor stepped out to unfold a simple, human story. Mistress Frankford had betrayed her husband with his best friend, Master Wendoll. With the help of a servant, the husband surprised the lovers in his own bed and decreed that his wife should live in a manor separated from him and their child. Full of shame and repentance, she quickly pined away and on her deathbed was finally forgiven by a husband who regretted having killed her with too kind a sentence.

Copeau's objective was clear: adultery treated as a serious theme, as a family tragedy with which people everywhere could identify. This was a far cry from crude melodramas and facetious farces performed by ham actors. Furthermore, by producing an obscure Elizabethan dramatist, Copeau could stigmatize even more the exaggeration and vulgarity served up for French audiences to joke and giggle about.

Mme. Blanche Albane played Mistress Frankford; Roger Karl her husband; Charles Dullin the servant; Louis Jouvet, Mme. Suzanne Bing, and the rest of the company had minor roles; and Jacques Copeau, who staged the play, made his perilous debut as an actor, as he himself recalls: "in the impossible role of Wendoll the seducer. . . . I was very badly dressed. An elaborate wig shaded my face, giving it a curious, sickly pallor under my soft, oversized felt hat. I greeted people as little as possible, fearful lest I remove the wig along with the hat."[2] As a result, Copeau was forced to move awkwardly, speak in a dying voice, and twitch his face nervously. In short, as one critic remarked, he acted like Molière, and no better.

When the curtain had fallen on the sad fate of Mistress Frankford, the same actors rushed to their dressing-rooms to change for Molière's *L'Amour médecin*. This three-act impromptu, conceived, written, rehearsed, and performed for the Sun King all within five days, was presented by the company with the verve and freshness of an actor's lark: song, dance, color, and the joy of living for an hour with the national poet and the Vieux-Colombier's patron saint. From the first moment, the actors were sitting so comically on a bench facing the audience—Sganarelle in his bronze-colored costume, M. Guillaume in yellow, M. Josse in green, Aminte in gray, Lucrèce in mauve—that all eyes began to twinkle. Then, when the two doctors appeared, the audience could no longer contain itself. Critic André Suarès "died laughing" at the fat, joyous doctor and the tall, skinny, stammering one. The happy quack was played by Lucien Weber, the other by Louis Jouvet, who that night acted the first of a series of successful comic roles.

Suarès wrote the very next day in *La Nouvelle Revue Française* that he had "never seen Molière better done . . . a minor miracle." Most of the audience agreed with him, but the few professional critics who eventually reported the opening of "that neat little theater of art and literature" gave vent to opinions that were far less enthusiastic. Paul Souday, for example, in *L'Eclair*: "The Vieux-Colombier insists upon forcing us to realize we're not at the Vieux-Colombier to have fun." Molière was almost completely ignored in favor of Heywood, and Copeau was roundly rebuked for bad acting, which risked endangering his efforts as a director, and for choosing a moralizing drama. The critics were more than mildly annoyed by a theater that dared to open its doors with nothing more sensational than an English dramatist, and not even Shakespeare but a relatively minor contemporary who could not possibly move a normal French audience.

Nothing sensational took place that night, it is true, but three unusual events did. The first was "out front," where the ushers neither solicited nor accepted tips, in keeping with the management's express request. (But it still cost twenty-five centimes at the entrance to buy the program in which this "request" was made.) For the first time, a Paris theater permitted its patrons to go straight to their seats without slowing down to fumble for small change. Secondly, a rare quality in French staging made its appearance: simplicity in the place of display and exaggeration. The third feature was the astonishing degree of devotion shown not only by the actors and stage workers, but by the unpaid personnel as well: working in the checkroom was the novelist Roger Martin du Gard, whose book *Jean Barois* had recently been published. The new theater's prospectus that the audience carried in their pockets had been addressed in the hand of Léon-Paul Fargue. In the prompter's box shone the round, bespectacled head of Georges Duhamel; and backstage the indefatigable Hélène Forestier (Mme. Roger Martin du Gard) was feverishly sewing away at last-minute seams, having had the needle in her hand for thirteen hours. The role of friendship and loyalty in starting the Vieux-Colombier on its way was enormous, decisive in fact, and the man who inspired such confidence was Director Copeau.

Jacques Copeau, the critic, editor, playwright, director, actor, and founder of the Théâtre du Vieux-Colombier, could lay claim to no theatrical or literary tradition in his family. He was born in Paris on February 4, 1879, at 76 rue du Faubourg Saint-Denis. His mother was a provincial bourgeoise and his father a small industrialist from a hard-working family. Still, a genuine, simple love for the theater did have its place in the Copeau household, for they had a small library of melodramas by Dumas, and these caught the boy's imagination. As he grew older, he was regularly taken to see them in the big boulevard theaters.[3]

It was not long before the serious Lycée Condorcet student became a stagestruck lad with but a single idea: to act. It all started when his grandfather used to radiate with the honor of having once played a game of dominoes at the Café de la Porte-Saint Martin with his favorite actor, Frédérick Lemaître. Young Jacques decided to follow in the footsteps of the great Lemaître—until the day he stole into a theater to see an actor rehearse the part of King Lear. The king had trouble keeping the beard out of his mouth and was in a wretched mood. Suddenly he left his throne and walked down into the orchestra, shouting at Copeau, "What the devil are you doing here?" Terrified, the boy fled and so did his ambition to act.

The thwarted would-be actor turned to writing for consolation. At seventeen, he wrote his first play, *Brouillard du matin (Morning Fog)*, a three-act comedy that his fellow-students at the lycée put on for family and friends. At the end of the performance, Copeau was presented to his classmate Edmond About's godfather, Francisque Sarcey, celebrated critic and champion of the "well-made" play, who congratulated the youthful author for taking Alexandre Dumas *fils* as his model and wrote a flattering review in the next day's *Le Temps*.

This took place in 1896, when André Antoine's naturalism and Lugné-Poe's symbolism were not yet strong enough to displace Dumas *fils* and his followers. The latter still held Sarcey's worshipful eye and controlled his powerful pen. Three years later, the respected critic died and the reign of Dumas *fils* began to falter. In 1900, Antoine's ideas finally won over the producers who ran two of the largest theaters in Paris.

By this time, Copeau too had outgrown the younger Dumas. He was at the Sorbonne (1897–1898), studying for a degree in literature and philosophy in preparation for the Ecole Normale Supérieure and the career of a university professor. But the young student neglected his lectures. Instead, he spent as much time as his meager funds permitted at the Théâtre Antoine and at Lugné-Poe's Théâtre de l'Oeuvre, the only two theaters in the France of 1900 where the budding playwright could find encouragement and artistic inspiration to justify his literary pretensions. He read widely and lost no time in discovering Ibsen, who filled him with enthusiasm; the self-disciplined Flaubert became his master; and the symbolist poets Verlaine, Mallarmé, and Rimbaud were his daily bread.

For two years, Jacques Copeau lived in the rarefied atmosphere of love and devotion to these great men. He was still uncertain which branch of

4

writing to choose, but he knew that writing was to be his lifework. At twenty, he dedicated himself to "the cult of love and poetry. . . promising never to change."[4] He wrote a one-act play that year (1899) called *La Sève* (*The Essence*, unproduced), and two years later composed the first outline of *La Maison natale*, the drama that was closest to his heart (though destined not to be staged until the final season of his Théâtre du Vieux-Colombier, a quarter of a century later). At this point, a decision had been reached: he would write for the theater. But fate had not yet had its word. His father suddenly died, and he was forced to give up his studies and literary predilections.

Before settling down to earn his living, Copeau took a trip to Scandinavia. He spent a year in Denmark (1902–1903), where he married a Danish woman, Agnes Thomsen. He worked hard, giving French lessons to support himself and his wife. But this did not keep the twenty-three-year-old husband from his writing. By the end of the year, *L'Ermitage*, a Parisian periodical for the symbolists and the neoclassicists, had published several of his articles. The first was against the superficial, philosophical dramas of Paul Hervieu, another was in praise of André Gide's *L'Immoraliste*. Gide promptly acknowledged this by sending a letter to Copenhagen, urging Copeau to make a career of writing.

Three months later, he and his wife arrived in Paris. Full of enthusiasm, he went immediately to see Gide, who again encouraged him. He felt that this time nothing could interfere with his decisions. But once more he was stopped when he was unexpectedly asked to manage his late father's iron factory in the Ardennes. At first he refused to be enslaved, but the obligation was too strong and he had to yield. His exile from Paris lasted two years. In 1905 the factory fell into bankruptcy, and he could at last return to the capital, to his friends.

Gide found him, at twenty-seven, looking ten years older than his age, "his overly expressive face already fatigued by suffering. His shoulders are high and hard like those of one who endures a great deal."[5] However, Gide told him "I hold no great fears for you: I feel you well-armed," to which Copeau replied, "Yes, I believe so, too, and yet I am getting nowhere. Do you know what I lack? The right *milieu*. Yes, I do not have the right *milieu*. . . ."[6] He clung to Gide and to the group of young writers who clustered around him for guidance and encouragement, Henri Ghéon, Jean Schlumberger, and Jacques Rivière among them. This unique circle helped Copeau satisfy a powerful need to be with friends and to be understood.

He again thought of becoming an actor, but the completely commercial state of the theater revolted him. He could never work at an art that was concerned primarily with financial success. He turned to his friends for assistance, those he had won by penetrating articles he had written in the *Revue d'Art dramatique* and *L'Ermitage*. But there were only three who could help him find work to support his wife and two children and still allow him time for his writing: Georges de Porto-Riche, André Gide, and the painter Albert Besnard. The latter recommended him to the Georges Petit Gallery of modern art at 8, rue de Sèze, in the heart of the Madeleine district, as exhibition director and salesman. There he learned, in spite of himself, the meaning of commercial art. He even showed good business sense; his friends began to predict for him a career à la Beaumarchais, the author of two successful Figaro plays, *The Barber of Seville* and *The Marriage of Figaro*. Beaumarchais simultaneously conducted a thriving arms trade to help the American colonists in the Revolutionary War and set up the first Playwrights' Association to guarantee royalties.

The next four years he worked all day at the Gallery and wrote at night. He soon developed into one of the most challenging drama critics in Paris, launching one appeal after another: "dramatic technique . . . [must] be made the most powerful, most sensitive, most complex, most perfect instrument . . . that the art of the theater be led to the rank of a supreme art, be adapted to enfold life as a whole, and with this end in view, to utilize the different lessons of the past, both recent and remote."[7]

Besides the dramatists, he took to task his fellow critics, believing as he did that "a pitiless, competent, sincere, bold, artistic group of critics could help prepare a renaissance in the theater." He was vitally concerned with reforming the critic by making him aware of his creative function and worthy to share responsibility for his country's culture. Indulgence and partiality in criticism must give way, he said, to sincerity and severity. And just as he reproached the critic his indolence, so he rebuked the public for its frivolity and attacked producers and actors for placing questions of money far above any consideration for art: "originality, sincerity, truth, style and one's conscience, everything which makes the artist a philosopher, novelist, poet, is denied him as dramatist. The theater is a special *métier*, a business deal. He alone is the prisoner of conventions, of prejudices, of an abstract formula in which there is neither life nor change."[8]

These opinions were published in the pages of avant-garde periodicals alongside the forceful writings of Gide, Ghéon, Schlumberger, and others, but they reached very few readers. It was not until 1907 that the general public first began to know the name of Copeau. That year Léon Blum, already a militant socialist, left the post of drama critic on *La Grande Revue* and the editor, Jacques Rouché, asked Copeau to take his place. This was his first big chance and he took full advantage of it. His "gentle face of patience and meditation"—to quote François Poncetton in the December 1919 *L'Opinion*—was no reflection of his fiery, forceful mind.

He continued to attack mediocrity on all sides, the living and the dead, the small and the great alike.

His friends, for whom discipline and work were a way of life, looked to him for critical evaluation of their writings. Gide, particularly, had every confidence in Copeau's "supple mind." A visit from him would excite Gide to even greater efforts. To him Copeau was a "good doctor" and adviser, and he noted in his *Journal* (March 6, 1906) that he was "impatient to submit to J.C." the pages of his manuscript. For even with friends, indulgence played very little part in Copeau's criticism. More and more, therefore, he began to be considered a spokesman of real importance, especially in matters concerning the theater.

Copeau was not alone to cry out against commercialism and its destruction of the artist's independence, against the "dead things" produced. Romain Coolus, in *Revue Blanche*, went so far as to ask that the administrator of the Comédie-Française be hanged for its unbearable Molière productions. One critic had the courage to say, "We must fight commercialism and the absence of art in the contemporary theater." Another stated categorically, "The race of dramatic authors has almost entirely disappeared," and he questioned "whether it will be reborn." In 1903, Romain Rolland complained bitterly that the Paris theater had become "Europe's house of debauchery," and a few years later Henry Bordeaux denounced the theater as "the hospital of literary perversity."[9]

Observing a typical Paris season wend its carefree way, one could not help agreeing with these opinions. Even recalcitrant taxpayers became so accustomed to the box office–driven play that the state-supported Odéon could, with a clear conscience, produce *Rue du Sentier*, "a pretty comedy . . . [in the] ultra-violent style of the day." A high-sounding title like *Les Honneurs de la guerre* was nothing but an amusing, light comedy of manners in which the war was between a man and his wife, with all the conventional banalities of such a battle. This was at the Vaudeville and was followed later in the season by *La Dame du Louvre*. At the Comédie des Champs-Elysées one could see the more serious *Trouble-Fête*, on the theme of an unwanted child, embroidering in pleasant dialogue the most commonplace plot imaginable. The Théâtre Réjane thrived on *La Reine des roses*, and some of the other Paris houses were filled by *Les Roses rouges* (Renaissance), *La Saignée* (Ambigu), *Les Travaux d'Hercule* (Apollo), *Monsieur le Juge* (Cluny), *Non . . . Mais!* (Cigale), *Cocorico*, *Deux Canards*, and so on. Such was the tenth-rate collection of dramatic offerings that boulevard theaters exhibited. For all these plays told the same sad story: the theater was a commercial enterprise that lived as any business did—by pleasing the public in the easiest and quickest way, taking no chances on the artistic visions of new, fresh, and imaginative minds. Since the public already liked one kind of play and one type of production and one brand of acting, the keepers of the box office preferred to wait until this public protested against their usual fare before changing. Meanwhile, ignorance was bliss and the coffers were full, so why change?[10]

Copeau accepted this challenge as an impetus and, strengthened by his numerous conversations with Gide, lashed out against the unbearable mediocrity of contemporary drama. For they both believed that "the theater is an extraordinary thing," and foresaw not "the decadence of dramatic art, but its renaissance. . . ."[11]

In 1909 Copeau collaborated with André Gide, Jean Schlumberger, André Ruyters, Henri Ghéon, and others to launch *La Nouvelle Revue Française*, and he grasped the opportunity to extend his fight for dramatic reform to the pages of this new periodical. When he later became its editor-in-chief he hoped that *N.R.F.* contributors, who in the words of one critic were models of "equilibrium, harmony and discipline" and whose names would soon read like a who's who of contemporary French literature, could be induced to create for the theater as well.

Again it was Jacques Rouché who gave Copeau, the critic-editor, his chance to write, this time for the theater instead of about it. Like all Paris, Rouché had been thrilled by the rich possibilities of stage painting and decoration, as revealed by Diaghilev's Russian Ballet. He promptly leased the Théâtre des Arts for the 1909–1910 season to experiment with modern scenic effects, and he asked Copeau to submit a play of his own. The would-be dramatist immediately left the Georges Petit Gallery, resigned as critic on the *Grande Revue*, reduced his *Nouvelle Revue Française* duties to a minimum, and leased a small house in the country at Le Limon, near La Ferté-sous-Jouarre, where he could write without interruption. He asked Jean Croué, a young, forward-thinking actor of the Comédie-Française, to collaborate with him in dramatizing Dostoevsky's *Brothers Karamazov*. Paul Souday, writing in *Le Temps* (December 1929), quoted *N.R.F.* writers who looked to the Russian as one of the greats. Some called him superior to Flaubert; Gide placed him higher than Balzac. Copeau regarded him as "unique" and extolled him as "the most man of men, the writer most imbued with the soul of humanity, the freest of men, for all life's forms and conflicts are to be found in him. . . ."[12]

Karamazov was produced at the Théâtre des Arts in 1910 and the press acclaimed it as a stage masterpiece. Jacques Copeau became the season's revelation, having disproved Antoine's theory that critics ought not to enter the sacred realm of creation "because they have the custom of writing about the plays of others."[13]

His future as a dramatist seemed promising and he looked forward to many years of peaceful writing at his quiet house in the country. He hoped to manage somehow to remove dramatic art from the box-office cage and place it respectfully in its rightful stronghold: the stage. From cage to stage was the short, immeasurable distance the drama had to cover if it were to recapture its dignity, its meaning, its art.

The obstacles to this utopia haunted Copeau. He knew there was more to the problem than the writing of plays. To start with, he sought a theater where works like his would be produced for what they were worth and not for what a boulevard producer or a one-style director wished to make of them. He wanted a leader with a vital stake in the future of dramatic art, and so kept looking for the director-messiah for whom the *Revue Blanche* had called out as long as twenty years before. The drama's two-hundred-year-old decline could only be halted by an all-round theater man, by another Shakespeare, Molière, or Goethe. Copeau saw the glimmer of such a man in Antoine, the fighter-founder of the Théâtre Libre and the little theater movement in Europe. But Antoine was not changing with the times. He had become the contented director of France's second national theater, the Théâtre de l'Odéon, and was resting on his "naturalistic" laurels. Nor did Copeau feel that Lugné-Poe was moving forward. The Ibsenian and symbolist mainstays of the Théâtre de l'Oeuvre had had their day. And while both men identified theatrical development with certain types of new writers, Rouché sought to revolutionize the theater from the visual standpoint, by considering stage sets all-important. To Copeau, these ideas were discouragingly incomplete. The problem was far greater than single-minded stage directors suggested it to be.[14]

Copeau thought he understood the predicament, but he saw as yet no single solution. There were too many different parts to the problem, and each was so segmented that the ultimate responsibility for the theater's gradual decline since the days of Racine and Molière could be attributed no more to poor plays than to the faults of actor, director, producer, stage designer, or public. One thing was clear: the theater was a cluttered, chaotic household, and "in chaos," as Stanislavsky wrote, "there can be no art."[15] There had to be a thorough cleaning. The stage, which is of necessity the art of coordinating arts, had to give each art a clear line of action if harmony were to be restored.

The classic rationalist in Copeau recognized this need for general order. But he had no esthetic doctrine like Rouché, no preferences for foreign or avant-garde plays like Lugné-Poe, no formula like Antoine. He had no revolutionary theater to offer, no striking manifesto to proclaim. What he wanted was the elimination of artificiality and blind imitation from every phase of the creative process.

More and more, Copeau and those around him began to despair of seeing such a theater in France. Finally, in the winter of 1913 (when it was still possible for a few people in a small room to create and nourish an art movement), he and his friends, with their typical ardor, youthfulness, and spontaneity, decided to look to themselves, just as they had when they founded the *Nouvelle Revue Française*. With their magazine growing artistically and prospering materially, the time had come to look towards new horizons. This was the moment Copeau chose to express their indignation "against the commercialization of art which degraded the French theater and turned away its cultivated public . . . against entertainers on sale . . . against speculation and pettiness . . . against bluff, greed, disorder, indiscipline, ignorance and stupidity, against scorn for the creator, against hatred of beauty, against useless productions, against indulgent critics, against a misguided public."[16]

Nor would it be enough merely to repair the theater that caused this indignation. The task ahead was one of reconstruction, and all agreed that Copeau, whose "calm assurance and exaltation . . . terrified" Gide, was the man to lead them. Therefore, with both *La Nouvelle Revue Française* and friends like André Gide, Charles Péguy, and André Suarès standing firmly behind him, with supporters like Jean Schlumberger, Gaston Gallimard, and Charles Pacquement working with him, the moment had come to take the great step: to found a home for his utopia-theater.

After much inquiry, he heard of a playhouse that was available in the Latin Quarter. It was the old Athénée-Saint-Germain at 21, rue du Vieux-Colombier, midway between the church of Saint-Sulpice and the department store Au Bon Marché. In 1905 it had been considered as a likely spot for a theater but was disapproved by the authorities because the contemplated price scale of seats was too low and "would attract an audience detrimental to good morals." Of more recent date, it had been used as a neighborhood playhouse to exhibit the usual run of melodramas and then, in 1912, served as the residence for a month for René de Camp's Théâtre de l'Art Libre. The interior, with its elaborate Louis XV *pâtisserie* style, was all that Copeau abhorred most. Yet he rented it at once.

This medieval Street of the Old Dove-Cote satisfied Copeau's sense of history and tradition. It was on the Left Bank, the one nearest the heart of all artists living in Paris. It was in the midst of the capital's center of culture, its university and academies, where the kind of theater Copeau envisaged would have most appeal. On this same street, about two hundred years before, Boileau received Molière, Racine, and La Fontaine at his home. The street was not easy to find; it was far removed from the noisy boulevards and so might give the new theater a better chance to be heard.

Copeau named the playhouse after the street, Théâtre du Vieux-Colombier, and had Francis Jourdain reconstruct and redecorate it to be the kind of home in which he would not be ashamed to bring up his family of artists—the family he had yet to find.

The model company, according to Antoine, should have thirty players of equal ability, ordinary talent, simple personality, and the capability of working as a team. Copeau agreed, but could pay no more than ten or twelve to start with. His goal was to obtain a "perfect ensemble of actors" comparable to those at the former Théâtre Libre. The glamour of a star had no place on the Street of the Old Dove-Cote.

One spring day in 1913, in the grayish light of Charles Dullin's small Montmartre studio, Copeau called for auditions. Most of the players were poor and little-known. He did not try to determine their talent. "I sought," he said, "to discern each one's natural, inner self. More than their ease at reading, a smile, a natural movement or a word, all off-stage, told me what I wanted," he recalled nostalgically in his *Souvenirs du Vieux-Colombier*, published in 1931.

Mme. Barbieri and Roger Karl had been singled out for praise five years before in a Copeau notice, Barbieri for her suppleness and sense of nuance. Karl had more recently been applauded for his fervor and conviction as Dmitri in the Copeau-Croué version of *The Brothers Karamazov*. Charles Dullin was acclaimed for his penetrating portrayal of Smerdiakov, old Karamazov's illegitimate son. Copeau could never forget Dullin's power "to make the horrible in man poetical."[17]

The buoyant and charming Blanche Albane (married to Georges Duhamel) was first approached to join the new theater by Dullin, with whom she had been acting at Rouché's Théâtre des Arts in her husband's play *Le Combat*. A second-prize winner at the Conservatory, she had acted with Lugné-Poe and at the Théâtre de l'Odéon under Antoine, who loaned her to Sarah Bernhardt to replace that great lady in Rostand's *L'Aiglon*. However, she told me in an interview, she had two good reasons of her own for wishing to join Copeau: first, she knew through her husband the whole *N.R.F.* group of writers and was familiar with their aims and their struggles, so akin to her husband's; and second, she had attended a reading by Copeau of Ibsen's *The Wild Duck* that left her "limp with emotion." In becoming a member of the troupe she expected, and was to lead, "a marvelous life."

Jane Lory went straight from the Conservatory to the Vieux-Colombier. "Someone had advised me to go see that Monsieur Copeau. The day I presented myself and was, to my great amazement, selected from among many contestants, I had not eaten for forty-eight hours."[18]

Louis Jouvet, in 1911, had attracted Copeau's attention in Henri Ghéon's *Le Pain*, prompting him to remark that Jouvet's "bearing, sobriety and depth heralded an artist."[19] In 1913 he went backstage of a small theater where Jouvet was playing in a melodrama and asked him to join the Vieux-Colombier as *régisseur*, not as an actor. The stage manager did have bit parts, but he was essentially everybody's assistant, including the chief usher's. Jouvet accepted.

The task of choosing actors done, Copeau depended upon attractive artistic inducements to make them follow him. His theater, he said, was to be a "shelter for future talent." The young men and women who wished to become part of it needed this protection, for they were not yet "drunk with glory, nor degraded by life . . . (but) were thirsty only for expression," as one supportive critic put it.[20] This was the fresh start they all wanted. Charles Dullin, for example, whose phenomenal success in *Karamazov* had brought him tempting offers from the boulevard, probably voiced everyone's feelings when he said, "At a time when I needed to believe in what I was doing . . . Copeau brought me what I was looking for."[21]

The fact that the Vieux-Colombier was to be a repertory theater, with at least three changes per week, was an effective argument. All knew that they would have the chance to portray more characters in one season on the rue du Vieux-Colombier than they could possibly perform in ten years on the Boulevard des Italiens.

Their director had nonetheless a good deal of convincing to do. He could afford to pay his company extremely little. One young actress asked for 300 francs a month (about $60 in 1913). Copeau tried to bring it down to 250. She lowered her eyes, thought hard, and then blurted out: "All right, monsieur, I accept . . . provided I don't have to supply my own costumes." It had recently taken her four months of acting to pay for one that she had worn in a boulevard production. Still smarting from the lash of a dressmaker's bill, she made Copeau atone for the sins of others. This player was Suzanne Bing, who became one of his most devoted collaborators. He agreed to her revolutionary suggestion and welcomed this chance to break with a demoralizing tradition of the French stage. It became a fundamental policy to furnish the cast with their stage wardrobe. This way an actress could dress to suit her role and not (as had sometimes happened) overdress thanks to private sources of income, or underdress for lack of funds.

Copeau now needed general methods for the reeducation of his troupe. He groped about for guidance and remembered that in preparing his first season of repertory at the Moscow Art Theatre (1898), Constantin Stanislavsky had taken his actors out of Moscow for the summer and into the country, where they rehearsed in a barn. Or did he recall that Stendhal had seen a comedy well-acted only once in his life—in a barn, and by unknown actors? Antoine, after fifteen years of experience, warned that "the metteur-en-scène must be able to manage his actors, and they are 'strange animals to lead,' as Molière said. To get the maximum out of them in effort and result, you must know them, live with them."[22] Stendhal, Stanislavsky, Antoine—they all pointed to the path leading out of Paris and into the country, where director and actors could live and grow together. "The work of the drama," explained Copeau, "requires quiet concentration difficult in a great metropolis."[23] The older, more experienced Gide had written ten years before that each time art languishes one should send it back to nature, as one takes a sick person to the baths.

At the end of June, *le patron* took his group to Le Limon, not far from his own country house. The company boarded with farmers and worked in Copeau's big garden surrounded by high walls. Each bush became a stage prop, and when the weather was bad, rehearsals were continued— in the barn, of course.

Although the troupe had talent and some experience, they had very little training for a season of repertory. A strict schedule was therefore maintained. For five hours each day, they rehearsed the plays of the coming season, alternating as much as possible to avoid monotony. Then the group was divided in half and each devoted two hours to sight readings and to the analysis of classic and modern plays, most emphasis being placed on the classics. In addition, one hour was spent on open-air exercises, swimming, and fencing. The evenings were given over to improvisation.

For ten weeks, the group maintained this full schedule in the strictest solitude. There were no appointments, no urgent personal affairs, no duties to be performed outside their circle. They lived and worked together in the most fraternal fashion. Copeau himself was the focal point in this atmosphere of fellowship, and the result was a wholesome, untheatrical relationship that he believed would eventually lead his players to act together more easily, more naturally, and more truthfully. All in all, "they learned," said Waldo Frank, "some simple and almost forgotten things. They unlearned most of what was Law in Paris. Then, they came to Paris."[24]

On September 1, Copeau and his company walked down the rue du Vieux-Colombier for the first time. Sincerely, frankly, modestly, the capital's latest stage director introduced the theater's newest group of artists as "an attempt at dramatic renovation." He chose that very day to publish an article in the *Nouvelle Revue Française* explaining his attempt.[25]

First, he stressed that the Théâtre du Vieux-Colombier had to live. Therefore, it would be run on the most economical basis: small annual salaries, low rental, limited general expenses, fixed expenditure for initial installations and stage sets. Costumes and décor would be made at minimum cost by a technical staff right on the premises, in old sheds that had been transformed into workshops behind the playhouse. To assure its economic security further, the repertory would be in constant rotation. This meant that at no time would the little theater's material success depend upon one play. Such a plan would also help maintain the high standard of plays, for some of them could only succeed if shown at intervals over a period of time. Without the advantages of repertory, works of outstanding quality might die for reasons entirely unrelated to the play itself.

Second, France's youngest theater wished to show particular respect for the classics, both past and modern, French and foreign. It would offer them as an "antidote to false taste and esthetic confusion," as a standard and a lesson for critics and dramatists. Instead of stooping to the use of "routine tricks of certain actors and the distorted practices of a so-called tradition," the Vieux-Colombier would try to make its audiences feel once more how the plays were originally conceived and first acted. Also, modern revivals and unproduced plays would be welcomed regardless of idea or style, providing they attained the required dramatic level. In this respect, the Vieux-Colombier would differ radically from Antoine's Théâtre Libre, which had been limited to a revolutionary school of writers. Indeed this new theater did not at all see the need for a revolution: "We do not believe in the power of esthetic formulae which are born and die each month. . . . We don't know what the theater of tomorrow will be. We proclaim nothing. But we do pledge ourselves to fight the baseness of the contemporary theater. In founding the Théâtre du Vieux-Colombier we are preparing a shelter for future talent."

Thirdly, if the fight should prove successful, it would be due in no small measure to "its young, enthusiastic, unselfish actors whose one ambition is to *serve* the art to which they devote themselves."

Finally, in discussing staging and sets, Copeau recognized the international aspect of his theater. He had followed closely the work of Stanislavsky, Dantchenko, and Meyerhold in Russia; of Reinhardt, Littman, Fuchs, and Erler in Germany; and of Gordon Craig and Granville-Barker in England. He found them all in agreement on one point: they all denounced the unimaginative realistic set and preferred the suggestive power of the synthetic set, which he, too, would use, but "with the moderation of our French taste." Here again, as in repertory, he would follow no one formula in preference to another, for that would tend to stress the outside of theatrical art, and he was concerned with the inside. There would be no trickery of any kind on his stage. "Old or new, we reject it all. Good or bad, rudimentary or perfected, artificial or realistic, we mean to repudiate the importance of all machinery." This was part of Copeau's cleansing process, part of his conception of the future theater. "We must not confuse," he warned, "scenic conventions with dramatic conventions . . . for the new drama, let us have a bare stage!" This did not imply that the "bare stage" would be a lecture platform from which to hear unactable plays of deep literary, poetical, or philosophical import. Copeau stressed that "we want to be above all else men of the theater, aware of all its characteristics and inherent difficulties and resolved to avoid none."[26]

He closed his article with an appeal to his prospective audience of students, writers, artists, and intellectual foreigners living in the Latin Quarter around his theater, not only to approve the work of his group but to encourage and defend it with their presence, their criticism, and their "active understanding."

14

The seats would be within their means, for the Vieux-Colombier was to be the lowest-priced theater in Paris. Subscription pads of twelve performances each were available to teachers and students, while anyone who could afford it was requested to buy a season pass at 300 francs. For non-subscribers, prices ranged from 2 francs 50 centimes to 6 francs. There were also two boxes with four and six seats at 10 francs.[27]

These low prices were established primarily because the audience had a major part to play in Copeau's plan for "a renovation of French dramatic art." Along with author and actor, it had to become familiar with an art it knew very little about. Copeau's task was "to tear it away from its habits, to develop and inspire it, to create it . . . then to transmit it" to the future. It would take time to do what a devoted theatergoer like Dorothy Thompson called "create a taste."[28] But Jacques Copeau was as patient as he was determined. He had a method and he had a will. He was an artist who loved his art more than life itself and he knew that he must win his audience or lose his art.

Mimeographed subscription blanks were dispatched to all prospective subscribers, explaining in detail (seven full pages) the function and goal of the joint-stock Company of the Théâtre du Vieux-Colombier. The company had a capital of 200,000 francs ($40,000), divided into 200 shares at 1000 francs each. Its object was clearly set forth: "Exploitation of the theater location in Paris on the rue du Vieux-Colombier and in a general manner, all enterprises directly or indirectly concerned with dramatic art." The company's lifetime was established for twenty-five years, a somewhat naive, optimistic estimate to commit to print, but one that emphasized the seriousness of the undertaking from the business, as well as artistic, standpoint.

The "Company" had no secrets from its shareholders. All was minutely listed:

Initial Expenses:	Annual rent	15,000 fs
	Theater repairs	15,000 fs
	Sets and costumes	12,000 fs
	Publicity	8,000 fs
	Formation of Company	3,000 fs
Annual Expenses:	Rent	15,000 fs
	Mortgage (38,000)	5,100 fs
	Interest on rent in advance	600 fs
	Insurance	2,000 fs
	Telephone	500 fs
	Administration	20,750 fs
	Permanent Personnel	6,650 fs
	Utilities	14,800 fs

Publicity	18,000 fs
Acting Company	38,000 fs
Production	15,936 fs
Sets	11,505 fs
Supplemental for matinées	8,200 fs
Total annual expenses for 270 days	157,051 fs

With a maximum daily intake of 2,175 francs, the total income would amount to 274,762 francs after certain taxes and authors' rights were deducted. The annual profit was then established at 90,721 francs. After a five percent reserve fund deduction and another five percent for interest on capital, the profits were to be divided as follows, giving each share a dividend of 17 francs, 70 centimes:

33% to shareholders	25,395 fs
33% to artists and administrators	25,395 fs
33% to a reserve fund	25,395 fs

The immediate response to these appeals went beyond Copeau's every expectation. Encouragement came from all sides. Among the first to answer was Eleanora Duse, whose subscription arrived from Viareggio on September 6, five days after the new theater's founding was announced. This was the kind of spontaneous support Copeau had hoped for to strengthen him and his fellow-workers during the last feverish days of rehearsal, and on opening night there were 300 paid subscriptions.

Since the company's arrival in Paris on September 1, they had been constantly at work. Sixteen plays were scheduled for the season, ten full-length and six one-acters. Considering that Stanislavsky's initial season at the Moscow Art Theater had six plays and that any Broadway or West End comedy requires at least four weeks of intensive rehearsing and then goes on the road for two or more weeks of tinkering, Copeau's array of productions was ambitious for a young company after only two months in the country and six weeks more in Paris.

There were, however, three important reasons for offering a broad repertory. First was the insatiable desire to experiment with various styles of plays and with different methods of staging. Copeau believed that practice makes perfect and wished to spread his practice over as many works as possible, hoping to learn and teach his art through the vitality that comes with variety.

Secondly, the Théâtre du Vieux-Colombier was unknown and had to make more than just a passing favorable impression if it were to last. Copeau could have enlisted the services of a star performer to give his theater more financial stability from the very start. But his fight was against the star system. He substituted a varied choice of plays to exhibit what he and the troupe were capable of. But it would not be enough merely to interest the blasé city of Paris, where new theaters were no novelty. Interesting productions à la Lugné-Poe with lukewarm support from general audiences would not establish the Vieux-Colombier as necessary to the French public. The city would have to be forced into noticing this unpretentious handful of theater workers.

How could Paris be made to feel that it needed the Vieux-Colombier? Copeau hoped he might achieve this by means of original, genuinely artistic, straightforward productions of the classics and the moderns, even though most people had lost interest in the first and lost faith in the second; artistic because, as Voltaire advised, he would allow good taste to precede reflection, and straightforward because the text alone would be stressed, not the scenery or the actor, stage mechanics, or director.

The third reason for choosing a large repertory lay in the nature of the French theater itself. Audiences were accustomed to seeing two plays on the same bill if one was a classic.

If the size of the repertory concerned only Copeau and his companions, its selection was bound to invite severe censure, for the classics were almost the exclusive property of the Comédie-Française. But Copeau was buoyed by the prospect of competition between the "House of Molière" on the rue de Richelieu and what he hoped would be the home of Molière on the rue du Vieux-Colombier. Richelieu and Vieux-Colombier represented all that was different between the splendor of Versailles and the simplicity of the Old Dove-Cote. In the first, Molière was forced to act up to his glamorous surroundings. In the second, Copeau wanted him to be himself, simply at home, in bedroom slippers and easy chair, relaxed and natural.

It was no light assignment to compete with France's First Theater and its hierarchy of talented players. For the sake of dramatic art, however, Copeau wanted his theater to be compared to the Comédie, which was too often overcome by its own glory to suit the taste of sincere theatergoers. That glory had drowned out for generations the true voice of Molière, since everything had to be subordinated to acting in this house of actors. Now, a little Left Bank theater was ready to protest against this deformation of a great man's heritage. Copeau had faith in the public's ability to distinguish the real from the imitation.

The aspiring director would welcome comparison with his country's national theater for yet another reason. He did not have confidence in its recently named administrator, Emile Fabre, the Théâtre Libre dramatist who, Copeau complained, "knows men, not man." This appointment gave Fabre free rein to make the Comédie a European stronghold for elaborate, realistic sets that would result in its actors' ignoring the script even more than before. Copeau could not overlook such artistic heresy. He was proud to defy stubbornness and false traditions with freedom and fresh-ness—freedom from fixed schools of thought, and freshness in method and approach with all writers, old and new.

These guiding principles, Copeau confided, gave birth to "lofty but vague ideas," bound together by friendship, work, and enthusiasm. And if Goethe was right that "enthusiasm alone can create great epochs," the future was indeed bright.

2

The First Season's Struggle (1913–1914)

"OUR PROGRAM WAS A PROGRAM of work," Copeau repeated to one and all. This was the leitmotif of the Vieux-Colombier's first season, which, it was hoped, would assure artistic performances. He had this in mind when he chose Thomas Heywood's melodrama. For here was a play with a commonplace idea and no style to speak of—negative qualities, to be sure, but they answered Copeau's purpose at that time. From the start, he wished to stress his theater's guiding tenet: to put new life into forgotten classics and revivify the unknown works of the past and the present.

Copeau never expected to achieve this goal in a single evening or even in a whole season. His theater was a long-range project. That is where he differed with the critics, for they anticipated seeing something sensational pop out of the Left Bank that very night. How could they know that the sensational side of the Vieux-Colombier lay in its spontaneous teamwork and not in the artificial theatricality so prevalent on the boulevard? How could they know that originality at the Vieux-Colombier was to be the artistic result of hard work and not of clever professional tricks? Two or three critics saw beyond the usual first-night mishaps and recognized the troupe's sincerity and strong *esprit de corps*. But the public at large was not touched by favorable comments in small magazines. It almost completely ignored this new theater, and so *A Woman Killed With Kindness* averaged 511 francs gross ($102) an evening for its twenty-six performances.

Critics and audiences remained aloof from the next production as well. But there was no time to brood. Copeau was looking ahead, a searching, eager apprentice who was far too busy working and in no mood to worry about lack of material or even moral encouragement. His season had a definite program, minutely planned for the needs of author, actor, director, and audience. The schedule would be faithfully adhered to because each play had its part in the general scheme of things. Nothing would be allowed to interfere with the artistic expansion of the Vieux-Colombier, neither box office nor critics, neither small nor large audiences.

If the first play of the season was an old-fashioned Elizabethan melodrama, the second one, *Les Fils Louverné*, was a new work by a new playwright, Jean Schlumberger. Writing for the theater had been his first preference, but the boulevard producers, in refusing to stage his plays, had forced him into other literary forms. When the Vieux-Colombier was founded his interest was revived and he willingly became a member of its executive board, just as he had earlier been a founder of the *N.R.F.* (In fact, the magazine's first number bears his address, 78 rue d'Assas.)

By choosing Schlumberger's work, Copeau hoped to encourage those outside the theater to write for the Vieux-Colombier. Its stage offered them the one practical way to eliminate faults of the unproduced playwright who wished to learn the technique of this medium. Only a theater willing to experiment with new writers as well as new methods could attract discouraged dramatists. With an honest, unbiased director eager to show works without regard for box-office appeal, novelists and poets, essayists and even philosophers might be drawn into the ranks. That was part of Copeau's method for renovating and rejuvenating, and Schlumberger was his first example. But this four-act conflict between two brothers over money and love met with a lukewarm reception.

One week after *Les Fils Louverné* opened, the Vieux-Colombier enchanted its followers with Alfred de Musset's fairylike *Barberine*, three acts full of love, poetry, and knights. This addition to the repertory stressed the company's versatility in acting. One of the main reasons for choosing Musset was that "the actor and text are completely revealed" and put on their own. There were no props and no sets to hide an actor's weaknesses, just a chair, a table, and a cushion. One of the actors complained, saying that he did not like the classics "because in those plays . . . well, there's nothing to do." Copeau agreed that there was "nothing to do but act what was written, no more and, if possible, no less."[1]

This virtue of the bare stage was recognized by the few critics who remained to the final curtain. They spoke of the new troupe as "already in the service of art." *Barberine* won for the Vieux-Colombier a more general audience, intrigued by the idea that a classic could be made so alive with such simple means. The London *Times* correspondent wrote home that Paris was now witnessing the most important event in the French theater since the Théâtre Libre. He considered the Vieux-Colombier "more significant than its predecessors by reason of its greater comprehensiveness."[2]

This comprehensiveness became even more apparent when Molière's *L'Avare* made its appearance exactly five days after the opening of *Barberine*. To go from Musset to the plenitude of *L'Avare* was a perilous jump for a relatively inexperienced group. But this one had Charles Dullin, who portrayed the old miser Harpagon as both the type and the character, revealing "the symbol, the man and the clown." The renewed vigor of this production, and Dullin's success, evoked a good deal of interest from the Right Bank, but not enough to bring it to the Left.

A few days later the first of twenty-four *Matinées Poétiques* was launched to help promote cohesion in the audience. (This was an imperative need if there was to be a dependable nucleus from which to expect criticism, encouragement, and support.) These lectures and readings familiarized Vieux-Colombier patrons with the development and past achievements of poetry, and showed how poets of the day had been influenced by Mallarmé and Verlaine, through the symbolists. The audience at these matinées perceived more clearly the aims of the Vieux-Colombier: why it leaned so heavily on the classics for guidance, why it shunned imitations of art and strove to attain the real thing, why it needed a homogeneous audience to collaborate with it on the difficult road ahead. These well-attended gatherings, inaugurated by Copeau for the first time in any theater, were conducted informally by him and the company. Whenever possible the poets themselves came to recite their works.

All this time, during November and December, new one-act plays were being introduced into the repertory: Jules Renard's *Le Pain de ménage*, Georges Courteline's *La Peur des coups*, Molière's *La Jalousie du barbouillé*, for example. While most of these had been in rehearsal before the season began, Paul Claudel's *L'Echange*, the next full-length production, had not. This was to be the first real test of a director-executive: to keep his theater going every night while increasing its repertory.

When Copeau had announced the year's schedule in September, he foresaw at least one major casting difficulty. He had to find the right actress to play Léchy Elbernon, Claudel's light-hearted seductress, and there was no one for the part in the company. He put a notice in *Comœdia* calling for actresses, and then lived through the sad spectacle of seeing "the proletariat of the theater" march before him: "unemployed and unemployable players, *grandes coquettes* worn out by ten years on the road, forty-year-old ingénues, . . . teachers, society matrons." At the third series of auditions, just as *le patron* was about to call it a day, "a tall young girl swept on the stage like a gust of wind, head high, majestic," acting in a clear, supple voice a scene from Victorien Sardou's *Patrie*. The scene did not suit her; she shouted her lines and overacted badly. Yet Copeau was impressed, feeling that there was in her a human being overflowing with "youth, life and a kind of deep, incoherent will." He called before him this beginner without make-up and read her the most exacting passages in Claudel's play. She didn't seem to understand a thing, but burst out like a real trouper: "I'm made for the part, it's all in me!"[3] Copeau smiled and engaged her as a member of the company—but not to play in Claudel. Another actress, Mlle. Marion, was chosen to act Léchy Elbernon, and it was not until two months later that the Vieux-Colombier programs carried for the first time the name of the exuberant beginner: Valentine Tessier.

Written twenty years earlier in New York and Boston where the author was in "administrative exile" as French consul, *L'Echange*, a nostalgic drama of thwarted loves, had never been performed. It had an ordinary theme, for to Claudel (as he wrote in the theater's program), "the interest of a drama must go beyond the anecdote it relates; it must say something." This "something" was transformed by the author into a touching conflict by the simplicity of his ideas, the near-childish naiveté of his two principal characters, and by the unconventional setting and mood in which he enclosed them. Louis Laine (Charles Dullin), the youthful dreamer, and his jealous wife, Marthe, live in a seashore cabin on the property of the boisterous, money-mad Thomas Pollack Nageoire (Copeau) and his actress wife, Léchy Elbernon. The proprietor tries to make love to Marthe, while Léchy takes Louis from his wife for a time; and when he wishes to return to his first love, Léchy causes his death.

The play had been widely read and highly rated as literature, but no producer had ventured to invest in it. There were no huge profits, it seemed, to be squeezed out of a lyric tragedy telling of unfulfilled hopes concealed in four restless hearts. As if to seal its doom, it was composed in Claudel's special kind of free verse.

What the commercial and even art theaters would not attempt, Copeau deemed a privilege and a challenge to offer. In an interview with Frédéric Lefèvre in *Nouvelles littéraires* (February 19, 1927), he described Claudel as "unquestionably the greatest dramatist of modern times. . . . Claudel's art alone is today sufficiently total, sufficiently synthetic and at the same time sufficiently eternal to serve as a basis and foundation for the most recent experiments." The script was difficult, for everything hinged on the director's and actor's ability to materialize accurately the author's unexpressed intentions. The actor, especially, had to achieve thorough mastery of a certain rhythm peculiar to Claudel's poetry if the results were to clarify the drama's inner conflict. The poet realized the problems he had created for the actor's talent and technique when he stated that the player's "aim is not to interpret a text, but to impart life to a character."[4]

Besides being a test for the company, *L'Echange* would also be one for the audience. After a hard time with Heywood and Schlumberger, Copeau was not reassured to see his little house become a temporary haven for audiences enchanted by the wit of the elusive *Barberine*. He wanted people he could count on—people who, like the theater itself, would accept all types of plays and not merely the lighter ones.

After Copeau persuaded the author not to change the script as written in 1893, he invited Claudel to supervise the staging of the entire production. On January 15 the green curtains parted on *L'Echange* to show once again a bare stage: a backdrop depicting the sky and in the foreground, a tree. The costumes were colorful, but stage effects were simplified in order to focus attention on the action. The company faced its task squarely and did its best to follow Claudel's instructions regarding clear delivery and the music of the voice, which he considered second only to the conveying of emotions.

The literary world was intrigued. Its curiosity had already been aroused the preceding season by Lugné-Poe's production of *L'Annonce faite à Marie*. But on the whole, the critics agreed that *L'Echange* represented about fifteen percent of the author's achievements to date (1914). For the next few weeks, they kept telling Claudel what a fine writer he was, and in the same breath rebuked the Vieux-Colombier for giving such strange plays instead of "collaborating in the rebirth of French taste." Copeau himself was praised for his acting, while the other three players were reproached for poor delivery and for falling into a monotonous, sermonizing tone; and the sets "until now so happy, have grown sad." Copeau, it was concluded, ought not to throw his "artiness" in people's faces.[5] Henri Ghéon was the only one to raise his voice in praise, but the clamor against Claudel's drama was too strong to maintain it beyond its sixteenth performance.

With a clear conscience and a diminishing audience, Copeau launched the next double bill, consisting of a modern classic and a new, unproduced play, both of them realistic in genre: Henri Becque's *La Navette* and Roger Martin du Gard's *Le Testament du Père Leleu*. Charles Dullin and Gina Barbieri excelled in bringing alive the cleverness and truthfulness of Martin du Gard's principal characters. In jumping within one month from the romantic lad in *L'Echange* to the sly, wiry old fossil Leleu, Dullin firmly established his position as a character actor.

Copeau tended to reject realistic and naturalistic works except, as he wrote in his theater program for the play, when they came from a master-critic of society like Becque, "whose wit, keenness and cruel irony made of *La Navette*," he wrote, "a delightful satire on lovers and their mistresses." Maurice Boissard, drama critic for the *Mercure de France*, confessed (in May 1914) that after years of reviewing plays, he never admired dramatic art enough to write for the theater. He changed his mind upon seeing this revival of *La Navette*: "the theater can indeed be a very attractive art, even an exciting one, equal perhaps, to the art of writing a book." And he went on to regret that this feeling had come to him so late in life.

What had been one writer's disappointed hope became reality that very day for another. Along with Becque's play, Roger Martin du Gard, who had so devotedly helped in the checkroom when the Vieux-Colombier opened its doors, was making his debut as a dramatist with *Le Testament du Père Leleu*. This Berrichon peasant farce, inspired by the Vieux-Colombier, revealed a talented and highly promising author of Molièresque comedy. Like Schlumberger, however, he loved the theater but would not write for it so long as art played second fiddle to the box office. Both required the assurance of an artist-director's leadership before they would consent to create for the stage. Both feared being misunderstood and possibly ridiculed, as so many of their illustrious predecessors had been. Both cherished—when it finally came—the fresh, unlabeled kind of theater the Vieux-Colombier represented. Both had confidence in Copeau and in his integrity as an artist.

The Vieux-Colombier was now in mid-season. It had unfolded a good deal of what it stood for—enough, at any rate, for Boissard to say: "We have three theaters in Paris; the Odéon (under Antoine), Le Théâtre du Vieux-Colombier, and Lugné-Poe's Oeuvre." But most critics were far too busy with boulevard *générales*[6] to indulge in the "charming audacity" of an evening on the Left Bank. Even a serious drama critic like Henry Bordeaux, upon returning from the Orient, wrote in January that he had heard much favorable comment about the new theater and would soon get there "if I have some evening free." That free evening came three months later. His colleagues on the *grandes revues* dropped in about as regularly, and when they did, it was rarely to sit through the whole play. (Was it because the old seats were not very comfortable?)

Copeau next revived his own version of Dostoevsky's *Les Frères Karamazov*. During the two years since Jacques Rouché's production, the play could be seen in Brussels, London, Austria, Czechoslovakia, Italy, and Serbia, while this season was to find it performed at the Lessing Theater in Berlin, the Burgtheater in Vienna, and in Frankfurt, Dresden, and Munich. This revival came as a welcome addition, for it required a minimum of preparation at a moment when Copeau was pressed for time— he had just accepted the invitation of the French Institute in London to give several performances in England. Since he had assisted in staging the original production, with sets and costumes generously loaned by Rouché, and with Dullin there to repeat his role of Smerdiakov, the play was soon in running order. It reached the public the second week of March, now with Copeau as the philosophical Ivan Karamazov and Paul Oettly making his debut as Dmitri. Valentine Tessier made her successful entry as the seductive Grouchenka. This was a tribute to the discernment of an inexperienced *patron*. He had admired in her "that harmonious violence, that dazzling freshness, that flame." With her Russian blood (through her mother), the role suited her admirably. Her previous stage experience had been limited to four rejections at the Conservatory (in spite of studying with Paul Mounet, celebrated Comédie-Française actor) and a few bit parts at Lugné-Poe's theater. In fact, the latter sent Copeau a letter of recommendation for her, at her request, but which Copeau did not receive until after the audition—fortunately enough, for relations between the two directors were not friendly and Copeau might well have rejected her for that reason.

The play met with the same success at the Vieux-Colombier as it had at the Théâtre des Arts. At this point, no praise could have pleased Copeau more than to read novelist-critic Abel Hermant's comment that at times he thought he was listening to a work of Paul Claudel's. It could easily have stayed on alone for the rest of the season if the box office, receiving money bearers with the same independence with which it offered them its wares, had had anything to say in the matter.

A few days after this successful revival, a company of fourteen met at the Gare du Nord and set out for Calais and England. There were MM. Copeau, Jouvet, Tallier, Bourin, Bouquet, Roger Martin du Gard; Mmes. Blanche Albane, Valentine Tessier, Suzanne Bing, and Jane Lory. Georges Duhamel (Blanche Albane's husband) accompanied them as a prompter, along with Mme. Didi, the wardrobe mistress, and a stagehand.

Their first performance took place in Birmingham on Tuesday night, the day they reached England, at John Drinkwater's Repertory Theater. The French Institute was eager to give England and its up-and-coming writers like Drinkwater an idea of what the contemporary French theater was striving for. At the Institute's request, the company played *Barberine*, *Le Pain de ménage*, and *La Jalousie du barbouillé*. Wednesday morning they left for Liverpool and gave two performances at the David Lewis Club Theater. Then they went to Manchester where a large crowd, gathered for the next day's races, came to see the French actors at the Midland Theater.

When they reached London, "England's Antoine," Sir Herbert Beerbohm Tree, placed His Majesty's Theatre at their disposal. Its huge stage was reduced in size to accommodate Copeau's sets, and the company again played the same three works. The English did not enter into the spirit of Molière's *La Jalousie du barbouillé*, which they regarded as a vulgar farce. But *Barberine*, whose wistful fantasy was so close to Shakespeare's comedies, evoked a good deal of laughter and much praise. The drama critic for the London *Times* saw in the Musset play a revival of "the spirit of the romantic movement . . . interpreted with an art and refinement such as could only be attained by actors to whose natural aptitude the most careful training has been superadded."[7] So impressed was the *Times* critic with the acting that he wrote: "The charm of the performance, indeed, lay not so much in the graceful comedy of the poet as in the excellence of the ensemble of the company and the perfect diction of its individual members." Such comments from foreign listeners would seem to justify the troupe's hard work from Le Limon onward, especially after the harsh verdict of Paris critics who had reproached the actors for poor diction only one month before.

The question, however, was not whether English critics were better judges of French diction than their French counterparts. The latter, accustomed to the exaggerated enunciation of the grand style, were reluctant to accept the more natural pronunciation called for by Copeau's methods of direction.

The English tour was a great success, morally as well as artistically. It increased even more for Copeau and his comrades the potentialities of their teamwork. They were becoming a force of considerable promise in the reviving of theatrical art in and out of France. The Vieux-Colombier stimulated its fellow idealists in the repertory theaters of Manchester, Liverpool, Birmingham, and London, and was in turn encouraged and strengthened by their reaction. There was no longer any doubt that new blood was now coming into the theater, and these artists were determined to keep it fresh through constant work, discipline, and experimentation. Otherwise, as Sheldon Cheney stated at the time, the "untroubled stagnation" of former years would surely return.[8]

While the French troupe was making its reputation in England, Philip Carr, director of the Little Theater, crossed the Channel and had his company perform Sheridan's *School for Scandal* and Chambers's *Tyranny of Tears* on the Vieux-Colombier stage.

Back in Paris, Copeau put on another unproduced play, Henri Ghéon's *L'Eau-de-vie*, which was in rehearsal in France during the English tour. Just as Claudel's *L'Echange* remained twenty years in print before reaching the stage, this "people's tragedy" on the devastating effects of alcoholism had to wait almost as long. When Ghéon's first play, *Le Pain*, was put on at Rouché's Théâtre des Arts in 1911, it aroused new interest in realistic subjects treated in a lyrical style, and made Copeau urge a director like Antoine to stage *L'Eau-de-vie*. He never dreamt that he, himself, would be directing it only two and a half years later.

L'Eau-de-vie was produced for the very same reason as *L'Echange*: to show that a lyrical style could be used for an ordinary, everyday theme. Like Claudel, Ghéon wished to construct his play note by note, as one builds melodies in a musical score. In fact, Copeau chose the script in great part for what he calls its "musical fullness" as another challenge to the vocal techniques of his actors.[9] This time, they met their task with greater flexibility, but audiences found the degenerate orgies in the play so repulsive that, according to Copeau, they "were put to flight." This made the author exclaim with pleasure, "Bravo! That's what I wanted."[10] Some critics, however, appreciated this attempt to achieve "a reconciliation between scenic realism and poetry."[11]

The play set much literary ink flowing, but the public stayed away. *L'Eau-de-vie* chugged on through twelve performances, the shortest run of the year for a major production. Yet George Jean Nathan, a young drama critic back in early 1914, praised this particular work as well as others he saw at the Vieux-Colombier.

The outlook was not bright at the beginning of May, the final month of the season. Fifteen plays had been given, nine full-length and six one-acters. Two of them, those by Schlumberger and Martin du Gard, were out-and-out discoveries, with the latter fairly successful. Claudel and Ghéon had first performances for old plays, which was Copeau's way of expressing indignation that there were good writers in France who had precious few producers. The modern one-act revivals of Courteline, Renard, and Becque proved highly popular. So did *Les Frères Karamazov*. The classics with Heywood, Musset, and Molière came in for much attention and some praise. But in all this varied collection of comedies, tragedies, farces, and melodramas, not one stood out as either a great play or an out-and-out revelation. This was the Vieux-Colombier's strength and its weakness, too. It took pride in reaffirming its status as a modest "shelter for future talent" and not as a showcase for startling novelties. But it also had to face hard realities, for without something unusual, something truly new that would appeal directly to an audience, it might not be able to survive this period of public indifference.

Copeau's staging was found to be attractive, frequently original and artistic. It was felt however, that the "gray, dull atmosphere . . . [was] harmful to works chosen with intelligence and taste . . . [making them appear] sad and poor."[12] But sobriety was a principle at the Vieux-Colombier even before Antoine was forced to resign from the Odéon because of ruinously luxurious sets. Quite aside from financial considerations, simplicity of décor was part of the plan to set off the acting along with the script. This obliged the actor to look to himself and not depend on outside help to hide his weaknesses. In this way the player was induced to reach the ultimate goal of his profession: to have at his disposal a finished technique in order to give his characterization the widest possible range for a complete, truthful life. The troupe was well on its way to achieving this end, but they were only on their way, and the public was reluctant to pay to see them when it could applaud instead the brilliant Sarah or the flamboyant Coquelin. The "literary and artistic public" to whom Copeau had addressed his opening appeal early in October did not come in large enough numbers. True, art leaders such as Rodin, Verhaeren, and Bergson came, and Claude Debussy was an inspiration to the troupe when he quietly appeared in their theater three nights in succession. But most of the hoped-for followers showed themselves about as eager as the general public. There was apparently no such thing as a ready-made elite to support art. There were just audiences, some more interested in art than others. But all had to be won over.

Copeau had hoped that by May he would have attracted a permanent audience, one he could count on for the next season. But Paris still remained aloof and there was only one month left and one more play to put on. With Antoine out of the Odéon, the Vieux-Colombier was the only place in Paris where dramatic art had a future. But what plans could Copeau make for a theater with a future but without an audience? He decided to postpone all decisions until after the opening of the final production.

There was a great deal of activity at the theater around the middle of May. So much depended on this last play and it was so late in the season. The company was completely exhausted. They could barely reach the theater for rehearsal after working all the previous day and giving a performance at night. Just before the opening, Copeau and Jouvet sweated through forty-eight hours without a break. It seemed as if work would never end. The opening had to be postponed. Despair had the upper hand everywhere. Finally, lest they all crack under the strain, the play was given a definite *générale* date. Ten minutes before curtain time, Duncan Grant, the English artist doing the costumes, covered from head to foot with his paints, was still running after the actors armed with brush and palette in order to add a finishing touch to their costumes. A sudden hush fell on all this last-minute excitement as the violins began to play and the Duke of Illyria stepped out on the forestage to deliver his lines in Shakespeare's *La Nuit des rois* (*Twelfth Night*): "Si la musique est la nourriture de l'amour, qu'elle reprenne. . . . Cette mesure encore! Elle avait une cadence mourante. . . . Assez, ne jouez plus: ce n'est déjà pas aussi suave que tout à l'heure." (If music be the food of love, play on, . . . That strain again;—it had a dying fall; . . . Enough; no more; 'Tis not so sweet now as it was before.)

As the Duke slipped off to the left, a slender form covered with pink veils appeared on the right with a palm-branch in her hand. It was Viola, played by Suzanne Bing, asking of the captain: "Amis, quelle est cette contrée?" The captain's answer: "C'est l'Illyrie, Madame." (What country, friends, is this? . . . Illyria, lady.)

In a few seconds, she too was led off to the left by the captain. Backstage, Copeau followed tremulously those first few minutes: "And then, at the end and at the height of these two scenes which have served but to prolong the musical impression of the prelude, themselves being like two movements of the same note, then only will the curtain part to reveal the complete stage, bathed in light, and the action in full swing."[13]

Jane Lory and Romain Bouquet were Maria and Sir Toby Belch. (From then on, Bouquet was called Toby by his fellow actors.) In a moment, Louis Jouvet as Sir Andrew Aguecheek joined them and became one of the outstanding comedians of Paris. Lucien Weber played the clown, Cariffa was Fabian, Blanche Albane the Countess Olivia, Oettly was Antonio, and Copeau the Countess's steward Malvolio.

Gone were despair, doubts, and fatigue. The actors were overjoyed at what they saw happening that night on both sides of the footlights. Even when they left the stage they could not leave the play. "They remained suspended in that enchanted world by an invisible thread," said Copeau. It was like "the discovery of an unknown land . . . a feast at which one finds everything."[14] They all felt that this last play of the season had captivated Paris with a direct appeal to its most susceptible and elusive self: its imagination.

The arch-traditionalist René Doumic, on the contrary, "was not very much amused . . . [listening to] one of the most boring plays I know."[15] Otherwise, delight prevailed and the happy news spread just about everywhere. The new French star was not another Sarah Bernhardt nor a writer with a sensational message. It was a whole production, a whole company, a whole theater, almost deliberately poor in means, but completely and proudly conscious of its creative power.

The critics did not know what to extol first, script, actors, sets, costumes, or themselves for enjoying the whole thing so much. The surprisingly faithful translation by Théodore Lascaris, done at Copeau's request when others were found wanting, was praised by the press and scholars alike for being tinged with just the right tones of archaic expressions to give the play its special coloring. Novelist Henry Bordeaux summed up the French version as "charming, clear and harmonious,"[16] while only ten years before, a critic had called Shakespeare "a barbarian who must be cleaned for the French theater."[17]

The troupe, all agreed, was truly a homogeneous unit, proving the superfluity of stars. Copeau showed once and for all that simple, relatively inexperienced actors played Shakespeare better than old-time professionals. Great actors, he said, can lead us into the depths of character; highly stylized ones bring out the form of the work; but simple players let loose most of the charm in a Shakespearean script: "They hardly step between us and the poet, giving our imagination every kind of liberty and pleasure."[18] Copeau's simple players did this, forcing Granville-Barker to admit that there were now French actors who played Shakespeare better than most English ones did.

More than text and actors, Copeau's staging of the whole production accounted for most of the enthusiasm and made him a factor to be dealt with in all future revivals of the classics. What he did not succeed in making the public appreciate in a contemporary play such as Claudel's

L'Exchange, he did with a three hundred-year-old foreign comedy: "the fusion between fancy and reality," Léon Daudet observed on May 27, 1914, in his reactionary royalist paper *Action Française.* The successful projection of this fusion brought audiences close to the Bard: "The tiny Vieux-Colombier stage performed the miracle of evoking for us in the twentieth century, in Paris, the stage of Stratford-on-Avon."[19] Claude Debussy, whom Antoine called "that messiah of good taste," wrote Copeau that when the curtain fell on the last scene he "was astonished not to see Shakespeare make his appearance at the end of the play,"[20] so complete was its rejuvenation and so alive was its new stage life.

To Copeau, all this seemed right and overdue. "Much too long a time," he wrote, "has Shakespeare been disfigured by adapters who, under pretext of having him profit from the 'progress' of our [stage] mechanics, altered the design of his works and slowed down its movement by changes of set." He further pleaded that "we must not fear to lead the stage back to a primitive expression . . . to an austerity in staging" which had been the rule for all the best periods in dramatic art. Only then, he concluded, would the contemporary theater be in a position to rediscover great style and inner power. In this manner he attempted to release the flow of human emotion locked up in the pages of Shakespeare's manuscript. He sought to reproduce Elizabeth's England with all "its extraordinary vitality" and he succeeded completely in returning a well-nigh forgotten freedom to Shakespeare, "the unique example of a great poet on the stage, in whom the stage curtails none of his liberty." By this, Copeau did not mean to propose staging Shakespeare as in the sixteenth century. This, he feared, would risk falling into a scholarly mise-en-scène and into a "laborious coldness."[21]

After the past eight months of trial and error, the Vieux-Colombier had become a Paris prodigy on its own independent terms and its own artistic standards. Throughout, it had offered only those works considered representative of dramatic art. There were different genres, starting with Heywood's Elizabethan melodrama about a conscience-stricken adulteress, then continuing with Musset's romantic drama on Barberine's fidelity, Claudel's symbolist tragedy on man's flight from reality, and ending with Shakespeare's ironic fantasy of love and life. This combination of classic, romantic, realist, and symbolist plays, French and foreign, all under the same roof, could have resulted in a heterogeneous clutter. The fact that they had all been done at the Vieux-Colombier gave them a "family resemblance . . . thanks to a higher law of harmony" that ruled there.[22] All were universal human themes projected in the simplest and most natural way by the cohesion and unity of sets and players under one man's direction.

The Vieux-Colombier was pointed out to new dramatists as a place where they could learn how to equal, not imitate, the classics by bringing out in their own works "the painting of human feelings, the vision of their time."[23] Copeau's results took on the proportions of a miracle, for never before had Shakespeare, in French, encountered such complete success. Thanks to *Twelfth Night*, dramatic rejuvenation left the realm of idea and speculation to become an integral part of practical theater work.

The future looked bright this May of 1914. Copeau and his friends of the *N.R.F.* had every reason to be pleased and proud: the magazine had reached a new high with three thousand regular subscribers, and the Vieux-Colombier—which had, in Gaston Gallimard, the same conscientious business head as the *N.R.F.*—counted four thousand prospective subscribers. (This was the number of requests on file for program-postcards, a fashion that Gallimard introduced into the theater world because there was no money in the Vieux-Colombier treasury to pay newspapers for the usual type of advertising.) Invitations for guest performances began to pour in upon the eight-month old theater. The Vieux-Colombier was requested to inaugurate Cologne's New Theater in September—1914! The *Journal de Genève* credited Paris with only two theaters: the Vieux-Colombier and the Comédie-Française.

All this surprised Gide. In his *Journal* for June 18, 1914, he writes: "This triumphal success almost embarrasses me, so greatly have I grown accustomed to predict non-success for merit and to transfer the recognition of our virtues to the other side of the grave."

With press and public completely won over, the five-hundred-seat theater could not possibly accommodate the crowds that tried to squeeze in. Nevertheless, a few days after the play's opening, the Vieux-Colombier, faithful to its schedule, closed its season in the faces of those clamoring for a view of the real Shakespeare. On May 30, Copeau and his troupe went on tour to Alsace, playing in Mulhouse, Colmar, and Strasbourg, and the little Molière bust was taken from its pedestal in the theater's lobby and put away for safekeeping.

3

Three Years of Silent Life
(1914–1917)

THE VIEUX-COLOMBIER LIVED IN "complete isolation" during its first season, Charles Dullin wrote in 1923, at least until *Twelfth Night* focused upon it the attention of *la ville-lumière*.[1] Then, Belgium, Italy, Switzerland, and Germany became eager to witness how this latest movement in dramatic art had recreated and restored "the dying art" of theater. They invited Copeau and his company to tour their countries. But he was too busy working on plans for the next season with which to convince Paris that *Twelfth Night* was not a happy accident, but the result of months of experiment and apprenticeship. He was searching for "a stage life which would not be inferior to the poetic life of a drama, and which would be faithful to it."[2] This ideal he hoped to approach more closely during the Vieux-Colombier's second season, when . . .

Tours, plans, writers, actors, directors, all were thrown to one side as war swept every able-bodied man to the frontiers of France. Dullin left for the Lorraine front in the dragoons; Jouvet, who was a graduate pharmacist, became an assistant in the Medical Corps; Copeau was drafted for limited service, reporting to *Les Invalides* in Paris for medical treatment. All the others either volunteered or were mobilized. And the theater itself, "the shelter for future talent," became a shelter for refugees and soldiers on leave.

Copeau tried to adapt his particular talent to wartime needs. He would have liked to reopen the Vieux-Colombier immediately for plays and other special productions suited to the emergency. He was disappointed with the general tone of war articles in the newspapers, even with those of Maurice Barrès, and believed he could do better himself. Gide, to whom he spoke of this, agreed wholeheartedly, "at least for the first few articles that he'd write." At this time, Copeau looked much younger to Gide, "more like Diderot than ever, embracing each new project with all his strength and heart . . . his energy (I ought rather to say: his excess of life) electrifies those around him."[3]

In this wave of patriotism, family loyalty to the Vieux-Colombier was not forgotten. Copeau urged Gide to translate Shakespeare's *As You Like It* while he himself took on *The Winter's Tale* for a possible 1915 production—"if we've chopped off the Kaiser's head," as he wrote to Louis Jouvet (November 26, 1914). Two weeks later his almost childlike enthusiasm stirred Jouvet: "After the war I believe we shall find inexhaustible good-will around us, from every standpoint, even financial. Not one day passes without some proof of this. My heart swells when I contemplate the future." So full of ambition and confidence was *le patron*, that he was even led to ask whether "this frightful truce" was not good for some purpose.[4] At the end of February, Copeau was still enthralled with the translating of *Winter's Tale*, and in addition he had almost completed his notations of the *Macbeth* mise-en-scène. Along with *Twelfth Night*, this would make three Shakespeare productions alternating on the boards. And Copeau wistfully remarked that he wished he had the time to finish his own play, *La Maison natale*.

On April 8, 1915, in an affectionately paternal letter to Valentine Tessier, Copeau repeated his hope that the Vieux-Colombier would reopen at summer's end. With the theater's closing at the outbreak of war, "la petite Valentine" had been left without any source of income. Using Copeau's influence, she obtained the post of diction teacher with the French Institute in London, where she and Jules Delacre, a Belgian refugee, eventually organized a little theater called "The French Players." Ever on the alert for new talent, Copeau asked her to have Delacre write him about joining the Vieux-Colombier after the war. He confided as well that he was "not very ill" but must nevertheless be "very careful" in the future, for both his lungs were infected with tuberculosis. Soon after, he was honorably discharged from the army and settled down in Le Limon for a period of rest. Two months later, although still not recovered, he was awaiting anxiously the arrival of Gaston Gallimard, also unwell, who was to stay with him for a couple of months to work out a sound administrative organization for the Vieux-Colombier.

This release from the army gave him the one and only period of leisure he was ever to have during his theater's lifetime, and he used it to digest fully the lessons of those first eight months. Practical experience had awakened his imagination to the endless possibilities lying dormant in the untouched corners of dramatic art. He wrote of this constantly to Dullin and Jouvet in the trenches, pouring out his dreams and his hopes. To Jouvet on August 25, 1915, he confessed:

> Yes, absolute communion, communion of the heart and one's whole being for a work as thrilling, as important, as sacred as that of the artisans of the middle ages (and like them, with simplicity, without pretension . . .). My ambition for our work has no limit . . . we must not accept the insufficiencies that habit imposes upon our fellow workers. I do not speak only of acting personnel, which I expect to reform from top to bottom by means of my school, but of the manual workers: stagehands, prop-men, electricians . . . there, too, we must start something, a real relationship must exist from us to them, they must be under control, and our words must really enter their hearts—really and not fictitiously. . . . You know well enough that I am not a utopian, a dreamer, a head stuffed full of literature. I hate that. I am the most modest and boldest of people. I deal only with men and things. The heart, two hands, a lot of courage in order to produce. Few ideas, but a rather vivid image of what is possible. I know what one can do and we will do it at the price of our lives. They can do nothing to stop us. We are giants if we don't give a damn about anything except reaching the goal of our work. No dealings with all those scoundrels who talk Art.

Now that he knew so much more about his craft, Copeau felt the need to study it and work at it objectively like a scientist experimenting in his laboratory. As the weeks went by his ideas became clearer and more precise until the day he decided to start his own laboratory—the School of the Vieux-Colombier. As early as 1913, he had planned to do this: "to create a real acting school, along with the theater and at the same time. It would be free. On the one hand we would bring into it very young people, even children, and on the other, men and women who love the theater and have an instinct for it which had not yet been deformed by defective methods. . . . Such a contingent of new forces would later make for the grandeur of our undertaking."[5]

At the time, his collaborators judged this plan premature and it was reluctantly left in abeyance until the theater could stand on its own. It was to become Copeau's sad experience that "someone who believes in something always appears childish."[6] Despite disagreement, however, he treated the Vieux-Colombier as a laboratory as well as a theater. To him, the School was a logical beginning to any attempt at dramatic renovation. He agreed with Goethe that "before doing, you must be."

Copeau felt that even intelligent, talented, and cooperative actors could not really create with inadequate time for rehearsals and under relentless pressure. They could not do their best without a calm, well-planned training, both technical and moral. Nor could mature men and women be expected to lose early habits and accept the new discipline as easily and as spontaneously as a group who had no previous contact with the theater. It was, therefore, not enough to gather together the best actors available. Copeau's dream was to develop a technique that would form them:

> [Just] as a business cannot do without its laboratory . . . art becomes impoverished or confused if it does not have the principles of a school to depend upon. . . . School or laboratory [is] indispensable to the theater which is both an art and a business. . . . [Stage] experience is worth what it is worth. If it begins to roughen, it is theory's job to smoothen it again. The stage alone makes the actor, just as it makes the author. But, it unmakes them, too.[7]

The future of the stage—principles, theories, workers, masters—could be found in two great artists: Gordon Craig and Adolphe Appia. Craig, the actor-designer-director son of Ellen Terry, was one of the pioneering geniuses of the contemporary theater in the development of the architectural set. Appia evolved the concept of the powerful role to be allotted stage lighting. Each was striving to make of theatrical art a composite, harmonious whole of all the arts.

Copeau was one of the few people in France to whom Gordon Craig was more than just a name. He disagreed with some of Craig's theories but admired the artistry and sincerity that motivated them. He esteemed above all the English artist's ideals, what Craig called "singleness of purpose and the power of not altering one's mind." He followed scrupulously Craig's dictum that "the thing is greater than the man . . . the work of art greater than the performer."[8] Above all, Copeau wished to emulate Craig's refusal to have anything to do with the theater unless he could work with people who had learned their craft thoroughly and from the beginning, under a real artist. When Jacques Rouché leased the Théâtre des Arts and asked the Englishman to direct it, he replied that if Rouché would consent to keep the theater closed for ten to fifteen years while craftsmen were being trained for it, then he would come to Paris. "Without a school or workshops in which I, the worker, can make and perfect a machine (and by that I mean a small well-organized army of workers), all the productions must be tenth-rate instead of first-rate."

Craig did not go to Paris, but in Florence three years later, just as the Vieux-Colombier was opening its doors, he was able to establish his School of Theatrical Art "to grow artists" who would scorn "the fake . . . for the genuine." In other words, he wanted his student-artists to develop into creative craftsmen and not into conventional practitioners.[9]

Before opening his own school, Copeau wanted to speak with the English artist. One day in September 1915, Copeau received a telegram inviting him to Italy. For a whole month, these two theater men saw each other almost every day, exchanging ideas and hopes as they strolled beneath the ancient arcades of Florence. Copeau absorbed everything and learned first-hand what had been done. The school had been divided into two classes. The first was made up of teachers and artisans learning Craig's methods and working under his direction. The second had paying students who studied various branches of theatrical art as taught by those in the first class. This school was essentially for scenic designers who wished to transmit and perpetuate the master's ideas with all the limitless vision of the true artist and all the stubborn narrowness of the high priest. Copeau's objective, on the other hand, was to found a school to train young people—and "untainted adults"—in all branches of theater but especially in acting, which he considered the cornerstone of dramatic art.

Craig's school in the little Goldoni Arena did not accept acting students during its brief career, from its founding in 1913 until it was "dropped" in 1914. (The word was angrily scrawled across a photo of the school hanging in the Paris studio-apartment where Craig lived in 1947.) Therefore, Copeau did not see his own type of school or even Craig's in actual operation, since he did not reach Florence until after its demise. But Craig was generous with his explanations, telling the young Frenchman how he expected to make artists of printers, designers, carpenters, electricians, woodcarvers, and prop-makers. Copeau visited all the ateliers, studied Craig's model sets and designs, browsed through his huge art portfolios and books and fondled the props, masks, and marionettes.

Even the city of Florence was a great source of instruction. He visited the libraries and museums and art circles, bookbinders and carpenters, paper shops, potters, dyers, and cloth manufacturers. He wrote Jouvet on October 3, 1915: "The tiny carpenter shops which clutter the little dark side streets would delight you. I shall bring back many photos, especially on architecture." And then he went off to the Boboli Gardens to act out for himself a bit of a Marivaux scene. For the moment, Copeau was indeed living a life apart. He had Gide musing in his *Journal* on September 27, 1915: "Card from J.C. last night, strangely out of time. He speaks of Florence, of Angelico, of Sforza. . . . Does all that still exist?"

Upon Craig's return from a week in the country, their friendship became much closer. In October 1915, Copeau gave Jouvet an enthusiastic plan for ways to adapt Craig's stage to their own theater:

> [It] answers completely the needs of our stage. It is absolutely beautiful, marvelously clear and 'made for us'. Entirely within our line of vision. We had already by ourselves found certain things. But here it is complete, colorful. In working with this material we should perhaps find improvements of detail, but as of this moment it satisfies all our needs. In brief, Gordon C. offers me on the basis of friendship the privilege of French rights for his 'screens' . . . and I become

the representative of his ideas in France. In addition, he showed me a system of lighting which gives admirable results and seems marvelously simple and practical on the model. The question is whether it would be so on the stage. It is the complete elimination of footlights and lanterns.

The "colossal" Craig was about to leave for America to stage, in a specially constructed theater, Johann Sebastian Bach's *Saint Matthew Passion*. He asked Copeau to go with him but Copeau had his mind set on other things. And as yet, he had no taste for the gigantic and the spacious.

During their many talks, Craig gave superb proof that art recognizes no boundaries. Spontaneously, and "on the basis of friendship," his vast store of knowledge and experience was made available to a French artist, as it would most likely have been to an artworker from any other country. It is to this Englishman's credit that no question of artistic jealousy or financial prerogatives entered into the picture. This lesson was not lost on Copeau who, a few years later, encouraged associates in and outside France to take over his own ideas.

Copeau learned from Craig that his theater had "a real reputation" throughout the world as "a living and aggressive thing." And when he left Florence, Craig's warning against the theater's fatal weakness rang in his ears: "hasty reforms, hasty preparations, hasty ideas hastily carried out."[10] Soon, Copeau would be hearing the same thing from Adolphe Appia: that only slow, sure work with youth "would bring joy back to art."

Copeau had hoped to see Eleanora Duse while he was in Italy. She wired him from Rome and invited him to come and see her there. But he was on a very strict budget and did not have the money for this additional trip. He left for France via Geneva to discuss with Jacques Dalcroze the stage possibilities of rhythmic coordination between body movement and stage characterization. He was greatly impressed with what he saw and, to a certain extent, integrated the Dalcroze system in his own school.

Dalcroze then introduced him to Adolphe Appia, "the man of cubes," according to Copeau, whose ideas had a profound influence on him. This Swiss artist saw the actor as a three-dimensional theater element with whom a three-dimensional stage must be made to harmonize. He wholeheartedly approved Copeau's idea of a school, if only for one reason. He looked upon technique as "a principle of order on which are founded all progress and reform."[11] There was, however, no one kind of school that he could suggest to Copeau as an infallible guide. The teaching of modern stage technique was in its formative period and could only develop by experiment. No one had as yet found a model: Stanislavsky and Reinhardt had schools and were trying to work out the actor's salvation; Gordon Craig's school lasted only one year; the old Paris Conservatory was little more than an elocution school, covered with a crust of conventional traditions. From Appia, therefore, Copeau learned that he was breaking into virgin territory, and he left Switzerland with a pioneer's vision of hope.

Back in Paris, with Suzanne Bing helping, he started the Vieux-Colombier School with a dozen teenage boys and girls. They met on Thursdays only, their day off from lycée. By molding young people into artists of the future theater, he hoped to clarify and develop his own ideas on acting techniques, to become a better director for his actors when they came back from war, and to have a fresh acting reserve to draw from with confidence. Only with a renewable personnel, he felt, could the theater remain alive.

Copeau believed that the school could answer "the need for a style in drama." He agreed with Craig that actors of the day had none and that without style there can be no art. But he would not go so far as to follow Craig's choice of the marionette as a substitute for the living actor. Craig felt that "the marionette is more than natural; it has style, that is to say, unity of expression; therefore the Marionette Theater is the true theater." Yet, he was too great an admirer of his mother, Ellen Terry, and of his early master, Henry Irving, to lay this down as an unalterable dictum: "They [actors] must create for themselves a new form of acting, consisting for the main part in symbolic gestures. Today they impersonate and interpret; tomorrow they must represent and interpret; and the third day they must create. By this means style may return."[12]

The Vieux-Colombier troupe had tried to answer this need for a style by working to become a homogeneous ensemble. It had actually realized a certain "unity of expression." With untrained children, however, Copeau hoped to obtain better results, since there would be no breaking-down process as was inevitably the case with professional actors. Everything would depend on how effectively he built, not on how completely he destroyed.

The school had one basic principle: a student-actor had to learn how to use, practically and objectively, the one medium of his art—himself. To begin with, Copeau did not let his students speak or sing. They were taught to control and color their voices by first uttering only the sounds of animals or the elements, such as the wind or the rain. "For his own sake," wrote Harley Granville-Barker, "the student should be kept from premature achievement."[13] Their bodies, in turn, were required to symbolize forms, like trees, before conveying emotions or ideas. Dalcroze's system of rhythmic dancing, already being taught in German and Russian acting schools, was drawn upon to restore movement to the drama and in that way complete thoughts too deep for words alone. Lines were the very last thing students were shown; that way they would not be guided by words they had memorized and which had no emotional root in them as in the dramatist. So important did Copeau consider the actor's physical education that it took on the holy aspect of a rite. Once, on a transatlantic liner, when he was auctioneer for the Seamen's Fund, a somewhat tipsy fellow-passenger, seeing how agile he was, offered him $100 to turn a somersault. Copeau refused. Not even for the poor would he belittle an essential element of the actor's art by making a showy spectacle of it. Incidents such as this started the myth that Copeau was no mere human, like the rest of his fellow artists, but a sort of Knight Templar of the theater, a high priest who regarded dramatic art in much the same way Moses looked upon the Sacred Tablets. Exaggerated as such opinions generally are, there was nonetheless a good deal of truth to this one: Copeau was proud and sensitive, impatient with stubbornness and scornful of hostility.

After learning the value of an obedient body and controlled voice, the actor moved gradually "from gymnastics to the idea of an internal rhythm, to music, the dance, masks, voice, elementary dramatic forms, conscious acting, improvisation, to poetry." Each of these elements had its raison d'être, not because the actor had occasion to call upon them as separate tools, each to be used at the right moment, but because each had its own nuance to add to the whole being which is the actor: "body, brain and voice, the man you see before you on the stage." And more than all others, improvisation usually gave Copeau his best effects. In this he was encouraged by the great heights attained at the Moscow Art Theater, where the actor made his every word and movement come forth as "the result of the right life of his imagination," what Stanislavsky called "the magical, creative *if*," the basis for all improvisation.[14]

Copeau had in Molière, whom Benedetto Croce called "the *commedia dell' arte* poet," his real master of improvisation. From the very start, when *L'Amour médecin* shared the opening night bill in 1913, Molière had been the Vieux-Colombier's most popular author with both public and actors. He guided the troupe's early steps, giving it its first lessons in acting. Copeau found in Molière "elasticity, ease, movement, diversity, constant preoccupation with acting," and above all, "simplicity." He wanted to train his actors so that they would surprise Paris as much as Molière's own actors had with the "newness, ease, liveliness and sharpness of their action." These qualities would restore to his comedies "the zest and gusto . . . not there since Molière himself taught actors how to speak his lines."[15] Copeau sought to project this zest through a judicious use of rhythmics, for he found in Molière strong elements of the dance and called his genius one of rhythm. In fact, lines often seemed the direct result of gestures and pantomime. He hoped, therefore, that by disciplining his students to achieve the movement and rhythm required of actors in a Molière play, the words would not have to be learned—they would come spontaneously. That was Molière's art and that was the supreme value of improvisation: the planting of spontaneity and spirit in the very soul of the actor.

Besides improvisation, Copeau had his young students make considerable use of the mask: "We say an actor gets into the part, under the skin of a character. Perhaps this is not correct. It is the character who approaches the actor, asks of him what he needs and little by little gets under the actor's skin. The latter tries to give his character free rein." In this, the mask played a vital part: "It symbolizes perfectly the actor's position in regard to the character (he is to play) and shows in what way a fusion takes place between the two. The actor playing beneath the mask receives from this cardboard object the reality of his character. He is commanded by it. He obeys it irresistibly."[16]

Copeau was attracted to the mask because it had style, "its own style," without which an artist could not be convincing. He wanted his student-actors to spend three years with him learning to discipline "the anarchy of muscles" and the other aspects of their *métier*. Talma, Irving, and Forbes-Robertson, in whose day there was no concentrated developing of technique, had proclaimed a twenty-year minimum to learn the art of acting. With them, Copeau was appalled at the obstacles an actor had to overcome:

> There he is, that man, exposed on the stage, offered as a showpiece and judged. A movement by his colleague or someone in the audience, a latecomer, a noise in the wings, too bright a light, the fold in a carpet, an error in staging, a forgotten prop, a costume mishap, a lapse of memory . . . without speaking of his health, mood, the weather, everything . . . each can deprive him of what he thought he had mastered after much work, each can separate him from the character he had composed.[17]

Indeed, twenty years would not be too much to master an art that in 1915 had no more than three or four schools, while painters and sculptors had scores throughout the world to teach them their craft. If there had been reliable workshops or studios for actors, comparable to what painters, sculptors, architects, and musicians had, would Talma have specified twenty years? Copeau was inclined to believe not. Considering, however, the small doses of their art that actors had to gulp down at odd intervals, in the greatest haste, with little preparation and even less reflection, it was no wonder that twenty years were needed. It was no wonder that theatrical art was in a state of chaos. It was no wonder that Eleanora Duse had said that to save the theater, the theater must be destroyed, the actors and actresses must all die of the plague. It was no wonder that Gordon Craig wanted to rid the theater of actors and replace them with marionettes. It was no wonder that Copeau wanted a school before having a playhouse: "to raise a generation of theater artists who would be initiated in their art as of their formative years, and who would receive in the theater, not that exclusively technical training which deforms and denaturalizes them, but a complete education which would harmoniously develop their body, their mind and their character as men."[18]

These two years of assimilation and experiments between 1915 and 1917 were amongst the fullest and most gratifying in Copeau's life. Ideals that had been dreams of a twenty-five year old had taken root ten years later when the Vieux-Colombier was founded and were only now, in quiet retreat and patient study, beginning to take shape in his mind and before his eyes. The year 1915 was replete with visions and plans for the school. By 1916 his dozen fledglings, with his own children amongst them, were eagerly following their master's precepts while he stood at their side watching the results and experimenting further. These were the all too few glorious days with no deadlines, no exhausted actors, no first nights, no critics, no successes, no failures: just work, honest, steady work.

Copeau hoped to find the necessary funds to go off into the country with students and teachers, to set up the school on a firm basis and work unmolested until the end of the war and the reopening of the theater. "Such is my plan" he wrote Jouvet on December 25, 1915:

> and you know . . . when I have a plan I stick to it. . . . Last night I said to my wife: I have a feeling we will make our fortune playing Shakespeare and Molière. Excuse this profane thought. It expresses well my faith in the future. *Fortune*, do you hear? *It can not be otherwise.* But for that, we must have actors, that is, people who do *absolutely not* resemble the rascals one sees on the boards today. And that is why, first of all, *the School* . . . Do you understand?

More and more Copeau became certain that the School must be the salvation of dramatic art. Roger Martin du Gard, on first hearing these ideas, thought Copeau had gone mad. But gradually he too began to understand.

Jouvet's enthusiasm matched that of his *patron*, particularly when the subject of improvisation came up in their correspondence. Both agreed it was the only way to break bad acting habits. This exchange of views on improvisation led Copeau directly to his "grand project": how to reintroduce improvised comedies on modern subjects. He sought an authentic rebirth of the popular genre. The old French and Italian farces were no more than restorations. He wanted creations, living, new creations. For this, he proposed (in a letter to Jouvet, winter 1916):

> *to invent* . . . about ten *modern* synthetic characters of great breadth, representing characteristics, foibles, passions, the moral, social and individual absurdities of today. Invent their outlines, invent their costumes, always identical, modified according to circumstances by a certain type of prop.
>
> These ten characters of an autonomous comedy which includes all types from pantomime to drama, confide them to ten actors. Each actor has his character which is his *property*, which becomes him-

self, which he nourishes from himself, from his feelings, his observations, experience, readings and his inventions. There is the great discovery (so simple!), the great revolution or rather the grand and majestic return to the oldest tradition. A brotherhood of farce-players always playing together, improvising together, authors and actors, singers, musicians, acrobats (the clowns alone of our time are a survival of that . . .). These ten characters enter into all possible combinations. This is infinite, constant renewal, it is satire and gaiety reborn. . . . *Voilà*. It's not any more clever than that. . . . (No sets. Always the same props with their physiognomy unchanging as with the actors.) I already perceive three of these characters: the *Intellectual* (doctor, philosopher, professor, etc.), the *Representative* (deputy, minister, electoral agent, food merchant, etc.), the *Adolescent* (the child in his family, the schoolboy, lover, artist, soldier, and finally the 'idealist', grandson of Pierrot, white face, etc.). . . . Am I mistaken? It seems to me that it's a goldmine. And a thing which no one else will be able to take from us, to imitate, to disguise. We'll need two or three years to prepare for this step.

In noting this projected rebirth and modernization of the commedia dell' arte, Gide concludes in his *Journal* (January 21, 1916): "If this plan is realized, I predict and wish for a participating audience, exciting, exalting the actors."

Travels, Craig, Appia, Dalcroze, the school, *Macbeth*, *The Winter's Tale*, second act of *La Maison natale*, stimulating ideas: all were part of a closed theater's silent evolution. After a conversation with Copeau, Gide, coming from his charity work in a refugee center, could barely understand how one could still want to build anything. He had forgotten that ten years earlier, in his journal for December 25, 1905, Copeau had told him: "the most serious accidents can never distract me [from my work] more than two days, three days, not more."

From all sides, Copeau was urged to keep planning. His coworkers lived only for the war to end so that they could return to *le patron*. Valentine Tessier wrote from London how much she missed France and wanted to know when she should come back to the Old Dove-Cote; Paul Oettly wrote from Morocco; poor Tallier was wounded and penned notes from his hospital bed; soon Cariffa was to fall in battle and the young actor's father sent a pathetically devoted letter to Copeau; Dullin corresponded faithfully from his trench on the eve of each bloody offensive, and then, ten days later, with the push finally over, jotted down a tired "I am spared!" and rushed it off to Copeau.

Jouvet, of course, was his constant solace. Each was necessary to the other, and each gladly avowed his need. "Your two letters of December 31, 1915 and January 10, 1916," wrote Copeau to Jouvet on January 26, 1916, caused me more than joy: a veritable happiness, a quickening of the heart. . . . Now that we have understood each other to the bottom of our hearts, every word we say to each other will of itself be intelligible, clear, full of sense. And I will see that all you tell me comes from the depths of your being. We shall no longer ever be able to disappoint one another. From the beginning, I watched each of your movements, each of your steps toward this kind of state of grace. I was aware of your love even before you had become conscious of it. . . . And I find all of you in that sublime sentence where you tell me that you could no longer even be flattered by approval, and that your every desire, your whole ambition is to serve, to devote yourself to a task, our task in common, this work which can be done only by us. Yes! a work of love—there is no way of naming it otherwise. . . . I tell you with the simple assurance of faith that nothing in the world can break our force, our start, when our work is based upon such an understanding, on such love. And little by little other beginnings will come to us, we shall bring about new conversions. Such is the primary condition for the reform, for the renovation which we are attempting. It is because others have not understood it that they have done nothing.

Nor was understanding for Copeau's work limited to the inner circle alone. Complete strangers stepped forth to express their solicitude. When *le patron* sent out a mimeographed appeal on December 15, 1915, for relief funds for Vieux-Colombier artists at war and for his unemployed actresses, the reply was spontaneous and generous. A total stranger, an American, called on Copeau and contributed 200 francs ($40). "Monsieur," Copeau quoted him in a letter to Jouvet, "I have seen Shakespeare played in all Europe and in America. I have never seen anything which resembles even remotely your production of *Twelfth Night*." Copeau compared this incident to the famous cry addressed to *"notre patron Molière"*: *"Bravo, Molière, voilà de la bonne comédie."* And he added when writing Jouvet of this:

> We have a host of friends who speak to us in the same language and who are ready to help us with their money, their time, their lives. That is why we must be certain of triumphing, in a way and to a degree never yet seen. There you have my feelings. *And if two or three share this work with me, I ask for no more in order to stir up the world.* Actually one must be *understood* by twenty or thirty persons to overcome the rest of the world, to carry it off by brute force. *Mon vieux*, let us do with all our strength all that can be done. *Let us not stop for an instant preparing, creating the future.* I shall never forget Martin du Gard telling me: 'I do not wish that either my wife or I should say to ourselves in ten years: We were privileged to be present at the birth of so admirable a thing and we did not do all that could be done when it came to devoting ourselves to it.' There you have

the word of the believer. That impossible rationalist has been touched by grace. *Ah! mon cher grand*, how I like to think that our work is a work of love.

On April 18, 1916, Copeau left Paris for Geneva, where he staged three plays and remained three months. Gaumont Films called upon him at this moment to become their artistic adviser. Copeau promptly wrote Jouvet: "It's nice, isn't it? There would probably be a lot of money in it. But I refused." How could Gaumont and Company know that but a few days before, on Christmas Day 1915, he had written Jouvet: "Maxim: let us always have our eyes fixed on the grandeur of our task and let us recognize, with genuine modesty, what we are worth. In general one sees oneself too small."

This work in Geneva under very trying conditions showed Copeau once again the superiority of the Vieux-Colombier. In a letter to Jouvet on May 16, 1916, he disclosed the reasons: "How well I see the road, how sure I am of the goal and the means. With you, *with all of you*, my children, what can I not attain? *With all of you*, there is the basic truth, the great miracle. All rests upon beings, all depends upon souls." Here was the echo of Copeau's strongest fear, the lack of a milieu.

Upon returning to Paris, Copeau hurried to see the structural changes he had ordered at the theater to increase the number of dressing rooms and thereby permit a similar increase in the troupe. He did well to hurry, for in that summer of 1916, his treasured period of freedom was drawing to a close. He had been taking an important part in counteracting German propaganda in Switzerland; his recent staging of three plays helped considerably. He followed this with a circular letter, signed by hand, inviting a number of outstanding French writers to contribute articles, suitable for publication in neutral countries, to maintain Allied cultural prestige in the German-speaking cantons.

At this point, although he had been judged physically unfit to fight for his country, he was judged artistically fit to enhance its prestige amongst prospective allies. The Minister of Fine Arts asked him to reassemble the Vieux-Colombier and tour the United States. Copeau agreed if his actors could be released from the trenches, but the War Ministry objected. Instead, Copeau alone was dispatched across the Atlantic as ambassador plenipotentiary of French culture. His knowledge of the classics and his experience in contemporary art and literature made him admirably suited to acquaint Americans with the culture his country was fighting to preserve.

On January 20, 1917, Copeau sailed from Bordeaux on the *S.S. Rochambeau* and arrived in the United States the following month to tell America what profound truths were smoldering in the hearts of French poets, novelists, dramatists, painters, and sculptors, and with what sublime beauty Gide, Bergson, Rodin, Debussy, and the others were giving form to those truths. He talked about his own brainchild, the Théâtre du Vieux-Colombier, what it had done and all that still remained to be done. Not once did he shout warnings that America should beware of the "Boche." He spoke only about art and literature, quietly and earnestly.

From the very first moment, no one could doubt the depth of his sincerity. His voice was gentle, serious, and honest, with a strange mixture of simplicity and authority, of pride and modesty in his mission. His eyes were dark and pensive except when he had to express either joy or indignation; then they would sparkle with fire and energy. The slow gestures of his thin, strong hands were expressive and to the point. His austere forehead and his thin, sharp, clean-shaven face, his almost bald head, the clear-cut design of his mouth and his straight prominent nose made people see in him a close resemblance to Dante.

His American listeners were struck by his logic and his common sense, and were surprised to find in him "a revolutionist without mannerism," a man who was "earnest, simple, magnetic." He was the model of his own words: "The essential thing is to give oneself without hope of reward."[19] This sincerity, which at times was so complete that it aroused Gide's suspicions during their early meetings, made Jacques Rivière dedicate an essay to Copeau, "On Sincerity Toward Oneself."

Upon request, he delivered his first lecture at Harvard University before Professor George Pierce Baker's 47 Workshop, America's vital and promising nucleus in theatrical art, where the Vieux-Colombier was already known and loved. Ten years earlier Copeau had smiled indulgently as he wrote of his "turbulent brothers of the new world."[20] In 1917, he found his country's future ally working, like himself, toward more modern stagecraft. Now he would smile a different smile. He was speaking to kindred spirits.

American art circles in the theater welcomed Copeau warmly. And while some, following the example of many French critics, reproached him for the somewhat puritanical tone that permeated his ideas, and subsequently his productions, others quickly recognized and admired his keen sense of pure art. Copeau strengthened these artists in their fight "to help conserve and develop creative impulse in the American theater." (These were the words the newly launched *Theater Arts Magazine*, renamed *Theater Arts Monthly*, used to justify its existence.) But the new movement was on the whole no more than a promise, as Sheldon Cheney wrote in 1914—even as reflected in some of the best little theaters: Washington Square Players, the Provincetown Playhouse, Stuart Walker's Portmanteau Theater. But the so-called American theater—Broadway, stock and road companies—was essentially controlled by business trusts. The product, good, bad, or indifferent, was all that mattered to them, so long as it sold and was in demand. Art was something for poets and painters to starve on in their garrets.

Copeau's six principal lectures, delivered in French at the Little Theater, were a resounding denunciation of everything Broadway, so like the French boulevard theaters, stood for. In his very first one, "Dramatic Art and the Commercial Theater," he told Americans what he had already told the French. For, even though he was a guest on an official mission in a foreign country and ought not to antagonize his hosts, he had been sent as an artist to speak of art.

As the lectures went on, Copeau won the confidence of his audiences more and more. He spoke of "Le Théâtre du Vieux-Colombier," "The Vieux-Colombier School," "New Dramatists," "The Reviving of Scenic Art," and "The Problem of the Modern Theater." An additional lecture, "Spirit in the Little Theater," was his first in English. In all of them he continually evoked the picture of "the shelter for future talent," of which he called himself a delegate-worker and which he tried to describe:

> I shall tell you what is new in the "house of the doves," and pure ... and invincible: it is a new spirit. Now, how shall I define that new spirit? I dare not say a religious spirit, yet I know it is a spirit of love. Love for beauty, for simplicity, and for the modest task we wish to perform; love for that life which breathes forever in the masterpieces of the past, which slumbers in our hearts and will inspire the unknown works of art of tomorrow.
>
> These valorous young men on the battlefield are now risking lives dedicated to the service of art. They have faced the enemy for more than two years. But their thoughts turn ever to the house of the doves. They keep watch over it, while they defend the national heritage. Two have already fallen. One, who still risks his life every day, has just written me: "My dear and best friend, I am going to tell you what you must do; you must take everything upon your shoulders ... and calmly face the possibility of keeping up the work *without us*. I also may be killed. Do not be disheartened, as long as the Vieux-Colombier survives. . . ." Such is the fervor of the *spirit* which inspires them. No wonder I am proud to be delegated by them to tell our friends in America of our past efforts, of the hope and faith we have in the future of the Vieux-Colombier.[21]

Many an American artist understood Copeau and the spirit of the Vieux-Colombier; for they, too, even though Americans, were part of that vast fraternity that Paul Valéry called "European man" and whom he defined not "by race, language or customs, but by aspiration and the scope of will."

Copeau was hardly midway in the task of undoing the French theater's reputation for frivolity, which was an important goal of his mission, and to relate what had been done to restore art to the drama, when rumors began to fly. People were talking about a Vieux-Colombier season in New

York that very year, whereas Copeau's visit had until then been considered a prelude to a postwar tour. On March 4, 1917, the *New York Times* reported that if the Vieux-Colombier, "artistic wonder of the French stage," came to New York "we would have . . . a French theater fit to represent France in America." A week later, Alexander Woollcott added his opinion of the current rumor: "Copeau has been hailed as the Antoine of today, and whose single season at the Vieux-Colombier electrified Paris and drew interested pilgrims from all over Europe. . . . If he comes next winter, perhaps he will let us see his idea of *Twelfth Night*. At least we should be allowed to see here, what is new and alive, and of fresh inspiration in the French theater." Copeau, for his part, commented that he had come to America simply to deliver a few lectures, and that was all.

The first two months he was busy fulfilling his mission, speaking in a number of Eastern cities and universities. It was not until the end of March that the well-known philanthropist Otto H. Kahn approached him with an offer to bring the Vieux-Colombier to New York. Everyone urged Copeau to accept. He took a month to think it over and asked the Minister of Fine Arts in Paris whether it would be possible to obtain the release of several of the actors from military service. When this was promised, he accepted with one condition: "at the first true dawn of peace I shall have to go back to my own work [in Paris where] . . . the Old Dove has been sleeping."[22]

While Copeau was concerned primarily with the development of his theater and the Minister with the welfare of France, Otto Kahn, too, had his reasons for backing the Vieux-Colombier: "to bring the best of European achievements in dramatic art before the eyes of the public and the artists of America is to render a valuable service to American art."[23] He had already sponsored the American fortunes of Matisse and Diaghilev's Russian Ballet with Nijinsky. It now seemed the right moment to serve dramatic art.

Interest in the drama as literature had increased phenomenally since 1900, a factor that was due mainly to Ibsen. But the theater in the United States needed "a sane persistent movement to educate the public taste in drama and improve the mental tenor of the average audience." There was the promise of such a movement in the growth of little theaters from three to fifty within five years, but artistically only one or two approached the European little theaters, and these, tucked away in New York's Greenwich Village, rarely played to an average audience. They were all experimenting madly, reaching "crude and intellectually undisciplined [results]."[24] The few that had good plays and sets fell far below the mark in acting. There was no one theater to serve as a model for all this agitated good will.

By inviting Copeau to transplant the entire organization of the Vieux-Colombier to New York for the 1917–1918 season, Kahn wished to permit American artists and audiences to observe a group of foreign artists in the very act of experimenting and creating under the disciplined direction of "the *régisseur* of the one theater in the world which seems manifestly most alive." The Vieux-Colombier represented the principles that American Little Theaters needed most: (1) it was a repertory theater, called by a responsible writer like John Palmer "the only system" for a healthy theater, in spite of Mrs. Fiske's assertion that "no single company, even after years of preparation, could give five entirely different plays and give them all properly"; (2) it was an experimental theater in search of new modes of expression to promote the unity and harmony of its productions, and this, Sheldon Cheney insisted, was precisely what typified in the United States the insurgent movement's "effort to find a synthesis of all the forces of the theater";" (3) it sought to bring into the theater and develop native dramatists, and in this respect America was very weak; (4) it was a revolutionary theater in reaction to the commercial houses on Boulevards and Broadway, and American artists had yet to learn how to counteract Erlanger and his crowd; (5) it saw the necessity to create and build an audience, and the American theater, too, according to Clayton Hamilton, suffered "tragically from lack of constant patronage by people of intelligence and taste."[25]

Otto Kahn perceived all this when he made his money and his good will available to Copeau; while, on the other hand, the French Minister of Fine Arts was convinced that now, more than ever, it was important to impress Americans with French culture. He must have been reminded that the *Mercure de France* had judged the Vieux-Colombier's English tour in 1914 "more useful to French art than a hundred publicized tours of famous stars." And Copeau was shocked to hear American theater people refer only to Germany and Russia, and never mention France in terms of the theater of the future. Besides, Reinhardt's secretary was obtaining funds to build branches of the *Berlin Deutsches Theater* in large American cities. The German Theater in New York was considered by many as the best in town, while the incumbent French Theater, Alexander Woollcott complained in the *Times* (March 11, 1917), going into its fourth season with old boulevard "war-horses," "has been a pretty sorry affair . . . conducted without taste, without artistic impulse and with less than a decent minimum of theater wisdom." Some of the French living in America stated bluntly that if the United States was not yet at war with Germany it was because German *Kultur* was considered superior to French culture. With the Vieux-Colombier in New York, there would constantly be in the public eye a proud, indestructible part of French art, and good art would be good propaganda.

As much as Copeau loved his country and as much as he appreciated Otto Kahn's motives, the Vieux-Colombier was to him a public trust and an important guarantee of survival for French culture. He would do nothing to abuse that trust nor jeopardize its future, not even for propaganda purposes. Thus far, he had abandoned all thought of personal security and comfort to establish and strengthen that guarantee. It was therefore certain, he explained in an interview with the *Times* (May 20, 1917), that he would have declined Mr. Kahn's proposal if it had meant leading the Vieux-Colombier toward betrayal:

> Our friends will say the Théâtre du Vieux-Colombier is growing too fast, one foot in the Old World and now one in the New. To them I say that were I not certain of maintaining the absolute moral integrity, the very soul and spirit of the Théâtre du Vieux-Colombier as it was in the beginning, and so save France with our spirit, with the same atmosphere—and, may I say, virtue—which was lauded at the start, I would not begin this undertaking.

Copeau saw definite advantages by playing in New York. He hoped the American metropolis would give his theater new life. The Vieux-Colombier could pick up where it left off, for what Copeau said in 1913 still held for 1917: his theater had to live if it was to have any effect. All the lessons learned from the first season and during the last three years of reflection, study and experiments could now be put to the test and developed even more. Then, once the war ended, it would return to Paris with its experience enriched and its confidence increased, with the added prestige of its propagandistic mission and with greater financial stability.

The advantages for the Vieux-Colombier appeared to be so overwhelming that even obvious difficulties were either disregarded or seemed relatively unimportant. Was a New York audience of 1917 sufficiently prepared to follow Copeau's advanced ideas in staging? Would French-speaking actors be able to convey their nuances and power of ensemble playing to foreigners? Would its repertory be too exacting for an audience fed until then on Broadway and rarely, if ever, touched by an American counterpart of an Antoine or a Lugné-Poe? How would the New World react to an Old World theater whose program was essentially traditional and national?[26]

As was his wont, Copeau saw only those obstacles that pertained to his art alone. All others were considered so completely secondary that he had not the least desire even to think about them. The idealist and the dreamer in him had a tendency to ignore difficulties of a practical nature while he had so many vital, immediate problems as director, author, or actor. When material obstacles finally forced themselves upon him and sought to color his vision as an artist, then only did he fight back defiantly, and sometimes compromise, reluctantly and grudgingly. For he had heart and mind in but one thing, the Vieux-Colombier.

4

New York
(1917–1919)

ON MAY 17, AT A RECEPTION in the Metropolitan Opera House with Dr. Nicholas Murray Butler presiding, Jacques Copeau was formally presented to New York as the new director of the French Theater. To a distinguished group gathered to do him honor, he expressed the wish to make of it "a home for all the friends of France, a home where truth and beauty will reign, and where forever in your midst we may hear the sweet language of France." And he appealed to his listeners not to be dismayed if told that the Vieux-Colombier was "but a small thing": "I am proud of this. It is because it is small that it is pure; because it is small it is only spirit, and so it must be pure; and being only spirit it has not been broken by the commercial difficulties of wartime. We are more united than ever."[1]

Although he could not announce the season's repertory, since it depended on what actors were released by the War Ministry, he did say that all styles of plays would be represented except "the gross and the vulgar . . . and we will prove to you that French writers can deal with something besides the eternal triangle."[2]

Copeau was proud and flattered to have his Vieux-Colombier acquaint America with the high level of French art, but he asked the general public not to interpret his art as a sign of snobbishness and be frightened away even before the theater had a chance to show its work. This appeal evoked praise from the press. Pitts Sanborn of the *New York Daily Tribune* (July 8, 1917) called him "the most advanced figure today in the race for theatrical renovation . . . he is bound to achieve important things, not only for the French drama, but for American dramatic art in New York." *Theater Arts Magazine* (May 1917) commented editorially that if he "accomplishes all that we hope for, we shall see the phenomenon of a French Theater becoming the first true theater in New York." Circumspect artists and critics, it went on to say, looked upon Copeau's coming season as "a sign of the times . . . and the best sign we know."

European artists also added words of praise for the Vieux-Colombier and these appeared in a pamphlet, A New French Theater in America, which was widely distributed. Claude Debussy found the theater "so clearly a form of French beauty, it should be shown and appreciated outside France." Igor Stravinsky wrote that it "represents French art in its most authentic and living sense." To Emile Verhaeren it was "the Theater of Today" and to Paul Claudel it symbolized "the best type of dramatic laboratory and workshop." Jules Jusserand, France's ambassador-scholar to the United States, wired Otto H. Kahn: "Copeau's past is the best guarantee for the future."

While these encomiums were being showered upon Copeau, he was busy attending to preparations for the coming season. The board of directors of the reorganized Théâtre-Français des Etats-Unis—Otto H. Kahn, Robert Goelet, Nicholas Murray Butler, Paul D. Cravath, Theodore Roosevelt Jr., Cornelius Vanderbilt, and their colleagues—had offered him the new Bijou Theater, located right in the heart of Broadway, but he preferred the old Garrick Theater on 35th Street, between Fifth and Sixth Avenues, which was outside the immediate range of Broadway's artificial glitter and which he could remodel to suit his own needs. As in 1913 with the Athénée-Saint-Germain, he again had an artist-architect, this time Antonin Raymond, redecorate the house for the requirements of the new theater.[3] Leaving behind a general manager familiar with his plans, he set sail for France to reassemble his company, bag and baggage, for the sixteen-week season that was to start on November 20. Prior to his departure the name of the Garrick Theater was changed to the Théâtre du Vieux-Colombier de New York.

In June, Copeau was back in Paris organizing everything for as early a departure as possible. The ministries plodded slowly through his requests, so that it was not until the beginning of October that the first few actors were able to leave for America. In the end, the War Ministry refused to release one of Copeau's best actors, Charles Dullin. Louis Jouvet, however, was freed, primarily because he was in Paris on a two-month sick leave. Several other charter members were made available: Romain Bouquet, Lucien Weber, Suzanne Bing, Valentine Tessier, and Jane Lory. Blanche Albane chose to remain in France to be close to her husband, Georges Duhamel, whose training as a physician made him essential to the Medical Corps. Copeau also chose a number of very young players who wished to work under his disciplined direction: Emile Chifoliau, André Chotin, Jean Sarment (soon after, the well-known author-actor-producer),

Jacques Vildrac, Renée Bouquet, Lucienne Bogaert, and Madeleine Geof-froy. In addition, several well-established actors joined the Vieux-Colom-bier out of admiration for its work, among them François Gournac, Henri Dhurtal, Marcel Millet, Marcel Vallée, Paulette Noizeux, and Eugénie Nau. Mlle. Van Doren, an actress in whom Copeau had long admired "the equilibrium and spiritual force of a soul that never lost contact with daily life,"[4] was fortunately free to join the company as well. Gaston Gallimard, publisher of the *Nouvelle Revue Française*, continued as the theater's business manager. Jouvet resumed the functions of general stage manager as well as actor, and Copeau enlisted the services of costumers, designers, propmen, and dancing and singing instructors. Sets and cos-tumes, old and new, were shipped to New York, along with the little statue of Molière to be placed as usual in the lobby of the theater.

On October 10, the friends of the Vieux-Colombier gathered to bid them godspeed. From the stage of the theater, Copeau told them of his hope to see a Vieux-Colombier in every Allied capital. He also promised that the main one would remain in Paris, in the clean "little dairy shop" into which they were now crowded to hear the master's last words be-fore departure. At the end of October, Copeau set sail once more for the country that he described in a letter to Jouvet (February 25, 1917) as "the land of infinite possibilities . . . marvelously young, chaotic, and which does not know its very self."

During these four months, the American supporters of the venture were also busy, sometimes at cross purposes. A publicity campaign had been launched to assure the enterprise a successful season. Subscriptions were going well, $20,000 having been received by the middle of October. A newly organized Women's Auxiliary named special committees for Chi-cago, Boston, Philadelphia, and Washington to arrange for post-season performances. Also, Le Cercle des Amis de la France was formed by Mrs. Philip Lydig, who was Copeau's helpful guide during his lecture tour. Mrs. August Belmont, Nicholas Murray Butler, Miss Ida Tarbell, and others tried to transform the large residence at 261 Madison Avenue into a home for some of the actors and a meeting-place for those interested in French culture. Unfortunately, this project was never realized. To underline even further the Frenchness of the whole undertaking, musicians like Yvette Guilbert, Pierre Monteux, Jacques Thibaud, and Robert Casadesus, and the Society of Ancient Instruments, as well as the Capet Quartet, consid-ered the theater their headquarters. The Vieux-Colombier became the cen-ter and inspiration of French culture in America, even before its arrival.

Copeau, with his wife and three children, reached the port of New York on November 11. His liner, the *Chicago*, had been forced to aban-don its usual course, now infested with German submarines, and so lost several days. The opening was postponed to give the troupe much needed time for additional rehearsals. On the night of the 27th, a week later than scheduled, the first-night audience came to see not a glamorous star's virtuosity nor a boulevard playwright's latest concoction to tickle an audience—the Vieux-Colombier had none of these—but simply the escapades of the sly rogue in *Les Fourberies de Scapin.* "Molière reborn!" John Corbin exclaimed in the *Times* (December 2, 1917).

Suzanne Bing stepped before the curtain to offer a "greeting . . . and a smile from France in the midst of war." This salutation over, the whole company, from director to stagehand, proceeded in turn to be introduced, respectfully explained their task at the Vieux-Colombier and trusted that the people of New York would follow understandingly what they were trying to do. Copeau painted modestly the aims of his work and his co-workers: "I am simply a man who performs his job as best he can, learning it each day, and each day discovering something he did not know the day before. I leave to others the task of describing our Old Dove-Cote as a 'temple of art'. And I beg of you to believe that our modesty is not feigned when we say simply that we wish to make of our house a clean house, worthy of the public's respect and the poet's friendship."[5]

Copeau thus took New Yorkers to heart in his *Impromptu du Vieux-Colombier,* just as Molière had taken Louis XIV's court to heart in "*L'Impromptu de Versailles.*" The evening continued with Molière's three-act farce on the escapades and knavery of Scapin; and the festivities ended with the Crowning of Molière, in which the Spirit of Drama through the centuries, from Aristophanes to Shakespeare, Corneille and Beaumarchais down to the present day, addressed Albert Marque's little plaster statue of the patron saint of the house. Then, as with the ceremonial crowning of famous authors at the Comédie-Française, a wreath was placed on Molière's brow by Copeau's nine-year old son, Pascal, while the Orchestra of Ancient Instruments played softly in the wings. In this way the first performance came to a close, in homage to the man in whom Theater was incarnated as both art and institution.

Most critics regarded Copeau's *Impromptu* and the Molière crowning as so much "elaborate hocus-pocus," but in *Les Fourberies de Scapin* they now saw why Copeau had so strongly stressed the actor's physical education in his lectures of the past winter. Here was a play acted with the body far more than with the brain or the voice. Copeau's vigor and litheness in the role of Scapin surprised and delighted those to whom Molière had become an awesome national idol. Géronte, the old miserly father, was given a masterful characterization by Jouvet, who abandoned the traditional cane in favor of an umbrella against the strong Neapolitan sun. One felt that the commedia dell' arte had been revived in all its freshness and freedom. Copeau tried to give the play back its Italian tradition of violence and cruelty by means of movement, and by means of the mask, used to establish consistency of mood. The critics saw this, but were not impressed by what they called a "boisterous and primitive farce . . . which furnished no adequate test of the merits of the Copeau company." They surmised that any actor with good direction could do as much, which was "very little . . . [in this] two hundred-year old farce . . . tiresome in the extreme, viewed by modern standards."[6] Farce, which Paul Claudel called "the highest expression of lyric style," they looked on as nothing more than a Punch and Judy show.

The empty stage with its small platform in the center provoked more pros and cons than anything in New York for quite some time. Along with the usual bare stage to set off the acting, Copeau used the small platform to focus the audience's attention even more on the actor's movements. This was an innovation that some called "highly experimental" and successful "in the main," but most critics did not see the need for it at all, and Louis De Foe in the *New York World* even declared that "freak drama had obtained a new start in New York." On the other hand, Professor A. G. H. Spiers of Columbia University wrote in *The Nation* that Copeau's version was a revelation. The only other critical praise was John Corbin's appreciation (in the *New York Times* of December 6, 1917) of "the unfolding of a managerial intelligence as fresh and subtle as it is original." On the whole, the Vieux-Colombier attracted very small audiences to its opening bill, although Copeau considered it the finest, in many respects, that he had ever given.

One week later, the same critics marveled at the new bill's superiority. Even the "freak drama" man was impressed by the company's versatility in the colorful acting of the three one-acters, each of a different literary period: Becque's *La Navette*, Mérimée's *Le Carrosse du Saint-Sacrement*, and Molière's *La Jalousie du barbouillé*. Mérimée's play was the evening's delight, so vividly did Copeau animate a text that the French had ignored for almost a century as impossible to stage. The costumes, color, and lighting made of the Peruvian setting a tropical atmosphere that, combined with script and actor, revealed the author as a real dramatist and America's discovery. The *New York Times* called it "a rare triumph" already justifying the company's presence in the United States and urged no one to miss "one of the rare privileges of our theater." One could not help thinking back to the time when Musset's plays were discovered in Russia while they remained unplayed and neglected in the *bouquiniste* boxes along the Seine.

To start with, six plays—four of them revivals from 1913—were alternated during the first month in New York. On Christmas Eve, *Twelfth Night* made its bow with almost all the same actors in the principal parts as in 1914. Arthur Hornblow in *Theater Arts Magazine* called it "a gem of dramatic accomplishment," even though he found nothing Anglo-Saxon in Sir Toby or Jouvet's Sir Andrew, whose acting of the part he nevertheless acclaimed. In the English version, everything revolves about Viola, while Malvolio is painted as a conceited fool who is blind to the very end.

> The French people have shifted all these values. Viola and the Duke sink into second place, their scenes come as interruptions in the sparkling current of events. The plot gathers around a jest, the humor broadened to the hilarious spirit of low comedy. We see the novel spectacle of a classic, the translation following the text with admirable fidelity, changed from a poetic romance of unrequited love to a romping farce of invariable good-humored grace, in which a practical joke plays the star role.[7]

No one objected to this so long as there were so many hearty laughs. Producers contemplating Shakespearean revivals were urged by the *New York Tribune*'s drama critic (February 25, 1919) to see this *Twelfth Night*:

> They will find a performance of such freshness and spontaneity that it exhibits no signs of a resurrection. The roistering comedy was done last night as if for the first time on any stage, and with as much care.
> All the signs of a Shakespeare revival, the ancient scenery, the creaking mechanism, the pair of stars and the inferior company, were noticeably not present. . . . The *Twelfth Night* in French should be recognized as a blessing to English-speaking lovers of the living Shakespeare.

Everyone was almost unreservedly enthusiastic. French-speaking actors were no hindrance to understanding the play. On the contrary, John Corbin (*New York Times*, February 9, 1919) found that the performance had "an authenticity and integrity such as is seldom found in the performances of English-speaking companies," while Arthur Hornblow (*Theatre Magazine*, February 1918) stated that the French had "a nicer simplicity than the Granville-Barker revolutionary venture and thereby gained in distinct effect." As a lesson to stock companies in ensemble acting, in which Little Theaters were most weak, the Vieux-Colombier now became "the most assertive indication of the triumph of the Little Theater."[8] The sets, too, attracted their share of attention, but the public had already been prepared for this by the clever, tasteful use of draperies, curtains, screens, and lights in *Le Carrosse du Saint-Sacrement* and *Barberine*, which had been played just before *Twelfth Night*. The whole production proved to be in New York what it had been in Paris, a bottomless well for the imagination.

By the end of the first month, the Vieux-Colombier had reached its mark to the satisfaction of many of those concerned with the art of the theater. The public at large, however, did not appear interested in art. They wanted, as always, to be overwhelmed and pushed into adoration. Copeau's troupe had not yet been able to do this, even with *Twelfth Night*. The classics, French or English, were not popular enough in America to attract a large audience, in spite of Copeau's originality and recreative power in staging them. And the three principal productions thus far, *Les Fourberies de Scapin*, *Barberine* and *Twelfth Night*, were all classics. Copeau had no alternative, for there had been precious little time to rehearse new actors in an unfamiliar repertory of modern plays. But now, with the theater organized and working more smoothly, five modern plays, unlikely to be done in English, were scheduled for production.

The first one appeared on January 8, *La Nouvelle Idole* by François de Curel. Copeau was praised for finally producing the moderns, but his company, with its comparatively weak feminine contingent, did not delineate clearly enough the more difficult scenes. In any case, it was no easy matter to arouse a non-French audience's sympathy when ideas more than action constituted the play's merits. Those who were able to follow the plot felt it was dated and remote, but were glad, nonetheless, that the French company had at last broken away from the classics, and especially from Molière's farces, which the public as a whole considered an inferior literary genre compared to his more imposing five-act plays.

The big day for the moderns, however, came with the production of the play that had brought Copeau recognition in France and that was to leave its mark on America: *Les Frères Karamazov*. So immediate and popular was its success that after the first performance the small house had to install kitchen chairs in front of the first row to accommodate the crowds. Not only was it lauded as the highest type of melodrama, because truthful situations and deep psychological characterizations created its intensity, but the dismal poignancy of Dostoevsky and the Russian spirit of the play stamped it as one of the outstanding offerings of the New York season, on and off Broadway. The enthusiasm of a young theater artist like Rollo Peters, expressed in *Theater Arts Magazine* (February 1918), would seem to justify Otto H. Kahn's reason for bringing Copeau's company to America:

> In the last four years in New York, I can remember two magnificent symphonic productions in which the action and the actors were fused in a fusion incredibly suggestive of life: Emanuel Reicher's presentation of *The Weavers*, and now Jacques Copeau's production of *Les Frères Karamazov*. . . . Those who are skeptical as to the true value of what this French Theater has brought to us—something for the American Theater to feel and profit by: a sincerity, a mastery of a true technique—will forget a certain artificiality in the plays produced earlier in the season. Through the passion of this sincerity, out of the fusion of the individual actors, Life rises before us.
>
> Here is the epitome of art: not a comfort or a shallow myth, but the intensification of life itself. The faults in the production, in the

play, of the separate actors, become as the common faults of the World of Men.

To Jacques Copeau and to his confreres all thanks. He has reassured us, has given us strength to labor and to struggle for a Theater which will become stronger than the Church, in that it has league with Life.

This production gave the cast its moment for highly emotional acting, in which the French have always excelled. In spite of the fact that Dullin was not there to play Smerdiakov, the company as a whole was highly praised and rated as a unique homogeneous ensemble. In addition, old Feodor's house with its angular stairway, seen in the third and fifth acts, on which Smerdiakov moved up and down, now slinking, now darting, created the atmosphere before a single word had been spoken.

When the Vieux-Colombier played *Les Frères Karamazov* in Washington, it was denounced as "Bolshevik drama." Still, neither slurs nor slogans could break its attraction in New York, where it became as firmly entrenched on the stage as in fiction. And every time it was given, there was a full house, which was not the fate of the plays that followed it from January 31 to almost the end of the season in April.

With the success of the modern *Karamazov*, press and public alike smiled knowingly and said to Copeau, "See?" He began to wonder himself whether more modern plays, even if inferior to the classics, were not the best way of winning a public over to greater appreciation of the classics. Perhaps he should give in to public taste a little more? In France he knew his public, in America he did not. For the moment, then, he would give them such plays as *La Traverse* by Villeroy, *La Petite Marquise* by Meilhac and Halévy, and *Les Mauvais Bergers* by Octave Mirbeau. The latter's *Les Affaires sont les affaires* had been successfully produced in New York some years before. *Les Mauvais Bergers* fell flat. It was even reported that the opening curtain went up on a full house and by the time the last act came around, the only audience left was the ushers. The moderns, it seemed, were meeting with the same reaction as the classics, and not until almost the end of the season did "success" return.

Copeau managed to obtain Dullin's release from the army, but only after he had been wounded, transferred to the rear, and placed on sick leave. With Dullin back, Copeau decided to risk putting on *L'Avare*, a more serious five-act play, even though the short, lighter comedies of Molière had been so badly received. It opened on March 19, about two weeks before the end of a difficult season. By then, 182 performances had been given of sixteen works, of which but 26 performances constituted the only two real successes of the season: *Twelfth Night* and *Les Frères Karamazov*. When the final curtain fell on *L'Avare*, Copeau was pleasantly surprised to discover that it was being put alongside *Karamazov*

as a hit of the season, "raising the company to a height it had not hith-
erto attained in the minor plays of Molière thus far presented." The public
had resented being shown only the farces of a great writer instead of what
they had been taught to regard as his masterpieces. But watching Dullin's
powerful creation of Harpagon, even the *New York World* critic who had
lashed out at Copeau for "eccentric" staging admitted that in *L'Avare* the
"Théâtre du Vieux-Colombier easily touched the highest point of artistic excellence of its entire first season."[9]

Copeau could afford to smile. In May 1914, Shakespeare aroused Paris
to flock to the Vieux-Colombier. In April 1918, the poet is Molière, the
place New York—"*ce mortel et dédaigneux New York*," a well-known
French critic had complained fifty years earlier.[10]

That "deadly and scornful New York" nearly ruined the Vieux-Colombier's first season. Except for three or four plays out of twenty—that is,
56 performances out of a total of 202—audiences remained fairly indifferent to its "seventeenth century bric-a-brac," according to the *New York
World*. Few of the French living in New York were patrons, and Americans felt little attraction to a language they could not understand. This
limited audiences almost exclusively to students of French literature. High
society's interest in the Vieux-Colombier had dwindled quite early in the
season. But their sponsorship, as well as the higher prices prevailing there
compared to other theaters, which was remedied in mid-season, caused
Copeau to be criticized as a highbrow. He answered that his theater was
not catering to intellectuals and the rich. He would like everyone to come,
but begged people to appreciate why he could not make his theater into
a house that would appeal to New York's five million inhabitants. On
March 27, 1918, in an address before the Drama League of America, he
told them that was not why he had come to America: "Any misunder-
standing that may have arisen between the American public and myself
was due to unawareness of the spirit behind my work, and of the scope
of my struggle. Some people took me for a producer, and I am trying to
be an artist. They wished to make an opportunist of me, while the fact is
I am a fighter."

He warned and warned again against mixing business with art:

> America is a meeting-place for the seekers of fortune, the great
> consumer of sensational novelties. It must beware of this. Everything
> springs up too quickly in this virgin soil. The grain follows too closely
> upon the flower. A man becomes exhausted here more quickly than
> elsewhere. Now the artist, very slowly, discovers what God has en-
> trusted to him. If the notion of rapid and brutal success can be fruitful
> in the industrial or commercial world, it is absolutely disastrous from
> the point of view of art.

Those were the words of Craig, too, of Appia and Stanislavsky, of that
small family of seekers after the truth who always saw the many imper-

fections in their work and sometimes perceived glimmers of a more finished, mature art. There were Americans, like Rollo Peters, who needed desperately to have these words of leadership and encouragement. It was, therefore, to Otto Kahn's credit that he wished to see Copeau's words sustained and so assured him once more the necessary funds to continue on in New York for another season.

The second one, unlike the first, was prepared thoroughly, if not less hurriedly. The company had little more than four months at its disposal for work and rehearsals in the country, at Otto Kahn's summer home in Morristown, New Jersey, where they lived as his guests. As in 1913 at Le Limon, Copeau and his actors set out to develop a repertory of twenty-two full plays and six one-acters, of which nineteen and four respectively were new to the company. At least half the total number were more or less completely alien to the kind of works Copeau would normally choose to give, but public pressure was such that he had to succumb to the average taste, just as the revolutionary and independent Antoine of twenty years before had had to adapt his tours to provincial tastes.

Henry Bernstein's *Le Secret* opened the new season midst shouts of hallelujah from the critics, now that the Vieux-Colombier was meeting the public halfway. For Copeau it was more like all the way. Ten years before, on May 10, 1907, in an article for *La Grande Revue* on "amoral theater," he had roundly reproached Bernstein for "his taste for the picturesque . . . most trivial aspect of art." Besides, David Belasco, the man who stood for everything artificial and stodgy in the American theater, who represented the antithesis of what the new stagecraft and the Little Theaters were fighting for, had presented Broadway with the same *Secret* only three years earlier. To Copeau, this was an avowal of disgust with himself, with his public, and the critics, whose line of attack against the Vieux-Colombier confirmed that it was the new art of the theater and their Little Theater protagonists that were being flayed in the person of their closest representative to Broadway. Copeau had to give his American audience *their* plays if they were to come at all to see *his*. This was the kind of concession he never made in France and for which he never forgave America. After this experience, he never allowed the reins of control to escape from his hands to such an extent: the 25 percent of attractive box-office repertory in the first New York season had jumped to 75 percent in the second.

On Armistice Day, November 11, 1918, *Le Voile du bonheur* by Georges Clemenceau was presented; from February 17 to the 24th, an American play by Percy MacKaye, *Washington*, was produced in French. Modern love triangles and spy plays shared the place of honor. Erckmann-Chatrian, Augier and Sandeau, Brieux and Hervieu, Rostand and Capus, Donnay and the younger Dumas, each had his day during an inhumanely exhausting season that forced the theater to open every Monday night with a new bill. The usual three changes per week that the company had always adhered to had been dropped in favor of a schedule that people could remember more easily. They did. The house was full at almost each performance and the season provided a neat financial profit. Copeau played the box-office game and so did the public.

But he had to breathe a bit of his art if he were to survive the year. Beaumarchais (*Le Mariage de Figaro*) followed Bernstein's *Le Secret*, and so Copeau managed to clear the atmosphere a little. He created an evocative mise-en-scène for Maeterlinck's *Pelléas et Mélisande*, in which Suzanne Bing as Mélisande and Jean Sarment as Pelléas gave outstanding performances. Even Copeau's ten-year-old son, Pascal, was applauded as Yniold, the one and only role he was ever to act. Molière *(Le Médecin malgré lui)* and Ibsen *(Rosmersholm)* were barely enough to instill some fresh life into the blood of his theater after Dumas's *La Femme de Claude*. And so it went on until the bitter end, when Copeau tried to atone for his sins with a final grand gesture of thankfulness for having lived through a perilous voyage. His mea culpa was laid at the feet of one of Molière's most exacting works: *Le Misanthrope*. Copeau, of course, played Alceste, the man whose exaggerated sense of honor and relentless sincerity finally cause his downfall.

If, once and for all, Copeau learned his lesson, the critics, too, learned theirs. The cry for modern plays answered, they were soon forced to admit that "more satisfaction if not more enjoyment is to be attained from the classical plays than from the modern," to quote Arthur Hornblow in *Theatre Magazine* from December 1918. They even called satisfaction and enjoyment synonymous for those who liked the classics. The critic who had once shouted the loudest for Copeau to play the moderns and satisfy the public now wrote that the stage cannot progress by catering to the box office. Copeau's faith in the proven works of the past was amply vindicated, but too late to change matters. He had already become a disappointed and grievously pained man, waiting impatiently for the day he would return home with the Vieux-Colombier, back "to their poverty and to their perfection."[11]

On April 7, they gave a farewell benefit performance to augment their funds with which to start off again in Paris. Appropriately enough, the play was *La Coupe enchantée* (*The Magic Bowl*—to be filled with gold) by La Fontaine and Champmeslé. At the same time, an association of Friends of the Vieux-Colombier in New York was formed in appreciation for the theater's hard work.

The City of New York did not wish to be left out of the festivities. Editorials like the one in the *New York Daily Tribune* for April 9, 1919, ranked the Vieux-Colombier with "the highest artistic achievements in the city's history." Copeau was called the kind of leader by whom civilization was saved. Artists and critics chose this moment to express their thanks to Copeau for becoming the inspiration of American theaters with the same ideals as his. The so-called new stagecraft spoke up more proudly and more courageously than ever before. The Vieux-Colombier became "the stimulus," as *The Nation* pointed out on March 29, 1919, for all who demanded that the American theater "turn from the chase of dollars to join France's pursuit of dramatic vitality, simplicity and truth."

Copeau felt, when writing of this experience many years later, that he had jeopardized his "meager savings of creative force."[12] He was too upset and much too overwrought to realize that his work had not gone unnoticed in spite of tremendous handicaps. America's entry into the war and the decision to bring his theater to New York had coincided. For months, France's new, unprepared ally was overwhelmed by the everyday problems that reached deep down into everyone's time and energy. Then came peace with its new problems and decisions. From one end of this unsettled period to the other, the Vieux-Colombier, a small French company with no reputation in America, with nothing to recommend it but its spirit, tried to do in the New York of 1917 what it had done in the Paris of 1913. The fact that it went through two seasons was a miracle of courage and perseverance. The fact that at this difficult time it was so faithfully followed and appreciated by the art world and left such a lasting impression in America was no less a miracle. Through sheer grit and labor it had won the respect and admiration of Americans at one of the most tumultuous periods in American history.

5

Reaching the Parisian Heights
(1919–1921)

SPEAKING WITH JOUVET ON BOARD the liner that was carrying them home, Copeau reflected how bitterly depressed he had become from the semi-exploitation to which they had just been subjected. As if to add insult to injury, at the close of the troupe's tour in Chicago, Copeau's personal wardrobe had been stolen from his room in Sherwood Anderson's home. In addition, Dullin had decided to leave the company. Jouvet answered *le patron* by summing up the feelings of both: "In spite of it all, we never stopped working."[1]

The creative force that Copeau felt he had almost lost in New York had in reality flowered in the soil of America. Here it was that he tested and developed the multifarious ideas and visions culled especially from *Twelfth Night* in 1914, from experiments with his actor-students in 1915 and 1916, and from the staging of several Vieux-Colombier plays in Geneva in 1916. These were the stepping-stones that in 1919 brought him back to Paris to remodel his Vieux-Colombier while waiting for the opportunity "to build a new theater on absolutely intact foundations." For the first time, perhaps, Copeau saw where he was going and where he was to go, what he had to steer clear of and what he had to cling to. His new theater would be no artificial structure built on sand, with an elaborate outside and a deadly emptiness inside.[2] The foundations of his theater were to be set in place the hard way, through practical experience. Then he could at last build confidently as a master of his craft.

After a much-needed rest and leisurely but thorough rehearsals in the country, during which time he and Suzanne Bing began their Shakespeare collaboration by finishing the translation of *Winter's Tale* for the reopening, Copeau came to Paris to resume work. While in 1913 he had announced the birth of his theater in newspapers and magazines, in 1919 his first statement was not for the press. Late in November, he called together his ever-widening circle of supporters who had encouraged the Vieux-Colombier during the hard as well as the good times. He confided in them his hopes and his fears. He told them frankly that he did not want their financial help alone; he asked for their moral support first, then let them help, willingly and eagerly, and not as a gesture of charity for a worthy cause. He invited those before him to become part of a critical, constructive nucleus that could be counted on for clear, unbiased opinions. He clarified from the very start what New York had misunderstood. The Vieux-Colombier was not a theater for intellectuals; it wanted the unsophisticated to come to it as well. Nor was it an avant-garde theater that meant to thrive on its originality and a temporary attractiveness for the curious-minded. He again reminded his listeners that this was no revolutionary movement, since its strongest bond was still with the classics.

For six years Copeau had waited patiently to bare his soul in this way to an understanding audience. After the first talk, there was a second and a third, and with each communion came added strength and greater confidence to the man whom hostility so easily froze into bitterness and resentment. Again and again he told his listeners that his theater was the "enemy of all lies." His dream was a theater from which he would strike all artifice, awkwardness, compromise, and dishonesty. This time, he would not postpone what he had wanted to do in 1913. There would be organized a well-rounded Vieux-Colombier School, and its objective would be to establish the healthiest conditions possible for creation. This time, Copeau pointed out to Henri Ghéon, there would be no compromise: "We start from the bottom with dependable people to study the problems of actor, dramatist, critic and the theater."[3] Everything false and pretentious would be removed so that they would become a force in the resurrection of French culture.

The password was to be sincerity. Copeau warned that this should not be confused with impetuosity, generosity, or spontaneity. His kind of sincerity was the accumulated result of maturity, coming only after much reflection and many years of experience and experimentation. Such sincerity, he believed, could be molded without forcing one's nature or incurring the moral and artistic disaster of becoming snobbish and artificial. This "lifting up of the theater on another plane," in the words of Waldo Frank, bore the imprint of Péguy's moral influence, whose memory Copeau invoked constantly as a reminder of his theater's lofty and unselfish purpose.

This direct appeal to his countrymen for help bore fruit at a moment in war-weary France when everyone was in despair in spite of victory and peace:

> You have made the Vieux-Colombier. The War has not destroyed it. We don't have to repeat everything since you are here. All we do is continue. We haven't changed. We are the same people, we want the same things, and we want them even more. If you think we were right in 1913, if you think that in this loose and incoherent state where we see the theater after the war our work is more urgent and our influence more timely than ever, then . . .

At the end of 1919, in answer to these heart-to-heart talks, Les Amis du Vieux-Colombier became a formal organization, not of actors or writers, but of ordinary friends; and a few weeks later, they brought him the money he still needed to open his theater.

The essence of these talks was printed in the first number of *Les Cahiers du Vieux-Colombier*, entitled "Les Amis du Vieux-Colombier," a publication very dear to the heart of Copeau. He had conceived the idea during the war, and with the enthusiasm so prevalent during that "heroic time of beginnings" he had written Jouvet on August 25, 1915:

> There is one thing to which I should like you to attach importance . . . that is the great Vieux-Colombier periodical. Make it the book where every discovery of good artisans will be recorded . . . And all that takes place in foreign countries will find its place in it. I am beginning to acquire correspondents in every country. I want people to speak of this publication from the very start as much as one speaks of the theater. That is where we shall be in touch with reality, *mon vieux*. You'll see. . . . We must be in the first rank, superior to all the others; we must prove it . . . [by having a] stage and journal. Craig, the only worthwhile theorist, is incomplete because he has no stage.

This would require a more careful selection of repertory in order to assure the stage-to-journal idea its maximum influence. Once again Parisian kiosks bore lively red and green posters announcing that the Théâtre du Vieux-Colombier would reopen with Shakespeare's *Winter's Tale*. (This time the young playwright Marcel Achard was prompter.) Having ended its one and only Paris season with a resounding Shakespeare success, it now wished to pick up the threads of those pleasant memories with another Shakespearean fantasy. Copeau could choose no clearer way to assure Paris of its continuation.

The Winter's Tale was produced in approximately the same vein as *Twelfth Night*, but this time, the fixed architectural design of the stage caught the critics unawares. They found this type of theater entirely too unusual for their taste. They did not relish the idea of seeing a play performed on a bare stage with gray walls at the back clearly visible. They balked and complained but, unlike the critics of 1913, did not dare ignore the Vieux-Colombier. They were by no means convinced that, even if Shakespeare did write a play mainly interested in characterization, Copeau should limit his theater to that alone. One critic, Alfred Savoir, began to plead for a League of Protection Against Masterpieces. But if the set was found too severe, the costumes made up for this by their vivid colors and striking designs, as conceived by the painter Fauconnet. The text, an extraordinarily faithful translation, dragged in spots and lacked the archaic flavor of Lascaris's *Twelfth Night*. Yet Professor Albert Feuillerat, a Shakespearean scholar, gave it a place of honor as being in a "French form worthy of Shakespeare."[4] André Suarès once more praised the troupe's loving and absolute submission to the great works of poetry, and Antoine recognized in its sincerity an art center everyone ought to support. But Copeau was plainly disappointed by the predominantly lukewarm reception accorded a play into which he had poured so much love and exuberance, and which he had in 1915 felt to be "something wonderful."

The Vieux-Colombier, however, did not have to wait until its final production in order to win over Paris. Copeau was still experimenting, to be sure, but his apprenticeship, with its uncertainties and fumbling, was almost at an end. Now he knew what he wanted even if he was not always sure of getting it, and his next bill demonstrated this more than anything Paris had seen since Antoine had made the capital dance to his tune. On March 5, he offered Mérimée's *Le Carrosse du Saint-Sacrement* and Charles Vildrac's *Le Paquebot Tenacity*, a production that returned the Vieux-Colombier to its prewar status as the one hope of the French theater.

Paris, like New York, was amazed by the ingenuous atmosphere in *Le Carrosse*, created synthetically by four flower pots, a screen, two vibrantly colorful costumes, and a stage bathed in yellow light. Prosper Mérimée was greatly admired by nineteenth-century contemporaries for his short stories such as "Carmen," but completely ignored as a dramatist, except by scholars. *Le Carrosse*, for example, was buried in a volume of his plays called *Théâtre de Clara Gazul* and became a huge success in 1920, thanks to Copeau's artistic instinct and his keen perception of the author's sense of irony and "art for art's sake" aloofness.

The charm of this forgotten play capped what was already a brilliant evening. *Le Paquebot Tenacity* had opened the program, and in this drama of everyday life, where man's will does not control his destiny, Copeau achieved one of his greatest feats as metteur-en-scène. The idea of theater disappeared completely. As soon as the curtains parted, disclosing two young men making their future plans, the audience saw itself standing alongside the characters on the stage, sharing and experiencing their pain, sorrow, and joy, their doubts and their confusion. They listened anxiously to Georges Vitray's Bastien and Jean Legoff's Segard as one would to the story of a dear friend. For two priceless hours the audience lived the perfect life: the life of the imagination.

The story was more than just simple, it was touchingly naive. The strong-willed Bastien and his sensitive follower are on their way to settle in Canada. Their ship, the *S.S. Tenacity*, is being repaired in a French port while they wait in a workers' restaurant-hotel near the pier. Thérèse, the barmaid, played by Catherine Jordaan, easily wins Segard's love. Bastien, just as easily, wins over the girl and runs off with her to some corner of France to lead the kind of life he would have normally lived. Segard, left on his own, leaves for Canada, a little doubtful and somewhat afraid, but reluctant to give up the adventure.

The stage set is the counter of a bar, two tables, four chairs—the triumph of drama over display and Copeau's best proof thus far that a good play needed no decorative propping-up.

This feat was realized in Charles Vildrac's first play, *Le Paquebot Tenacity*, a work guided by the double concept of pity and love, of bitterness and optimism.

With this production, Antoine, whose critical eye recognized superior writers, proclaimed the Vieux-Colombier "the most artistic corner of Paris: I truly felt the other evening that the future is there. M. Copeau is finishing up the invention of a really new and unexpected instrument which we need for another stage revolution, and if he reveals works to us, it is over his house that the star will rise."[5]

Most critics could not fit it into one category or another, for it seemed to belong to several. It had a classic sobriety of language, the symbolist's pursuit of the unknown and the realist's slice of everyday life. No one could say exactly what it was, and so it was called "a kind of masterpiece." The critics treated it with the respect due a genuinely moving drama and with the professional skepticism due their readers when discussing a new type of play. But as others began to appear, Vildrac's drama took on the force of a precursor; the critics eventually evolved the convenient label of "the School of Silence," because emotions were usually evoked by the discreet means of subtle pauses and subconscious hints, never bombastic phrases or overt actions. Regardless of critics or labels, the public flocked to see *Le Paquebot Tenacity*.

One month later, Georges Duhamel exhibited what he had learned as a playwright while living in such intimacy with the Vieux-Colombier. He described to me this attachment in musical terms: a composer creates a harp concerto because there is a harpist he has in mind to play it. "The Vieux-Colombier was our instrument." Copeau asked for no better proof of his theater's influence amongst writers who had until then not been dramatists. *L'Oeuvre des athlètes*, was produced while the theater was being filled by *Le Paquebot Tenacity* and *Le Carrosse du Saint-Sacrement*. (Copeau had returned to the old rule of three changes per week.) Henry Bordeaux in the *Revue hebdomadaire* (April 1920) waxed enthusiastic over Duhamel's satire of an ambitious hypocrite who had a good deal of Tartuffe and Trissotin in him. He hailed it as "one of the most vigorously comic, most healthy and colorful plays we have had occasion to sit through for a long time." Most of the critics saw in Duhamel great promise as a dramatist and some even compared his play to Molière's comedies of the *Précieuses Ridicules* type. But the work did not maintain an even keel. It had some very funny scenes, a good second act and a poor fourth. It was well-acted, with Jouvet and Bacqué in the cast, and effectively staged by Copeau, but the audience did not take to it, in spite of its principal character, Beleuf, who had all the makings of a symbol ready to be placed next to those illustrious types created by Molière and Renard.

While the next major work of the season, Jules Romains's *Cromedeyre-le-Vieil*, was in rehearsal, Copeau revived *Les Fourberies de Scapin*. He hoped that Paris would erase the bitter memory of its sad New York reception. French critics accepted the platform within the stage with more understanding than New York—for they recalled that their own Tabarin had used the same idea—but they evinced the same skepticism regarding its value. The Comédie-Française, for example, which did not use the platform in its version of *Les Fourberies*, played the farce better than the Vieux-Colombier, according to Paul Souday. But no one chose to argue it out with Copeau, considering it a matter of sentiment. Paris applauded the company's energy, but on the whole, it was to a critic like Alphonse Séché, no more than a "praiseworthy effort, average result."[6]

On May 27, *Cromedeyre-le-Vieil* made its appearance as Jules Romains's debut.[7] This was a great year in drama for the literary phalanstery formed by some ten writers at the Abbaye de Créteil, of which Romains, Duhamel, Vildrac, and Chennevière were part, all linked in many ways to the destiny of the Vieux-Colombier.

Duhamel was the first to have heard Romains's play read in an actress's salon, and he hurried "home" to tell Copeau about it. With more than casual interest, the latter asked to read it, for Romains's unanimism—with its strong collective consciousness—had already established itself in his novels and poetry. If it could be projected from the stage, the same spirit of communion might be attained in the theater as in church. Copeau disclosed in his theater program:

> From the very first reading, we all had the feeling that Jules Romains's work, so spontaneous, so strong and so well constructed, would of itself resist, with implacable austerity, any trickery in acting. No actor's cleverness, no illusions of mise-en-scène could sub-

stitute themselves here, nor even add to a clear understanding of the text, to the profound and almost religious feeling of its truth, its beauty, its rhythm. It was less a question of a theatrical production than a secret poetic communion.

Copeau's interest developed into enthusiasm during the staging of the play. Through the unusual groupings of actors, he succeeded in conveying to his audience the rivalry between two whole towns rather than between two groups of individuals. Such staging answered every inner thought of the dramatist and gave the work a powerful impact.

The critics found the play bold, original, strong. Maurice Allem, however, contended that Romains's work was more of a poem than a drama and was certain that it would read better than it played. Already in 1911, after seeing the same author's *L'Armée dans la ville* produced at the Odéon by Antoine, drama critic Léon Blum (soon to become a militant Socialist leader) had wondered whether unanimism could ever achieve anything else but a new form of lyric description. But in 1920 Henry Bordeaux felt that it fully represented its time, since the war had given it a much wider appeal.

As the final program for the season, three one-act plays were produced: La Fontaine's and Champmeslé's *La Coupe enchantée*, Viélé-Griffin's *Phocas le Jardinier*, and a first play by Emile Mazaud, *La Folle Journée*. In these works lay much of the Vieux-Colombier's raison d'être; its sincere passion for the classics, its attachment to the mysticism of the symbolist poets, and finally its search for contemporary comedy. Mazaud belonged to this last group and was promptly compared with Renard and Courteline for his "style, humor, tenderness and gift for drama."[8] This threesome was a reminder that the 1913 aims were still being pursued.

Opinions varied, but one view prevailed with almost everyone in Paris, from Antoine to Vandérem. In a matter of five months, critics and public recognized that the Vieux-Colombier had made of a "small neighborhood theater the best theater in Paris. Not through magic, but slow work."[9] Mérimée, for example, was given his place next to Musset, while Viélé-Griffin joined the company of such ignored but recently produced living playwrights as Claudel and Ghéon. The classics of Shakespeare, Molière, and La Fontaine, and the newcomer Mérimée accounted for almost half of the total performances, 113 out of 234. But the phenomenon of the year was the quality and popularity of the four new dramatists introduced to the Paris public: Vildrac, Duhamel, Romains, and Mazaud.

During its first season of 1913–1914, 57 out of a total of 390 performances were devoted to newly produced modern plays. In 1920, out of a short season's total of 234 performances there were 105, with Vildrac alone played 61 times. These figures spoke more eloquently than theories or principles, for they reflected the popularity of new writers working for the new spirit in the French theater. To be sure, the current moderns bore some resemblance to their realist and symbolist forerunners, but their source of inspiration ran deeper still into the past, for they were often compared with Molière and his contemporary heirs like Courteline and Renard. Only one theater in Paris respected their works; that explained why the Vieux-Colombier had such a monopoly on the latest and best plays in France—just as its literary alter ego, the *Nouvelle Revue Française*, had with its reappearance in 1919 become a monopoly of a kind by bringing into the limelight such outstanding writers as Paul Valéry, Marcel Proust, Jean Giraudoux, and Paul Morand.

By the time the season ended in July, his theater was so firmly entrenched artistically and professionally that Copeau could make elaborate plans for the future. With successful modern playwrights in the repertory, with his superior staging of both moderns and classics, with his company considered amongst the leading actors of Paris, he was hailed for saving dramatic art in 1919 as Antoine had done twenty years before. The Vieux-Colombier was not only popular; it became fashionable to go there. Right after the war people avidly sought a new, fresh approach to theatrical art. Americans like Alexander Woollcott, visiting France, could find nothing in Paris to equal the programs or acting of the Vieux-Colombier.

There were full houses at almost every performance, yet the small size of the theater, now seating 363 after the remodeling, and the increased budget forced Michel Saint-Denis, Copeau's nephew and the theater's youthful treasurer, to announce in a letter of July 17, 1920, to Founding Members that the season's deficit had reached 116,000 francs (about $23,000). The following day Copeau sent word to a devoted benefactor of the French theater (and particularly of his), Auguste Rondel, telling him that the Vieux-Colombier must have the financial support of six hundred Founding Members for the next season, and pleading, "try to bring us new ones."

Profitable deals were proposed to commercialize his success. There were even prospects of financial aid from the government such as Antoine's Théâtre Libre had received during its heyday. But Copeau turned them away. "I don't want any . . . they would bind me. I don't want state funds, they would choke me."[10] He simply wanted to continue his work, to grow with it, as he explained to Les Amis in the theater's 1920 program:

> The organization of the Vieux-Colombier cannot, for the moment, be established on a commercial basis. In order not to allow its spirit to be altered nor deviated from its path, its growth must be progressive and natural, it must obey only the pressure of its inner force.
> We shall remain in our little theater of 300 seats until the day our public will have furnished us the proof that it is ready to follow us

elsewhere, and that it is sufficiently faithful, sufficiently numerous to guarantee the existence of an enterprise of identical nature, but of more ample means. That day, we shall build for the Vieux-Colombier the House it will have deserved. But so long as we remain in our little theater of 300 seats, the total amount of our receipts and our expenses will balance only with great difficulty.

The Vieux-Colombier is not a fantasy of amateurs or intellectuals concocted to tickle the curiosity of snobs and to win for itself the ephemeral favor of great philanthropists. It is a work of slow construction, open to all workers of the theater, and destined for the general public which must give it life. It is, essentially, a work of will, sincerity, cooperation. It calls for the friendship of a willing public, of a sincere public for which it is made, one whose moral and material support it needs.

He took the next big step in this direction by reestablishing the School of the Vieux-Colombier. He had been forced to discontinue it when his theater was transferred to New York, but even there it was not forgotten. During his lecture tour in America, Mrs. Philip Lydig had practically promised him that American funds would be forthcoming so that the school could be run on a financially independent basis. Much to Copeau's dismay, nothing more came of this. When the troupe reached New York, Suzanne Bing, his most devoted collaborator throughout the lifetime of the Vieux-Colombier School, occasionally visited Margaret Naumburg's Kindergarten, observing closely the children's games and mannerisms. One of Copeau's final lectures in America, delivered at the invitation of the Cleveland Playhouse in the winter of 1919, stressed his conviction that "the only hope we can have for the future of the theater is educating, developing, training children for the theater." No matter how young he had taken his actors, he confessed years later, they remained what they were: "always looking at everything from the standpoint of the actor, which is exactly against beauty on the stage. . . . I took them as young as I could, as unprejudiced as I could. I worked for them five years. I gave them everything I could. I tried to cultivate them. But with the exception of two or three, I failed, and I know now you cannot train them, you cannot cultivate them, you cannot educate them."

In 1920, his friends began more and more to appreciate his reasons for starting a laboratory in theater art. If he could perform such wonders with mature theater artists, then the school was indeed an indispensable element in fulfilling the Vieux-Colombier's destiny. Only in a school could author and actor, director and designer learn their art in the broad, experimental sense for which there was limited place in the theater itself. There was no such school in France in 1920 any more than in 1913 or 1915, and the need for one was just as great. He therefore set himself to the task of organizing it with more energy and vigor than he had ever applied to anything before. In contrast with the 1915 approach, this time the school would not be restricted to forming actors alone, although that was its most important object. Copeau wished to "study both together and separately all the essential problems of the theater."[11]

To help him achieve these ambitious aims, he asked Jules Romains to become the active director of the school. He confessed he "was groping in a badly explored region, full of surprises and ambushes," and needed a dependable, understanding assistant.[12] Romains sympathized with Copeau's problems and deplored with him that "people of taste, cultured people, artists . . . agree that the theater is either obnoxious or negligible." He admitted that the boulevard theater had cleverness and a host of average qualities, but he bitterly resented its lack of ambition, and consequently its lack of art. He believed that the solution lay in "the possession of a strong doctrine" and the development of a technique with the help of a master's teaching and a workshop: "so long as the artist remains what he is today [1918], either self-taught or the bored student of a broken-down discipline, so long as there are no 'schools' worthy of that name, a clear technique, which is the sign of glorious epochs, will not be realized."[13]

He fitted into Copeau's plans not only artistically but pedagogically as well. He was an established poet and novelist, and more recently, as author of *Cromedeyre-le-Vieil*, had shown dramatic skill. He was a former student of the Ecole Normale Supérieure and had taught philosophy. Moreover, his esthetic doctrine of unanimism was well suited to the kind of school Copeau wanted, which was an esprit de corps as closely knit as the blood relations in a family. Together, they planned the school's organization and its program. It opened in the fall of 1920 and the first classes were held in an old wooden shack in the theater's courtyard—not unlike a barn. But the quarters were too small and the school soon moved to 9, rue du Cherche-Midi, which made the town jesters mock Copeau's ambitious hopes by hurling at him "*Il cherche midi à quatorze heures!*" (he's on a wild-goose chase). Such causticity fell on deaf ears, for Copeau conducted the school on a highly organized and disciplined level. A special pamphlet was issued, outlining it to the public in the following manner:

Professional School of the Vieux-Colombier

Goal: This is a technical school to give students as methodical and complete a training as possible. For actors, playwrights and theatrical technicians. Free to students of both sexes. Limited Number. Ages 14–20.

Outside students will attend all courses and be subject to the same training as professional students. Limited number: 10.

Fee: 100 francs [$20] per month.

Auditors: Limited number: 20.

Fee: 150 francs for 3 months, 250 francs for 6 months.

Children's Gatherings: Thursdays and Sundays, 2 to 4 P.M.

> Songs, dances, costume parties, improvisations, charades, etc. Goal is to entertain children together and develop by simple and spontaneous games their taste, intelligence, imagination and faculties of self-expression.

Required Age: 8–12.

> Parents not admitted, to avoid giving gatherings the aspect of school performances.

Limited number: 30.

Fee: 50 francs per month.

Staff

Director: M. Jules Romains

Secretary: Mlle. Suzanne Maistre

Teaching Staff: MM. Jacques Copeau, Jules Romains, Georges Chennevière, Louis Jouvet, Mme. Suzanne Bing, Fratellini Brothers, MM. André Bacqué, Romain Bouquet, Georges Vitray, Mme. Jane Bathori, MM. Louis Brochard, Albert Marque, Mlle. Marthe Esquerré.

Course of Study (1920–1921)

Public courses: Vieux-Colombier repertory. Given by M. Jacques Copeau. Study of principal works, particularly the classics.

> Readings, commentaries and analyses from technical and literary viewpoint and in relation to acting and staging.

General courses:

1. Theory of the Theater. Greek Tragedy. Given by M. Jacques Copeau. Religious origins and social significance of Greek theater. Birth and development of drama, of the tragic form, of theatrical medium. Acting. Staging. Texts: Aeschylus, Sophocles, Euripides, satirical drama, comedy, Aristophanes.

    1a. Theory of Theatrical Architecture. Greek Theater. Given by M. Louis Jouvet. Study of Greek Theater from architectural and material standpoint. Relationship between audience and chorus, chorus and stage, stage and audience. Acoustics. Visibility. Light. Props, etc.

2. Course on Poetic Technique. Given by M. Jules Romains. Elements of general prosody. Ancient prosody. Theory of French classical versification. Theory of modern versification.

    2a. Practical uses of poetic technique. Given by M. Georges Chennevière. Practical analyses, demonstrations, exercises relative to general prosody, ancient prosody. French classical versification, modern versification. Correction of written work. (Must be taken with course 2).

3. Schools, communities and civilization. Schools and communities in Greek life. Given by M. Georges Chennevière. The country. Race. Spirit. General view of history of Greek civilization. Great men and

collectivities. Philosophical schools. Philosophical and religious communities. Literary and artistic schools. Associations. Daily life of individuals, groups and cities. How it expresses itself in poetry, music, Greek theater.

4. Singing. Given by Mme. Jane Bathori. Solfeggio and singing. Placing the voice. Choral. Solo.

Limited classes (open to students only)

1. Physical Education. Acrobatics. Conducted by Fratellini Brothers (clowns) at Cirque Médrano.
2. Music. Given by M. Louis Brochard. Corporal (walking, marching, movements to music). Vocal (solfeggio, choral, solo). Instrumental (flute, drums, tambourine, castanets, cymbals, string instruments). Poetry sung, ancient poetry (with help from M. Georges Chennevière).
3. French Language. Given by Mlle. Marthe Esquerré. Grammar exercises. Vocabulary. Script analysis.
   3a. Memory exercises. Given by Mlle. Marthe Esquerré. Rational training of memory. Script recitations.
4. Elementary course in reading and diction. Given by Mme. Suzanne Bing. Reading aloud. Mechanism of elocution. Diction. Study of types and styles. Declamation: ode, recitative, chant; individual and group.
5. Training of dramatic instinct. Exercises directed by M. Jacques Copeau and Mme. Suzanne Bing. The adolescent's cultivation of spontaneity and inventiveness. Recitatives, legerdemain, witticism, singing, dancing, improvisation, impromptu dialogue, pantomime. Application of different abilities acquired by student in the course of his general instruction.
6. Development of dramatic sense. Given by M. Jacques Copeau.
7. Diction and Staging. Given by MM. André Bacqué and Georges Vitray. Diction, Acting, Staging. Comedy. Tragedy. Drama. Study of repertory; in particular, complete study and staging of plays selected from Vieux-Colombier repertory, which will have been part of commentary in M. Jacques Copeau's public lectures.
8. Workshop. Practical study of stage elements. Workshop assistant: Mlle. Marie-Hélène Copeau. Technical advisers: MM. Louis Jouvet and Albert Marque. Geometric designs. Modeling. Casting. Painting. Work on wood, leather, cardboard. Cutting and dressmaking. These workshops will allow for a maximum of student initiative and personal spontaneity. They will alternate, depending upon opportunity, with readings, games, group walks, visits to museums, monuments, parks, etc.

There were only twelve apprenticed students in the closed courses, a number that Copeau rarely permitted to increase, for it would have defeated his purpose of developing cautiously a technique for each branch of theatrical art. It was more important to find this technique than to give incomplete training to large numbers of authors, actors, designers, and others. Besides, no one could enter the Vieux-Colombier School to specialize from the start in any one branch of the theater. There was a required program common to all, everyone taking courses in acting, writing, directing, designing, and so on. When a student showed special talent in one branch, only then did he get special training. Lectures on the history of theater were open to Vieux-Colombier audiences.

His main interest lay with the apprentice group, who ranged from fourteen to twenty years of age and were to remain under his tutelage for three years free of charge. He entrusted *les enfants* to Suzanne Bing, who supervised them in diction, dramatic exercises, and the technique of movement, the latter being a partial application of the Dalcroze method, modified and adapted to the instrument—the actor—in his relations with time, space, other actors, his environment, and the nuances of expression.

The faculty of the school, as seen, was composed principally of those in the Vieux-Colombier Theater. Copeau, in his technical course on directing and acting, gave his young people extremely difficult passages to read, then cut them short at their mistakes in order to teach them humility before a manuscript. Jules Romains's course on poetic technique sought to make the students fully conscious of the harmony of words and was then applied, after the lecture, in practical exercises under poet Georges Chennevière's direction.

Special lecturers were frequently invited to speak to the students and to the Vieux-Colombier public. During the 1922–1923 season, for example, the public courses consisted of forty-two lectures on criticism, the novel, poetry, and the theater by no less a "faculty" than Albert Thibaudet (six on "The Art and Profession of Criticism"), Benjamin Crémieux (four on "Evaluating Criticism"), Jacques Rivière (four on "Some Progress in the Study of the Human Heart: Freud and Proust"), Edmond Jaloux (four on "The Novel Today"), Valéry Larbaud (four on "Contemporary Spanish Novelists"), André Gide (four on "The Art of the Novel," after his six famous lectures on Dostoevsky), Paul Valéry (four on "Poetry in the Nineteenth Century"), Henri Ghéon (four on "Spiritual and Material Conditions of a New Dramatic Art, and Dramatic Art in General"), and Jules Romains (four on "Matter and Form of Drama"). In exchange for this priceless professional and educational training, far more exacting than the Conservatory (where the student's program of study was limited almost uniquely to the reciting of one scene after another, aiming at a prize and a job in a state-controlled theater), Copeau required students not to take classes outside his school; no acting on any stage but the Vieux-Colombier during school years. After the three-year course, if selected, they must accept to play at the Vieux-Colombier at lowest salary for one to three years. This was no deterrent; there were artists in Paris like Jean Legoff who shunned bulging boulevard contracts to play in the theater on the rue du Vieux-Colombier, and young actors like Dorcy, who actually broke his contract with the Théâtre du Châtelet to go to school on the rue du Cherche-Midi.[14]

Copeau's sense of discipline and order was the school's cornerstone, maintained steadfast in spite of the skepticism of critic friends who protested that a systematized education and training was artificial and dangerous in art. If they had spent one day at the school and viewed the results of that system in the growing self-assurance of the students as it was transmitted into their improvisations—for this was, as in 1915, the backbone for teaching the art of acting—they would have called it, as did Henri Bidou, "the only drama school in France." Granville-Barker, after seeing a student performance of a Japanese Noh, jumped on the stage to congratulate the young actors, exclaiming: "Until today I have never believed in drama schools, but you have won me over." And Adolphe Appia wrote Copeau: "Your 'little ones' are my only hope."[15]

The artist in him was so thrilled at finally seeing the school in full operation and so closely allied with the aims of his theater, that he proclaimed once and for all that the Vieux-Colombier would never abandon its ideals or its future in order "to enrich a group of capitalists or fatten up a bunch of State servants";[16] the boulevard and Comédie-Française were still anathema to him. Instead, he again appealed to Les Amis du Vieux-Colombier to continue their moral and financial support as they had earlier in the year. He specified six uses to which their money would be put: to pay fair salaries to his permanent staff of associates; to increase the number of actors and technicians so that the Vieux-Colombier might attempt more ambitious productions and send companies out into the provinces and abroad, which it had had to decline to do thus far; to have more time for rehearsals; to acquire more modern equipment and undertake technical research for future productions; to support the school; and to build a theater of their own from original plans answering new needs of drama.

The greatly increased interest in the Vieux-Colombier justified these elaborate plans. In November of 1919, Les Amis had 241 subscribers. When the first postwar season opened in February of 1920, there were 582. By October, there were 1,468. At this rate, Copeau expected that by the end of the 1920–1921 season, which was about to begin, there would be about 6,000 subscribers. He had a right to look forward—in spite of doubters—for even the French government, by decree of December 9, 1920, gave the Vieux-Colombier a subsidy of 5,000 francs ($1,000) with no strings attached.

There were still critics who derisively called the Vieux-Colombier an avant-garde theater. These few had not yet been convinced that it had no sensational ideas lurking in the wings and that once it succeeded in loosing them on the public, it would not quiet down and disappear. On the other hand, a large part of the public was still of the opinion that the Vieux-Colombier was warming up for a successful entry into the real—commercial—theater. But the so-called real theater was surprised at not having Copeau's actors and technicians accept its offers of higher pay, surprised at finding that not one of them considered their playhouse a stepping-stone to their own selfish ends. Boulevard producers did not yet realize that the Vieux-Colombier Theater was at the same time the Vieux-Colombier spirit. They could not touch the first so long as they did not understand the second.

With the future brighter than ever, the first complete postwar season began on October 14. Until almost the end of January, the repertory was limited to revivals, especially of Vildrac's *Le Paquebot Tenacity* and *Twelfth Night*. French critics, who had not seen Shakespeare's play since 1914, were again enthusiastic to the point of urging Parisians not to go and see *L'Atlantide* or *Le Roi* on the boulevard if they had not yet been to the Latin Quarter to view Copeau's revival.

On January 24, a modern *mystère* by Ghéon on the life of Saint Alexis, *Le Pauvre sous l'escalier*, received its first performance midst great applause from the first night audience. But the critics were, on the whole, quite bored. Besides, the play had the unorthodox quality of daring to combine comedy and tragedy in one and the same scene, a mixture for which the French had often reproached Shakespeare. To Copeau it was another experiment, this time to discover how close the theater could be brought to the church, whether people would attend the theater as they do a religious rite and then leave with the same exaltation and reverence as from a house of worship. François Mauriac, himself a devout Catholic writer, saw this possibility and expressed pleasure that where the converted Racine had abandoned the theater, the converted Ghéon became more attached to it than ever.

Schlumberger also contributed a play to the season, his ten-year-old *La Mort de Sparte*, which was a failure in spite of Mauriac's praise of the company. (He called each extra in the crowd scenes an artist.)

But by now everyone expected good acting at the Vieux-Colombier. What they wanted were good plays by new authors, and Copeau offered none this season, not until the end when he staged François Porché's lyric drama in free verse about adolescence, *La Dauphine*. It met with a *succès d'estime* but evoked little enthusiasm from the public.

True to form, the critics forgot the four successfully launched new dramatists of the previous season, Vildrac, Duhamel, Romains, and Mazaud, and grumbled that the Vieux-Colombier had given them too few new plays this season and not a single successful one in the manner of a Vildrac. They even accused Copeau of restricting his theater to a certain type of play, which some interpreted as a sign of vitality and others as a sign of decadence. But he answered frankly that he would not accept plays because they were different. He wanted good plays, not just new ones. Indeed the theater's posters for the coming 1920–1921 season said just that: "Submissive to the teachings of masters of the past, we advance toward the future." At this same time, Copeau, after reading one thousand manuscripts, complained to an interviewer: "Alas! Not one of the authors I've read seems to realize the liberty that the artist is given by a blank page. The liberty of creation! They all welcome the old clichés, outmoded formulas and obsolete rules. No one *dares to dare. . . .*"[17]

As a result of such criteria, only three new plays were put on this season, making 28 performances out of a total of 463. The classics alone accounted for 248, and this told the story: when there were no new plays that could stand up to the classics, Copeau, rather than yield to mediocrity for the sake of playing something modern, preferred to choose plays from the wealth of inspiring material he found in the past. He made them fresh and alive by his staging, eliminating the stodginess and respectful awe one found in other theaters, where the classics were usually played as a ritual. Nor did his moderns have any of the artificial glamour of a boulevard production where the value of a dramatist was in direct proportion to the money in the box office and had little to do with the quality of his work.

Even if the critics were dissatisfied, the public was more than happy to see the classics come to life under Copeau's touch as if they were new plays. The theater was full at almost every performance; everyone spoke of the perfection of a Vieux-Colombier production, a word that made Copeau smile, for he saw only its imperfections. These did not, however, worry him, for time and work would eliminate them gradually as they had been doing since 1913.

The Vieux-Colombier's ability to win over crowds was in itself a revolution in popular taste and proved to Copeau that art could attract the general public and hold on to it, since Paris had an elite audience of some five or six thousand people who were more than eager to give the Vieux-Colombier their attention. "We have made them exacting. Their reaction is . . . our most precious, most delicate means of control."[18] That audience resented the least sign of weakness on the part of their theater, thereby forcing writer, director, actor, and the rest to maintain the high standards expected. There was also another public of about thirty to thirty-five thousand who followed faithfully but with less conscientiousness than the first group. Together they were a powerful support.

So demanding was the Vieux-Colombier audience that they protested to Copeau the commotion caused in the theater and on the stage by latecomers at the opening of Romains's *Cromedeyre*. He was urged to do something about it and evolved a cure that caused many a disgruntled critic to quake with anger. As of the 1920–1921 season, no one was permitted to enter the theater except during intermissions, "out of regard for the public." In addition, the company requested the public "not to turn its back on the stage, but to remain seated until the curtain falls for the last time on the last act of the play. We do all in our power to satisfy the public and show it our respect. May we be permitted to count on its courtesy." While some critics fumed, audiences took the requests seriously, understanding the moral and artistic motives behind them.

Not only France but all Europe took notice of what was taking place in that little playhouse on the Left Bank. Foreigners, as well as the French, went there to view a genuine manifestation of European art. They recognized in it the kind of Western culture that is destined to last. "Of the new theaters thus far evolved," observed Kenneth Macgowan in *Theater Arts Magazine* (October 1921), "Copeau's is the most complete, studied and yet natural experiment . . . prophetic of a home for the new play."

Emblem of the two doves (*colombes*) chosen by Jacques Copeau for his Vieux-Colombier Theater. Copeau asked the symbolist poet Mallarmé to provide them with appropriate dialogue for the program: "Do you go to the theater?" "No, almost never." "Oh well, neither do I." (Author's collection)

Poster for the opening of the Vieux-Colombier Theater on October 15, 1913, with an appeal "to youth . . . to the well-educated . . . to all" for help to inspire and promote dramatic art. (Département des Arts du Spectacle, Bibliothèque Nationale de France)

Members of the Vieux-Colombier company in the countryside near Copeau's house at Le Limon, where they prepared for their 1913 debut in Paris. *Seated, left to right:* Charles Dullin, Jacques Copeau (wearing hat), Blanche Albane (wife of novelist Georges Duhamel), Suzanne Bing (with Copeau's dog Filou at her feet). Standing behind Bing is Louis Jouvet. (Département des Arts du Spectacle, Bibliothèque Nationale de France)

Scene from the 1914 production of *The Brothers Karamazov*, adapted by Jacques Copeau and Jean Croué. *Left to right:* Jacques Copeau (as Ivan), Charles Dullin (as Smerdiakov), and Louis Jouvet (as old Feodor, the father). (Département des Arts du Spectacle, Bibliothèque Nationale de France. Rights Reserved)

Jacques Copeau as Ivan, the philosopher brother, in *The Brothers Karamazov*. (Département des Arts du Spectacle, Bibliothèque Nationale de France)

Costume sketches by the English painter Duncan Grant for a 1914 production of *Twelfth Night* by William Shakespeare. *Left to right:* Viola, Sir Andrew Aguecheek (played by Louis Jouvet), and "Toby" (Sir Toby Belch). Copeau knew Grant through the Bloomsbury group and brought him over from London. (Département des Arts du Spectacle, Bibliothèque Nationale de France)

Poster created by the Nabi painter Edouard Vuillard for the Vieux-Colombier's first season in America, 1917–18. (© ARS, New York, 1998)

Jacques Copeau (center) in the title role in *Les Fourberies de Scapin* (*The Knaveries of Scapin*) by Molière, which opened the New York season on November 27, 1917. The raised platform within the stage caught the audience by surprise. (Département des Arts du Spectacle, Bibliothèque Nationale de France. Rights Reserved)

Jacques Copeau in the title role in *Washington* by Percy Mackaye, performed in French in 1919, during the second New York season. (Département des Arts du Spectacle, Bibliothèque Nationale de France)

The building in which Copeau established the first all-theater school in 1920, in the courtyard of the Vieux-Colombier. (Département des Arts du Spectacle, Bibliothèque Nationale de France)

The old-fashioned Athénée Saint-Germain Theater in 1913, as Copeau first saw it before renaming it the Vieux-Colombier. (Département des Arts du Spectacle, Bibliothèque Nationale de France)

Drawing of the Vieux-Colombier Theater as remodeled by Copeau's architect, Francis Jourdain, with its double stage frame opening on the proscenium. (Département des Arts du Spectacle, Bibliothèque Nationale de France)

Louis Jouvet in 1917, with the maquette that he designed for the New York stage and that Antonin Raymond, Copeau's Franco-American architect, built. (Département des Arts du Spectacle, Bibliothèque Nationale de France)

The 1918 New York set for *The Doctor in Spite of Himself* (*Le Médecin malgré lui*) by Molière, which called for the play's action to be concentrated on the platform elevated four steps above the main stage. (Département des Arts du Spectacle, Bibliothèque Nationale de France)

The Vieux-Colombier Theater in Paris, 1919. Louis Jouvet's permanent set featured four adjustable lighting projectors, known since then as "jouvets." (Département des Arts du Spectacle, Bibliothèque Nationale de France)

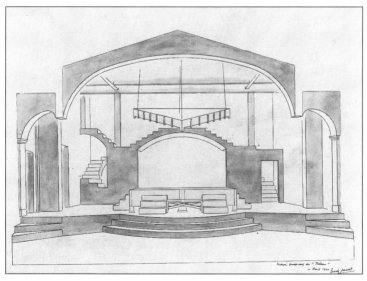

Louis Jouvet's perspective drawing of the 1920 Vieux-Colombier stage. (Courtesy of Lisa Jouvet)˙

Costume sketch by Guy-Pierre Fauconnet for a harlequin clown, from *The Winter's Tale* by William Shakespeare, which opened the 1920 postwar season at the Vieux-Colombier. (Département des Arts du Spectacle, Bibliothèque Nationale de France)

Costume sketch by Fauconnet for Autolycus blowing a horn, from the *The Winter's Tale*. (Département des Arts du Spectacle, Bibliothèque Nationale de France)

Costume sketch by Duncan Grant for the High Priest, from the 1922 production of *Saül* by André Gide. (Département des Arts du Spectacle, Bibliothèque Nationale de France)

Members of the cast of the 1927 New York production of *The Brothers Kara-*
mazov. *Left to right*: George Gaul, Alfred Lunt, Morris Carnovsky, and Edward
G. Robinson. (Billy Rose Theatre Collection, New York Public Library for the
Performing Arts, Astor Lenox Tilden Foundation. Photograph by Vandama)

Jacques Copeau in 1927, on board ship after staging *The Brothers Karama-zov* for the Theater Guild in New York. (Département des Arts du Spectacle, Bibliothèque Nationale de France)

6

The Ways and Means of Copeau's Art

COPEAU WAS THE UNUSUAL TYPE of metteur-en-scène who remained impartial to author, actor, scenic designer, and audience. For that reason, all looked to him as their master. Charles Vildrac called him "a real and precious collaborator."[1] René Benjamin dedicated *Les Plaisirs du hasard* to him. Even a highly successful boulevard playwright like Edouard Bourdet who never had his work produced at the Vieux-Colombier wrote that it was to the author's best interest to efface himself at production time when the director was as brilliant as a Stanislavsky or a Copeau.[2]

This impartiality, which derived from discipline and devotion to the moral and artistic premises of his theater, made Copeau the kind of patient perfectionist who proceeded carefully and gradually from one problem of theatrical art to the other. Step by step, he experimented, going from one turning in the road to another: it was the freshness and originality of the staging of *Twelfth Night* that established the reputation of the Vieux-Colombier and of Copeau as metteur-en-scène, giving the French a rare, authentic glimpse of Shakespeare; it was the riot of color in *Le Carrosse du Saint-Sacrement* that helped reveal the dramatist in Mérimée; it was due in great part to Copeau's faith in the art of improvisation and its intrinsic physical style of acting that Molière was so astonishingly rejuvenated. And what theater in France could have, or would have, given Vildrac's *Le Paquebot Tenacity* the simple and natural acting it received at the Vieux-Colombier, the unaffectedness of Copeau's direction, the honest, unadorned set that allowed the play to stand on its own? All this and more were the results of successful experiments on the stage and with the stage.

Copeau belonged to that fellowship of dreamer-workers that the commercial theater envied and dreaded, because instinctively the boulevard and Broadway knew—but dared not admit—that "the theater," as Lee Simonson wrote in *Theater Arts Monthly* (July 1933), "remains alive by remaining a workshop," and a Copeau mise-en-scène was always a workshop experiment that he alone conducted without regard for the box office. And in this conscious, planned, unselfish leadership lay the great secret of Copeau's art. Artistically and intellectually, he was aware of all aspects of his *métier* but feared its possible effects on his fellow workers. He wrote of this to Jouvet on February 5, 1916: "I should like *to place all books under lock and key* to keep you from using them. . . . You'd never have anything before you but graphic documents. *I* am the knowledge of the past, I who shall absorb it, who shall digest it, who shall clarify it and who shall transmit it to you little by little, *all fresh, all new*, pell-mell with my own discoveries and my personal knowledge. *No restoration*. A creation. Life."

This forceful drive towards perfection was one of the most distinctive facets of the Vieux-Colombier, for it governed not only Copeau but each person striving to unfold words, action, line, color, and rhythm under his direction. In France, this collective effort in drama first took on the appearance of a mature art under Copeau at the Vieux-Colombier, which was referred to as a school for metteurs-en-scène. It achieved full recognition in 1936 when the nation placed Copeau, Jouvet, Dullin, and Baty in charge of staging at the Comédie-Française.

This quarter-century of theatrical reform was, at its inception, directed in France almost exclusively by Copeau, who had the rare capacity, in Paul Valéry's imagery (*Nouvelle Revue Française*, July 1, 1936), "to multiply what he knows by what he knows," thereby achieving a maximum effect in each production. Eventually, his formulas and principles became a veritable manual on theatrical art.

These began to take practical form the moment Copeau removed the gilt decorations of the Athénée-Saint-Germain and installed in their place the simple, buff walls of the Théâtre du Vieux-Colombier. In 1913 he started the break from Antoine's "fourth wall" theater and sought to establish as close a link as possible between audience and stage. With this in mind, he eliminated the distracting ornamentation that had been a part of playhouses since Louis XIV's time. The elaborate *pâtisserie* curves became straight panels. All flourishes on the proscenium were chiseled off and a flat black surface took their place. Instead of the ugly yellow houselights, there was a subdued glow that created a velvety sense of softness and quiet. And the gaudy, painted curtain, moving from the floor up, was replaced by a deep emerald green cloth one that lay in gentle folds and opened gracefully from the center as a discreet separation between actor and audience.

Direct contact between stage and audience was an essential and original aspect of Copeau's mise-en-scène, which he further developed in New York in 1917. He made the 910-seat Garrick Theater an intimate little playhouse of 550 by shutting off the second balcony and eliminating the boxes located on the sides. He had other boxes, however, put at the rear center of the orchestra parallel with the last two rows. The closed balcony facilitated problems of staging and was transformed into a large rehearsal room, workshops, and offices. This made it possible to rehearse two plays simultaneously, a necessity that Copeau had fortunately foreseen long before it had been decided to change bills every Monday during the second American season.

From wall to wall, the New York stage was seventy-three feet long. It had a twenty-six foot opening and twenty-eight feet of depth. The first few rows of the orchestra were torn out to permit a much larger apron, where the play's action could continue in front of the curtain. The stage was linked directly to the audience by means of steps leading down to the floor of the orchestra and by the complete elimination of footlights. Broadway's gilt and tinsel were replaced by sixteenth-century lath and plaster. The result was a stage extolled by Clayton Hamilton in *Bookman* (January 1918) for its "simplicity and quietude of tone." It suggested to him a medieval inn-yard in Warwick or Beauvais. In 1919, when Copeau and the troupe returned to Paris, these same innovations were reproduced on the stage of the Vieux-Colombier. In its final form, this stage became a model "ten years ahead of its time," wrote Kenneth Macgowan in *Theater Arts Magazine* (October 1921).

Yet, Copeau's plans went through their seven lean years of evolution before taking on a semblance of permanency in 1920. In 1913, for example, a small backdrop depicted the changes of scene for *A Woman Killed With Kindness*, something that he would never tolerate in 1917. By then he had ended his "incomplete and brutal apprenticeship," climaxed by *Twelfth Night*, and discovered the architectural stage, which he had evolved with a sharp eye on Shakespeare's own manner of production.[3]

The first experiments with this type of stage aroused great interest, for now Copeau had made the architect, along with the poet, the actor, and the director, another element in the organic whole of dramatic art. The stage was stripped to its bare walls. In the rear was a balcony with three bays; these were raised on four columns and could be curtained off when not in use. This balcony with its stairways, bridges, and system of interlocking cubes could be compared to a child's building blocks. To answer Copeau's constant need of experimentation, the combination of movable units made it possible for him to treat the stage with the same imaginative approach that the playwright applied to his script, the director to a new piece of business, or the actor to a change of intonation. The stage, therefore, became a fluid counterpart of the writer's imagination, as subject to change during rehearsal as any other element of dramatic art.[4]

Another ingenious device was the two towers on either side of the proscenium, each containing a door, a staircase and a window. At the foot of each was a small platform or auxiliary stage where boxes were normally found. These, added to the movable apron over the orchestra pit just below the level of the stage, had been designed to obtain a variety of exits and entrances and to assure the actors a maximum of playing space on different levels. Although Molière was the spiritual leader of the Vieux-Colombier, its physical structure resembled more closely that of Shakespeare's theater. The obvious purpose was to get the actor on and off as easily as possible. Everything on this stage seemed plastic and pliable, with very little to restrict the poet or the actor.

All this came as the result of much investigation. Even before his visits to Craig and Appia in the fall of 1915, Copeau, with the help of his friend "Théo" (the Belgian artist Théodore Van Rysselberghe), was feverishly studying the innumerable stage possibilities of the architectural set. Knowing its scope and limitations, he wrote to Jouvet in August 1915:

> There are difficulties which I have not yet solved. Two of the principal ones are, in fact, *solidity and assemblage*. To guarantee solidity, I believe it difficult to have cubes of different weights. I believe that in order to be limitlessly practical they must be unrestrictedly interchangeable. What we must find from the standpoint of assemblage, besides the practical gadget to make it stick together and give a perfect assemblage, is the *common divisor* . . . [to this use of cubes, Copeau would add] architectural elements to introduce the necessary variants of color and style. . . . And these supplementary elements, like every element of detail, in order to make a form or a period precise and take on artistic value, will have to be made by hand, *beautiful*. . . . There could be a certain type of stage set for Molière's comedy, one for Greek tragedy. . . . The *judicious use of curtains*, a few props and columns would easily soften (with lighting) the geometric, fixed, cubic aspect of this arrangement. . . . One very important thing is to find *the practical means for keeping these solid parts together and attached to the stage floor without ever hammering a nail into it.*

And in a P.S. to this letter, Copeau laid down the principle: "For the construction that we dream of, we must not rely on what we shall have to construct. We must seek out the most practical, the simplest, the characteristic *architectural elements*, with the help of which everything can be constructed. *Voilà le principe*."

These innovations had been tested in New York, and when Copeau returned to Paris he instituted as many of them as his smaller theater permitted. The stage was once more stripped (to the dismay of the critics attending the Vieux-Colombier's 1920 reopening with *The Winter's Tale*), and became all stone, eliminating the drum-like resonance of the floors common to most small theaters. Another stage entrance was created, over and above the great number already discovered in New York: a trapdoor leading down from the apron to below stage. The enlarged apron and the steps linking stage and auditorium meant that several rows of seats had to be removed, thus lowering the theater's seating capacity from 500 to 360 and reducing its income by thirty percent. But the problem in Copeau's mind was completely one of art, not money. While in 1913 he had stressed the decommercialization of the theater, in 1919 he wished to "detheatricalize the theater."

Besides the dignified simplicity of the auditorium and the architectural design of the stage, the Vieux-Colombier's lighting system rounded out its physical structure. Lanterns were concealed behind the outer and inner proscenium arches and lighted the mainstage, while the forestage and other playing areas received light from lanterns artistically hung in the theater's ceiling, on each side near the proscenium. These were manipulated on pulleys and their colored gelatins were easily turned. There were also flood- and bunchlights and a single border placed upstage. Thanks to Craig, whom England remembers as the man who would have nothing to do with footlights, there were none at the Vieux-Colombier either, a successful innovation that Copeau first tried out in New York and that Paris welcomed in 1920. This system of lighting, developed by Jouvet and since called "les jouvets," was integrated with Copeau's mise-en-scène; it spoke an impressive stage language that strove to be in complete harmony with the poet's lines and the actor's playing.[5]

Copeau also provided the Vieux-Colombier with a material self-sufficiency that would assure its permanency. In the courtyard next to it were the administrative offices, archives full of manuscripts and photographs, and a publicity department. There were the same old sheds used for making scenery, constructing props and furniture, and designing and painting costumes and masks. Under the theater's lobby was a storeroom for electrical equipment. The lobby itself contained, besides the perennial Molière bust, a large checkroom and a display of Vieux-Colombier literature, including the publications of Gaston Gallimard, who printed its repertory in America and France as each new play reached the stage. Back to Paris with Copeau went his New York idea of making his theater a general center of culture by opening it to concerts sponsored by the *Revue musicale*. Next door to the theater there was even a Restaurant du Vieux-Colombier to give a finishing touch of independence. "Une petite cité," a small town, Suzanne Bing nostalgically recalled in 1946.

This material background had to be organized in 1913 and reorganized in 1920, and then be kept moving smoothly and economically if the theater were to function as a harmonious unit. The first and most important stage element that had to fit into this background and blend with it in its artistic and organic ensemble was the actor. Although the text was the guiding score for the entire production, it was the actor who was the dramatist's chief instrumentalist and the director's principal mode of expression in delineating his "design of a dramatic action," as Copeau defined mise-en-scène.

Drama being a plastic art, the human body—that is, voice and movement—took its natural place at the head of all theater components, each of which was set to accommodate the actor. That was why Molière had become the Vieux-Colombier's patron saint. He had been an actor, not only writing plays to be acted but himself acting to convey his ideas. It was therefore the actor who dictated to Copeau the kind of stage the theater should have. In this he followed Appia's principle: "Scenic art must be based on the one reality worthy of the theater, the human body."[6]

Because the actor is three-dimensional, so at the Vieux-Colombier the acting space was three-dimensional. This basic tenet governed every change evolved by Copeau, the most important of which was the permanent balcony, running the length of the stage, with its few adjustable parts. Every detail took the form of a solid: a simple screen designating the wall of a room was given a three-inch depth. But the structure that came closest to realizing Copeau's dramatic ideal was the steps that led from mainstage to forestage, and then into the auditorium itself. This created an active relationship between player and audience that made the player more natural, more accessible, and more direct, even when the steps were not used for the play's action as in *Les Frères Karamazov*. The result produced the first formalistic, presentational theater in modern times, for it completely eliminated the illusion of realism. Georges Vitray, one of Copeau's actors, told about sitting in a café one night after a performance of Molière's *Les Fourberies de Scapin* and hearing a man in a worker's cap marvel to a friend: "I went in because I thought it was a cinema. I bought a seat for three francs and *mon vieux*, you should have seen them, the people. Real society! I'm going to take my wife, and tell her to dress up. And then, *mon vieux*, you know what? They don't have stage sets. They sit right on the steps so you *see the words!*"

The Vieux-Colombier actor was never permitted to imitate reality. He suggested it. This was a sharp break from the manner of an Antoine or a Stanislavsky, who emphasized the actor's ability to transmit the physical and mental counterpart of his characterization. Yet what Copeau took from them, whose realistic staging he considered basically false and inartistic, was their actor's sincerity and naturalness. These he used to attain an objective interpretation of the character played, rather than the actual character as subjectively reproduced by a Stanislavsky. Copeau sought to transmit the image of reality, whereas most schools of acting pursued the reality of the image.

Essentially, Copeau's mise-en-scène was "the actor in movement on a surface."[7] A Vieux-Colombier production was one rhythmic whole, which had the effect of a visual symphony on its spectators. This was not only true of comedy, where rhythm and tempo—Ellen Terry called it pace— were all-important. Tragedy was also staged with rhythm, an interior, psychological rhythm. For example, in *Les Frères Karamazov* it was not enough for old Feodor to leave the stage at the end of his lines. Copeau made him start building up his exit in the middle of his scene so that when he finally left the stage, it was the result of a long prepared sequence and a contribution to the dramatic impact of the scene, rather than a character simply walking off on a line or action cue.[8] Such complete consciousness of rhythm, both physical and mental, led Waldo Frank (in *Theater Arts Monthly*, September 1925) to see in Copeau's staging a "fundamental law in the revised theater," and Harold Clurman (in the *Post*, January 8, 1927) to feel that Copeau's "grace and clarity . . . arise from his wonderful musical sense." Others were struck by the ballet-like precision of his mise-en-scène. But to Copeau it was simply the will to achieve freedom of movement, for he confessed to absolute musical ignorance.

The actor's freedom was further enhanced by the complete elimination of all devices that might monopolize an audience's attention. The first to go was the painted set. With the exception of costumes and furniture, the painter had no place in a Vieux-Colombier production. This was a revolutionary break from the eighteenth and nineteenth centuries, when stage decoration was limited to the art of painted scenery. Copeau followed Craig's principle that the stage be considered as so much space for design, and he adopted Appia's outline of that design by the use of volumes and lights. Yet he deviated from Craig's stress on lines as the most evocative style for the stage. He used curtains and screens effectively, but these never played the dominant role that they had in a Craig design. The Englishman also believed that the essence of a play evolved by means of the power of suggestion inherent in the scenic design. This doctrine led Craig to eliminate the living actor from the theater completely, in favor of the of the "übermarionette." It made the play a mere scenario to guide the designer but not to limit or control him. The Frenchman in Copeau revolted against such disrespect for two types of artist that France had traditionally upheld as amongst its greatest, the dramatic poet and the actor. In an interview by the *Christian Science Monitor*, November 12, 1924, he insisted: "The poet alone is the real origin and life of all drama, as Aeschylus was of Greek drama; and the director [metteur-en-scène] must catch the spirit of the drama's basic unity and incorporate its rhythm into his work. There must be no failure of coordination anywhere."

Craig and Appia, however, opened to Copeau the vastness of their vision, a vision that bespoke the need of a semi-religious creation of beauty and joy for the theater. He learned from them the limitless potentialities of a stage where atmosphere supplanted actuality, where synthesis and suggestion took the place of analysis and detail.

In order to achieve complete unity between actor and set, set and play, play and actor, the usual old-timer or faded star who supervised rehearsals at the Comédie-Française or on the boulevards would not suffice as the impartial master-builder required in this art of coordination. Therefore, in the best interest of the theater, wrote the distinguished stage designer Lee Simonson in his *Stage Is Set*, "revival of scenic design . . . coincides exactly with the emergence of the director as a commanding and necessary figure on the modern stage." Whether it be Granville-Barker, Tyrone Guthrie, Peter Brook, Fuchs, Erler, Reinhardt, Fehling, Jessner, Piscator, Stanislavsky, Meyerhold, Tairoff, Evreinov, Antoine, Copeau, Gémier, Baty, Dullin, Pitoëff, Jouvet, Vilar, Chéreau, Barrault—and these are only a few of Europe's past and present leaders—one man alone, assisted by his theater's manifold collaborators, controlled the path in both design and nature that was taken by a play's action.

Copeau himself defined the kind of man the metteur-en-scène had to be if he were faithfully to represent his calling: "sincere and modest, his virtues: maturity, reflection, choice; he does not invent ideas, he retrieves them—*il n'invente pas les idées, il les retrouve*! His function is to translate the author, to read the text, feel its inspiration, control it, just as the musician reads printed notes and sings them in harmony and at a glance."[9] Unlike Craig and Reinhardt, Copeau considered himself the poet's proxy, not his master. Dramatic creation and mise-en-scène were "two parts of a single act."

This made some of his most ardent admirers call him a literary producer. Samuel Waxman, for example, in his book *Antoine and the Théâtre Libre*, wrote: "Go to Copeau if you want to know if your play is literature, but go to Antoine to find out if it is drama." Yet Copeau himself never tired of criticizing dramatists for being literary. He did not deify the text; he merely allotted it the full place that any artistic conductor gave his score, classic or modern. And if he reproached the spectacle-loving Antoine, it was because the latter was given more and more to sacrificing the play to sumptuous sets. Also, Copeau perceived in the tendencies of the day an exaggerated devotion to means of expression and little feeling for that which was to be expressed. He stated bluntly that a new mechanical contrivance for the stage was not to be mistaken for a new art of the theater. Music-made moods he distrusted and compared to tasty sauces that hide the poor quality of the meat. (*Twelfth Night*, it is true, contained no less than eight musical sequences, but each was called for by Shakespeare in the actual dialogue and were authentic English airs.) And "decadence in the art of writing plays" he attributed primarily to "the era of scenic innovation and material display." For these contentions he was called literary, but those who worked with him and had occasion to observe him closely admired his constructive sense of theater and found him "a *Theatermensch* who was always excited over the theatrical truth."[10]

The way to such truth would lead to a dramatic renascence itself. Copeau pursued four principal criteria to achieve this: to have the actor think his part, to convince the poet to write for the stage, to offer the play the limitless visionary expanse of theatrical architecture, and to devise a profound over-all unity of production. In aspiring to these goals, the Vieux-Colombier School was the strongest link to the theater of the future. But each of the four received individual attention at the theater itself from the very start of its existence.

When, in the summer of 1913, the actors were taken to the country, one purpose was to create the unusual spirit that was eventually to inflame the imagination of both player and director, a spirit of freedom born, paradoxically, of discipline and hard work. Copeau's supervision of his actors' training, both mental and physical, succeeded to a remarkable degree in cleansing them of the personal rivalries and professional jealousies so prevalent in the theater. He felt he could not make true artists of his actors unless they were first of all made to be modest, forward-looking men and women, capable, among other things, of playing a lead one night and a supernumerary the next without grudges or mental reservations. (Such was the unusual tradition launched by the famous Düsseldorf Troupe.) Valentine Tessier, in 1914, did just that when she played Grouchenka in *Les Frères Karamazov* and then a bit part in *Twelfth Night*. Consequently, the complete homogeneity of Copeau's company was the wonder of Paris. Almost everyone saw this, but few could explain it without being aware of the unique spirit that pervaded the art of this community of players.

Le patron had not only to create this spirit of moral and professional integrity. He had, upon occasion, to guard it, and even fight for it. At the very beginning, difficulties had arisen. Roger Karl and Gina Barbieri, who both had established reputations as actors, did not take easily to Copeau's methods of theatrical reform. Karl soon left the company; Mme. Barbieri's husband did not wish to see his wife "go to school" and kept her in town while others rehearsed in the country in 1913. (At the theater she was a most devoted actress.) Jouvet used to become moody and irritable when he had to take part in rhythmic gymnastics. And while Valentine Tessier was acting in England during the First World War when the Vieux-

Colombier was closed, she aroused Copeau's fears when he learned under whose management she was playing. He wrote her on November 22, 1916:

> I was led to think that this prolonged stay in England had spoiled you. Nor did I hide my irritation from you. . . . Let us speak no more of that. I do not question your affection or your devotion. I trust that both will increase when we are once again together and undertake a long-range piece of work, a work which will no longer be hindered or stopped. Through this incident I believe you will have felt also how jealous I am of the attachment and devotion of those whom I consider collaborators in my work and a little like my children. Any wrong done to the nature of this attachment, of this devotion, is for me a wound which I cannot bear. I have had and shall doubtlessly continue to have other disappointments, which is why I am so touchy. But for now and for the future you must understand that I am completely devoted to all of you, that I shall always do everything for you, all that I can and even more; you know I am usually not brutal and that I want above all to be liked, but in return for these feelings, I demand and I am determined to demand in the future absolute loyalty and a veritable submission from those whom I wish to make artists and to whom I give all I can give.
>
> I hope, *ma chère Valentine*, that we shall never have to speak of this again. Do not think I have forgotten the qualities which made me appreciate you; I know that you are good and courageous, but do not think either that I am happy to see you work with people like [name of a minor foreign producer]. The mere fact that I had to telegraph him made me feel like vomiting.

The real test came later, however, after actors like Jouvet and Tessier became known. As early as 1920, the famous actor-manager Lucien Guitry (father of the equally celebrated Sacha) asked Copeau to lend him Jouvet for a role. Copeau refused outright. His actors' contracts specifically forbade them to act outside the Vieux-Colombier without authorization. This clause held for the summer months as well, when the theater was closed. Actors were placed on half-pay, 600 francs per month ($120), during summer recess. Valentine Tessier discovered this when she was on a summer road tour of forty-two cities with the Vieux-Colombier and being praised everywhere for her performance in *Le Carrosse du Saint-Sacrement*. One such word of praise came from a critic-playwright, Alfred Savoir, the same man who a few months earlier had pleaded for a "League of Protection against Masterpieces" in speaking of the Vieux-Colombier repertory. He suggested to the popular Valentine in the summer of 1920 that she "star" and tour with her own troupe. She casually mentioned this in a letter to Copeau, who lost no time in setting her straight:

> My dear Valentine, Your short note from Epinal reaches me today. It crossed the letter I wrote you a few days ago, and which an-

swered it so to speak. But I do not resist the pleasure of writing you again, although I have so many things to do.

I am delighted that you are meeting with success and being fêted, especially if you are strong enough to be wary of praise and remain the simple, charming girl that you are. At such times I should like to be near you, chat with you, tell you what I know of the world, to stir up in you that aversion which I have for all that is not simple, everyday work. *Ma chère petite*, do you know what an Alfred Savoir is? . . . the sum of all that we hate, of all that we have repudiated. The Vieux-Colombier and those who compose it have now reached the most dangerous moment of all when, along with the fashion of success, it is approached by those very persons against whom it struggles, who will never understand it in its essence and whose admiration would certainly be an insult for me if I did not know that never in their life will they ever be able to influence me. Valentine, don't let yourself be touched by those people. I do not know what truth their words or their intentions have, but I wish to tell you immediately that if they or others ask you to play as guest-star, I shall refuse them point-blank. . . . at no price do I wish to create a precedent which would inevitably bring us indiscipline and disorder. I don't want them to be able to approach Vieux-Colombier actors as they do the actors of those houses without doctrine and honor. . . . And I should like the mere word "boulevard" to fill my comrades with horror rather than envy. I shall not loan out one of my actors any more than I would one of my children. By our cohesion we form and shall continue to form more and more an invincible force. Those who find that the Vieux-Colombier is no longer suitable to them or does not satisfy their needs have only to withdraw. But I shall never accept the ambiguous system of actors on tour as guest-stars.

I tell you all this bluntly, my dear Valentine, but without an iota of anger against you. On the contrary, I have great confidence in your loyalty. And even if one day you feel like leaving me, I shall bear no bitterness. But I believe you would be wrong. And I am so sure of the future that it gives me both conviction and strength to invite you all to be patient.

This moral education of the actor was intimately linked with professional development. Copeau lived for this dual purpose. His acting was intelligent and sincere, serious and noble, distinguished and finished, a clear reflection of his theater's more general aims. As with himself, he required his actors to think their parts, for he believed that it was primarily in this way that he could eventually formulate the rules of a technique that had kept ticking in time with civilization at its highest moments of culture. By learning how to think his part, he had acquired an acting style as distinctive as his directing style. From the moment he stepped on the stage, that style impressed itself on the spectator. Of his Ivan in *Karamazov*, Harold Clurman wrote in the *Post* (January 8, 1927):

There is something inescapably incisive and defined in his performance, and the mystery of the character is not conveyed by any haziness or blurring in the means of presentation, but, on the contrary, by their very austerity and directness. There is something almost awful in Copeau's clarity.

Though Ivan is a highly emotional character, Copeau's portrayal of him is severe and hard. Even in his final-act mad scene, in which he attained great power, Copeau's emotionalism is largely a nervous emotionalism, always dominated by mind. Copeau's acting is contained, tempered. He has thought without aridity, effectiveness without trickiness, intensity without violence.

Technically, Copeau achieves his remarkable definiteness and relief not only by his admirable powers of concentration but by his unmatched diction, pure and precise almost to a fault. Copeau's speech, however, derives its magic not merely from its clarity but from his very keen sense of rhythm which communicates itself to his movements as well, and which is one of his greatest gifts as a director.

Arthur Hornblow, after praising this same Ivan, remarked in *Theatre Magazine* (March 1918) that many people "would go far to see him in *Hamlet*," which was a favorite way for American critics to place an actor at the top of his profession. But Copeau never played Hamlet. He preferred the more fantastic Shakespeare of *Twelfth Night* and *The Winter's Tale*. His Malvolio was compared by John Corbin in the *New York Times* (February 9, 1919) to that of Sir Henry Irving and described as "a cerebral effort rather than an instinctive and absolute creation." Clurman felt that his comedy could "stimulate and pique, but . . . not rouse or shake us. It is too mental for that." And when Copeau played Scapin in France, some saw in him the serious literary leader and "had all the trouble in the world to find him comic."[11]

This cerebral quality, however, was not intellectually dry. Having mastered body and voice, Copeau and his actors were able to transmit their characters sculpturally to the audience. Jouvet's Feodor Karamazov made people detest the old scoundrel of a father as soon as they got a glimpse of the curve of his back and the angle of his elbows. This lesson of sculpture, absent from the stage since Greek times, found its way to the Vieux-Colombier along with Rodin's return to the principle that expression and suggestion should precede actuality and thought. (This would explain the sculptor's admiration for Copeau's directing.) Copeau did not himself stress the caricatural vein in acting to the extent Jouvet did. Yet he followed along a certain line of exaggeration typical of the whole company. Ivan's insanity, for example, he conveyed by means of a tossing torso, feet beating nervously on the floor, a turning head and popping eyes. This appealed directly to the audience's imagination, for Copeau had no intention of imitating the actions of a real lunatic, as Macgowan and Jones pointed out in their *Continental Stagecraft*. Also, except for the gout and a different costume, Copeau's acting of the governor in *Le Carrosse du Saint-Sacrement* and his philosophical Ivan Karamazov were essentially similar. In both, his playing had its clear presentational note; the only difference was one of mood, created in no small measure by his beautifully modulated and clear speech. The total effect of his acting was that of a theatrical reading (he was considered one of the best readers in France), addressed to an audience and yet remaining realistically within the limits of the circumscribed stage area.

A cerebral actor left nothing to chance. Every move, every intonation was prearranged and set in its proper place. That was part of the Vieux-Colombier's discipline, and it succeeded in developing several of the most distinguished actors on the French stage. They were, by principle, respectful interpreters whose intelligence and theatrical instinct helped sway more than one writer to become a dramatist.

Once the new dramatist was won over to the theater, Copeau wanted him to plan his work for the Vieux-Colombier's architectural stage. This, he felt, offered the writer the limitless space he needed to give his imagination free play. He hoped the dramatist would thus learn how to use the freedom he had not had since Shakespeare's day. It did not mean that he wished to force the playwright to work only for this type of stage; but when the author required the scope of the universe to fulfill his vision, the Vieux-Colombier was here to give it life, as with the Bard.

Still, the permanent set had its complex and tyrannical side, too, abetted as often as not by Copeau's own principle of the bare stage. The cement floor could not take a nail to fasten scenery of any kind, and it had a dull, annoying sound under the actors' feet. With the theater walls themselves forming the walls of the stage, the acoustics were bad. Moreover, the only way to reduce the size of the stage was by the use of screens or curtains, which sometimes did not suit realistic plays like *Le Testament du Père Leleu*. Also, Copeau wanted no part of the stage designer's revolution that appealed to the eye and with which Reinhardt had softened a good part of the theater. He stood for no artificial, tricky mechanics that dazzle the spectator and transport him into a fairyland of unexpected vistas. The actor was his one and only player. Sets, costumes, lights, and props received attention, but only insofar as they supported the play and its interpreters. They never became a player along with the actor. They had their own language, but one that was spoken and never itself spoke.

The permanent stage, however, gave the Vieux-Colombier far more than it took away. It forced actors to give of their best. They dared not walk across the bare stage without projecting ideas clearly by means of their gait, gestures, and diction. They had to maintain the highest standards of their art on a stage where there were no visual delights to distract the audience's attention from an actor's weaknesses. The author, too, felt this same obligation to aim high. It was an inspiration and a responsibility to write for a stage whose same walls had received Molière the night before and would house Shakespeare the next.

Such a stage obliged the metteur-en-scène to remain constantly within the bounds of good taste; otherwise the simplicity and sobriety of his production risked appearing poverty-stricken. To forestall such a reaction and impress the spectator with the premeditated choice of this unpretentiousness, Copeau devised more ingenious ways of changing atmosphere than a boulevard producer ever dreamed existed. Indeed, the barer the stage, the more meaningful and the more creative he made the resulting mise-en-scène, appealing to imagination far more than to the eye. Not that the eye was ignored. A great deal of originality was shown in designing costumes; these were conceived in order to color the stage as well as cover the actors. Each costume was treated as a work of art whose role was to contribute to the play's action and not be just a decoration to set off a figure or a face.

Costumes were second only to lighting at the Vieux-Colombier. The permanent walls and panels at the back of the stage were painted in a light gray that some critics found dull and harsh. But that shade lent itself to myriad changes beneath the colored lights that were played on it, and it became green, blue, and purple in *Les Frères Karamazov* as easily as it turned bright yellow and orange in *Le Carrosse du Saint-Sacrement*. These lights did more to shift locale and create atmosphere than all props combined.

Charles Vildrac described a quick transformation of set, typical at the Vieux-Colombier:

> After the third act of *Le Paquebot Tenacity*, in which the 'bistro' atmosphere is very well realized, as soon as one takes out the counter and its glasses, the shelf and its bottles, the little tables and their stools, the main table, somewhat larger (the one which Jouvet and I, in the rush of a final rehearsal, had varnished with a walnut stain as Roger Martin du Gard looked on amused); as soon as the stagehand, with one pull, tears the upstage glass door, the real café door, out of its hinges; as soon as the electrician sends up to the ceiling a lantern and its zinc reflector; as soon as he gilds the stage with an intense yellow light and exotic screens and green flowerpots appear and frame the vast desk of Peru's Viceroy; as soon as a prettily colored cloth is placed upstage as a door-curtain, everything is ready for *Le Carrosse du Saint-Sacrement*, and La Périchole can appear in all her glory, for she will find the frame she needs for the voluminous hoops of her gown, for her Spanish mantilla and comb.[12]

These quick changes that switched the same stage from a French harbor café to the quarters of the Viceroy of Peru were made inside of ten minutes, but the planning and execution of all the details took weeks, even months, under *le patron's* critical supervision. It was his responsibility to study each moment of the production carefully and attain that degree of harmony that made his audience expect the best in theater art at the Vieux-Colombier. To obtain this he listed the multiple tasks he had to face: "to circumscribe the dramatic area, establish its space and form its volume, conceive sets, devise the lighting . . . imagine the actor's physical appearance and costumes, regulate mass movements, assign each object its place, give each actor his line of action, and seek out in a world of fiction the natural movements and infinite variety of life."[13]

In this way he hoped to make life on the stage equal and true to the drama's life off the stage. As soon as Copeau selected a play, he organized the whole production quietly in his study. (He once had a large model stage but it did not prove of much value.) Every detail was duly recorded in a large ledger. "I file everything to make work easy," he wrote Jouvet in 1916. Then, with company and friends gathered around a table, he read the script in his clear, expressive voice, which succeeded in revealing the character and tone of each role. After casting the play, he assigned a scene to be improvised along the line of action, then the actors would play it to form their own characterizations and supply their own lines. After a definite and spontaneous mood had been reached, they would see the script for the first time. Again they sat around the table and each actor read his part while Copeau explained the lines. The first stage rehearsal was not held until the whole company knew the script thoroughly, "to the last comma," according to Jules Romains. Then they would modify their interpretations to comply with the text and coordinate words and movements, retaining the spontaneity of the original improvisation.

Copeau, from the orchestra, directed rehearsals and whenever necessary jumped onto the stage to show what he wanted. He seemed to be everywhere at once, especially when he was acting a part as well as staging the play. He would be on stage to speak his lines, and while his fellow-actor was answering he was already at the back of the house to judge the effect. He gave the impression of wanting to run fast enough to see himself act. He never tried to dominate his actors, but preferred to let them find their own gestures and intonations. When he did correct them, it was with a smile, affectionately, jokingly, his hands on the actor's shoulders. Upon occasion, however, he knew how to use authority and persuasion, for he held that "leaving the actor too much liberty is dangerous." Charles Dullin, as actor, appreciated particularly in his former *patron* "the swarm of ideas which surrounded these [acting] suggestions."[14]

During rehearsal time he visited each of his many ateliers daily. Everything was within his range and based on personal experience and technical knowledge. If he was less than pleased with a costume Hélène Forestier (Mme. Roger Martin du Gard) had just finished, he saw at once what to do: "Hélène *ma chère*, let's put a pin here," or "let's use a blue ribbon instead of a green one, a bit narrower, and let it fall there."

In all this mass of detail that he had to transform into the harmonious synthesis seen on opening night, Copeau's constant preoccupation was to avoid the superfluous everywhere. The actor's slightest gesture and movement had to be justified and become a constructive, indispensable part of the production.

Copeau, man of principle and seeker of rules, master of discipline and finder of laws, was above all a conscientious artist who felt obligated to keep moving forward toward perfection, an achievement that he knew was unattainable under the prevailing conditions in the theater, even his theater. But try he would, and did, to restore to the drama some of its former luster as a truly evocative and emotional art, one whose salvation lay in the honesty of its craftsmen. With sincere, devoted helpers, he thought he could reach his goal. On the way there, he set in place and helped build the four principal "columns" that made the Vieux-Colombier a modern French counterpart of a Greek temple of art. The first was the complete supremacy of the dramatist's text; yet when no living writer submitted a play whose superiority was clear and unquestioned, in Copeau's judgment, there were always the classics to depend on. The second was the harmony of all the elements in a production: gestures, words, colors, sounds, and so on, all under the direction of a single brain. The third was the architectural conception of the permanent set, which spelled conquest over the elusive third dimension, creating an elasticity for the stage to match the plasticity of the actor. And finally, only the barest essentials constituted the set, and even those stage properties were unassertive; whether the set had to suggest wealth or poverty, the décor did no more than give the play its locale, evoke the proper atmosphere, and then become incorporated into the play and no longer noticed.

With these precepts, Copeau produced rich mises-en-scène for works like *Barberine* and *Le Carrosse du Saint-Sacrement*, simple ones for *Le Paquebot Tenacity* and *Le Testament du Père Leleu*, symbolic ones for *Twelfth Night* and *The Winter's Tale*, the plays of Claudel, Gide. . . . All styles found effective and faithful expression on the Vieux-Colombier stage. All were presented with utmost authenticity. All sought to stir the spectator's imagination. All were given as modest, sincere offerings of genuine artists who believed that "there is a great deal of grandeur in a little bit of truth."[15]

7

Bitter Fruits of Fame (1921–1923)

IN JULY OF 1921, EXHAUSTED AFTER the long season's work, Copeau left Paris for the country. He had gladly turned over to Jouvet and to his nephew and student-assistant, Michel Saint-Denis, the bulk of the theater's administrative duties for the summer months when it was on tour. He preferred to remain in his study, secluded in an old square tower in the midst of a garden. There he was happiest, far removed from the constant interruptions of Paris. There he planned and prepared, and studied at leisure the problems and solutions that were to delight Paris the coming winter. Occasionally, a writer would visit him to ask for help. (René Benjamin worked with him there on the weak spots of his *Il faut que chacun soit à sa place*.) Copeau, *le patron*, remained in this tranquillity as long as he could, and when he returned to Paris it was with a fresh store of energy and ambition.

The 1921–1922 season opened with *La Fraude*, a melodrama by Louis Fallens, a Belgian writer who had recently died. Copeau saw in it qualities similar to those of *Le Paquebot Tenacity*; yet it was the most complete failure the Vieux-Colombier had ever experienced. To the last man, the critics spoke of their disappointment and surprise. Their notices, however, were full of respect and admiration for the theater itself: "No one admires M. Copeau's work more than we," "there [at the Vieux-Colombier] is the secret of all art," "there is so much will for art at the Théâtre du Vieux-Colombier," "*la chère compagnie du Vieux-Colombier*."[1] They spoke of Copeau as if they preferred to ignore his present poor choice since there had been so many good ones in the past. They even placed the blame for their unfavorable notices on Copeau himself for having accustomed them to so much better.

The public shared the sentiments of the critics and flocked to see revivals of *Le Testament du Père Leleu, La Navette, La Nuit des Rois* (*Twelfth Night*), and *L'Avare*. *Cromedeyre* was returned to the repertory "to find its public, slowly, but irresistibly," Copeau explained in the play's program, adding that this would postpone to the following season Romains's new comedy, *M. Le Trouhadec saisi par la débauche*. *Les Frères Karamazov* was brought back this season to observe the centenary of Dostoevsky's birth and *Le Misanthrope* was revived to honor the tercentenary of Molière.

This last work offered Copeau another opportunity to present a classic so that a 1922 audience could see what a 1666 audience had applauded. Copeau acted Alceste as the tragic figure, while Lucien Guitry, doing the same role simultaneously at the Théâtre Edouard VII, stressed the ridiculous side of the character. Copeau even went so far as to weep on the stage, a most unorthodox and unforgivable display of emotion in French classic drama. The critics voiced their pros and cons, and the Vieux-Colombier filled its 350 seats at every performance. Jean Sarment told the story of the two Englishmen who said to a Frenchman on leaving the theater: "Played in that way, your Molière is as great as our Shakespeare. Never would we have believed it before."[2]

The season's new dramatist, René Benjamin, was produced on April 21, 1922. *Les Plaisirs du hasard* stamped its author as a comic writer of great force. The critics compared his satiric vein to that of Molière, Beaumarchais, and Courteline.

The last addition to the year's repertory was André Gide's *Saül*. Since 1901, when Lugné-Poe put on *Le Roi Candaule*, Gide had remained aloof from the theater, but continued nonetheless to consider it "an extraordinary thing." As early as 1904, in his lecture on *L'Evolution du Théâtre*, he had called upon the theater to be exactly and only what it is, theater. Stage theories on "the synthesis of the arts" horrified him. But, as with Martin du Gard, Schlumberger, Ghéon, and so many others, the Vieux-Colombier had reconciled him somewhat to the joys of writing for the theater, even though it bored him to step into one. Copeau, himself, was never in greater artistic accord with anyone than he was with Gide. He saw in the author of *Saül* a natural writer of comedies, if Gide could only overcome his repugnance for the theater. As a matter of fact, Gide wrote in his *Journal* on June 21, 1914: "The desire to write a comedy torments me every day and almost each hour of the day. I should like J.C. [Jacques Copeau] to give me a subject, as Pushkin gave Gogol the one for *The Inspector*. I believe that a good subject would thrive wonderfully in my head, but I cannot find the subject *in me* as I do my other books. That of a drama, if not given by someone else, must at least come from outside, be *proposed*."

Copeau sought to give his friend's five-act play the mise-en-scène he felt it deserved after a twenty-six year wait. (It was written in 1896 and published in 1903 by *Mercure de France*.) He called upon his students to design and make masks, and for the first time, allowed them to act as a chorus of little demons under the direction of chief demon Suzanne Bing. Arthur Honegger composed the score for the demons, which Gide, incidentally, found too conspicuous, fearing that it made them take on too much importance. All these matters were discussed by author, director, and Roger Martin du Gard during a three-day trip to the country at the end of April, just before rehearsals began.

The play opened on June 16 and met with a lukewarm reception, which may not have completely displeased its author. "Each time that 'success' came near me it made me grimace," he once said. Yet a critic like Henri Béraud (*Mercure de France*), who disliked Gide's writings, admitted that *Saül* was a "fine work." And Copeau's mise-en-scène was called the best to date.

The season had introduced a single promising playwright in René Benjamin, but the press protested less the dearth of new writers than in former years. Critics like Henri Bidou (*Journal des débats*) were disposed to explain away mediocre plays and speak of the Vieux-Colombier's more important qualities: its spirit and principles in art. Even Adolphe Brisson (*Le Temps*), whose column had ignored the Vieux-Colombier during its early years, now spoke of it with pride as a powerful nucleus of increasing influence. And Lucien Dubech (*Revue universelle*) pointed out the Vieux-Colombier as "the model, guide and initiator" of all art theaters in France.

Audiences at this time reached a high point of participation in "their" theater's life. Offering financial help no longer satisfied a large number of supporters. They asked to share as well in the actual artistic and spiritual life of their *maison*. Copeau invited them to appear on the stage as extras, in active collaboration with the entire production. In Beaumarchais's *Le Mariage de Figaro*, for example, a journalist—himself an extra at one time—reported that alongside Copeau, Boverio, and other professionals, there were reputable painters, sculptors, doctors, professors, and the whole staff of *Essais libres*, a Left Bank literary magazine. Rarely had audiences ever been so completely integrated into the inner life of a theater.

At the start of the following season (1922–1923), so loud were the clamors from the provinces and foreign lands to see his work, that Copeau formed a touring company with a few of his Paris actors, new ones and students, to alternate with the regular company in playing outside Paris. While this new company was gathering laurels elsewhere (provincials complained that they could never get a seat at the Vieux-Colombier when they were in Paris), Copeau launched a season reminiscent of the second one in New York. There were twenty-five plays, of which fifteen were major works, and four of these new to the repertory. One was Vildrac's *Michel Auclair.* By the sincerity of its tone it resembled *Le Paquebot Tenacity,* but it fell short of the latter's natural humanness and truthfulness in story and characterization. The playwright Robert de Flers, writing in *Le Figaro* (January 1, 1923) after seeing Vildrac's drama, recommended however "that actors go to the Théâtre du Vieux-Colombier to see how a play should be acted." And Henri Bidou in his review of the same play (in *Journal des débats,* February 3, 1923) noted that "whatever be the fortunes of a work, it belongs to theater history if it has been played within those famous walls."

The final production of the season, *Bastos le hardi,* came in time to forestall a growing flood of protests that in all the season's lengthy repertory, not one new play of real merit had been produced. This was a comedy by Léon Régis and François de Veynes, written specially for the Vieux-Colombier and dedicated to Jacques Copeau. "Without his work," the authors announced, "this play would not have been written."

There were no rave notices, but once more Copeau proved to be the host in a "shelter for future talent." Dullin wrote in the *Revue de l'Amérique latine* (October 1923) that the new play contained "the germs of that classic renovation which Copeau had been pursuing." Talk of the Vieux-Colombier's "artistic Jansenism" was quashed, and Henri Bidou (in *Journal des débats,* May 25, 1923) felt that with this latest work it was "on the point of being perfect." He congratulated Copeau for softening somewhat the "inhuman austerity" of his stage of earlier days. He thanked him for doing away with the platform within the stage and for not using the permanent set too much.

Financially, the end of the 1922–1923 season revealed the usual deficit, only this time it was bigger: 125,000 francs (over $25,000). And again Copeau had to write his friends for assistance, "if only to support my little school, of which I expect much for the future." Auguste Rondel, amongst others, promised 1000 francs, but three months later, with the money not yet received, Copeau had to write Rondel: "I am so poor that I am obliged not to leave unrealized any of my friends' promises and that is why I am taking the liberty of reminding you of yours." Rondel replied promptly with a check for 500 francs, which Copeau acknowledged (October 25, 1923): "I have just received your generous offering and I hasten to thank you. If I had three hundred friends to help me every year in similar proportions, I should never have any more difficulties or worries."

This two-year period from 1921 to 1923 made the Vieux-Colombier's reputation secure throughout the world. The alternate company was sent abroad on tour in answer to the numerous invitations received from Sweden, Italy, Holland, Switzerland, Spain, and Belgium. Copeau's idea of the permanent set found its followers throughout Europe: the Hollander Fritz Lensvelt, the American Sam Hume, the German Emil Pirchau. In Brussels, Jules Delacre opened the Théâtre du Marais, whose stage was designed by Jouvet himself and was a very close copy of the Vieux-Colombier stage in New York.

In 1922, Copeau was invited to send models of his work to the Universal Theater Exposition in Amsterdam as a representative for France and to speak, at the same session with Craig, on his mise-en-scène. Judging from the exhibits, it appeared that the modern theater was more and more adopting an architectural stage and going farther and farther away from realism. Even the avant-garde group at the Comédie-Française, Charles Granval, Denis d'Inès, and Jean Croué (Copeau's collaborator in 1911 on *The Brothers Karamazov*), was quite suddenly given its chance to experiment with the new staging in *Les Fourberies de Scapin*.

The repertory and spirit of the Vieux-Colombier were also bearing fruit. That same year, the Theater Guild in New York concluded arrangements with Copeau to put on his plays in English. In London the Little Everyman's Theater of Hempstead worked in the same vein as the Vieux-Colombier. Hilar's repertory movement in Czechoslovakia, intending to raise the level of the drama and public taste, was launched. The Municipal Theater in Prague produced *Le Paquebot Tenacity* in the same spirit as at the Vieux-Colombier and as well, according to Vildrac. In France, a new metteur-en-scène, Gaston Baty, had just opened La Baraque de la Chimère with the collaboration of a group of authors who wished to found a theater on "enthusiasm, faith, and voluntary poverty," three qualities that brought back vividly the Copeau days of 1913. At the Comédie-Française, the most recent addition to the company was Madeleine Renaud, who, to Henri Béraud, appeared as if she had been "loaned to the Comédie by the Vieux-Colombier." And Firmin Gémier, who had shown himself a partisan of many of Copeau's ideas on staging, was named the head of the Odéon.

Although most of these influences fanned out of the Latin Quarter across Europe and the ocean, there were two international events of great moment in the life of the Vieux-Colombier that took place on its own stage and strengthened its morale when circumstances had suddenly turned against it. The first was the touching visit paid the company by Eleanora Duse in the spring of 1922. The great Italian actress had followed faithfully from afar the progress of the Vieux-Colombier and had even attempted to create a similar theater in her own country. With that remarkable intuition that so many theater artists have wondered at, she would send Copeau a telegram or letter at the psychological hour to encourage him and express her admiration for his work: "that living and noble thing." In one of those letters, she told him that she would be in Paris and wished to speak with him. When she arrived, he went eagerly to meet her. He tells of the meeting in his *Souvenirs*: "It is an old, sick and unsteady woman whom I find in the Regina Hotel, but adorably majestic and whose glance recovers its fire as soon as she speaks of the theater. For she wants to return to the stage. She is almost without funds. She wants to play in Paris again. But theater life hurts her. She would therefore like to give her performances at the Vieux-Colombier."

For economic reasons, this plan did not materialize, but nevertheless, on Monday, June 19, Copeau and the Vieux-Colombier welcomed her. Copeau recalled the gathering:

> The curtain had been lowered. On the stage, softly lighted, I had assembled all the actors, the whole personnel of the house, a few close friends. Duse entered. She was leaning on the arm of my dear friend Croiza. . . . All present rose without saying a word. Our little students, in white dresses, stepped forward a little awkwardly. My daughter, in front, carried a bouquet of roses which she placed in the arms of la Duse. Then as she bent down to kiss the child, Duse's big aristocratic hat fell off behind her. Gina Barbieri said a few words in Italian, I, a few in French. Duse mumbled two or three sentences which her emotion rendered unintelligible. But that mattered little. We had her to ourselves, amongst us: her eyes, her hands, her voice. On the stage or in life, she was one of those creatures whose mere presence affects you as a blessing. Our short ceremony had not lasted more than fifteen minutes. Upon returning to her car, Duse said to Croiza: "That will be my best memory of Paris."

A few weeks later she sailed for America, where she died. An Italian naval vessel brought her body home for national mourning.

The second event of this period of success—and impending disaster—was Stanislavsky's first visit to Paris, in 1922, with his Moscow Art Theater. Copeau met him at the Gare du Nord on his arrival. Then, with Antoine, he welcomed him on the stage of the Théâtre des Champs-Elysées, where his troupe was to play for two weeks. Some years before, while directing in Geneva, Copeau met an acquaintance who had seen the Moscow Art Theater and predicted a brilliant future for the Vieux-Colombier. With a neophyte's enthusiasm, Copeau commented upon this in a letter to Jouvet: "For that he had to go to Russia!" Six years later, after attending a Moscow Art performance, he heard one of his best actresses, Valentine Tessier, complain to him: "I ought to go to the country and grow cabbages." He answered: "Patience. Wait until you've acted like them, together for thirty years."[3]

The two men met as often as their work permitted, and on Thursday, December 21, 1922, at midnight (after the strain of the opening night of Vildrac's *Michel Auclair*), the Vieux-Colombier received on its own stage the Moscow Art Theater and its director, "consecrating by his presence the place of our work." Copeau hailed him that night as the master of them all: "by the nobility of his character, loftiness of spirit, knowledge and authority. . . . He bears on his face the marks of a man who has dreamed very much, loved very much, struggled very much, searched, suffered, and who, on the threshold of old age, still seeks, has not stopped learning and has not stopped hoping."[4]

In his talks with Copeau, the great Russian director kept repeating: "Our art of the theater is extraordinarily behind all the others arts of our times. But it is a fraud to apply to it artificially the methods of these other arts. We must not pretend to express what we cannot express." At times, he would place his hands on Copeau's shoulders and say to him sadly: "Believe me, we artists of the theater, we who believe in our art and live only for it, from all the countries in the world, we ought to unite and work together instead of being consumed and exhausted uselessly for people who don't want us."[5] Craig had once spoken the same way to Copeau, and Copeau had in turn been trying to convince his own associates of this.

During these talks with Stanislavsky, he yearned desperately to confide to him—but did not—the problems that were besetting him at that very moment. Even so close a friend as Gide could not make him open his heart: "Went to see J.C. [*Journal*, December 30, 1922] whom I find weary and very somber. He complains of that solitude for which he had so obstinately worked. He has rejected all advice and done his best to make his best friends leave him. 'I shall hold out until the end; but do not speak to me.' At the moment he needs people to talk to him. . . . He feels himself quite abandoned. One cannot not abandon a mystic."

In the fall of 1922, a few weeks before Stanislavsky's arrival in Paris, Jouvet had left the Vieux-Colombier to become metteur-en-scène at the Comédie des Champs-Elysées. Jules Romains, Georges Duhamel, and other early friends had grown impatient with Copeau's ideals and his adamant aloofness to commercializing his ideas. Even Les Amis du Vieux-Colombier, the friends of 1919, were withdrawing their patronage. The paradox of the situation was that they should choose to do so at the moment their theater was at the height of its reputation both at home and abroad.

The reasons for this break between Copeau and his friends were based in two fundamentally different conceptions of art as applied to the theater. The first was held by Jouvet: "*there are no problems in the theater but one: that is the problem of success. . . . the theater must first be a business, a flourishing commercial enterprise, then only is it permitted to impose itself upon the realm of art.*"[6] The second conception was Copeau's and Craig's, which Stanislavsky had put into words: "The very least utilitarian purpose or tendency, brought into the realm of pure art, kills art instantly."[7]

Jouvet's outlook was human enough. He was ambitious. As early as

1910, according to his friend Maurice Boissard (drama critic of *Mercure de France*), the young Jouvet wondered in amazement why he wasn't getting anywhere and said so in *Revue de la Quinzaine* (May 1, 1920): "It's curious! I can't understand it! I've written a good deal. I'm on good terms with all the right people. I go wherever one ought to go to be seen. I say as much good as possible of everybody so that they may say the same of me. Well, you won't believe me, but I am getting nowhere!"

Continuing in the same sardonic vein—though with Jouvet there was usually a good deal of truth along with the banter—he offered to pay M. Boissard a monthly fee for the use of his column in the *Mercure* to tell producers about the new dramatic art they persisted in ignoring. Three years later, in 1913, Jouvet joined the Vieux-Colombier. As the years went by, he worked more and more with Copeau on the mise-en-scène until he became a veritable jack-of-all-trades, with his finger in every atelier and his person in almost every play, whether as actor, designer, electrician, or stage manager.

Then, with the phenomenal success of the short 1920 season, thanks to Vildrac, Mérimée, Romains, Duhamel, and Mazaud, the Vieux-Colombier became the most dynamic theater of Paris, through its staging as well as its plays. But when the 1920–1921 season brought no new successful playwrights and Parisians continued to fill the theater anyway, it was obvious that Copeau's evocative, simple mise-en-scène had been accepted and belonged to the new order of the day. Offers were brought to him to move to a larger theater. Some business heads were even willing to build him a new one, seeing in the Vieux-Colombier a good investment. But Copeau answered that he was not yet ready. When asked how much time he still needed to develop his art, he would answer, as Craig once did: "Oh, ten years!" The capitalists shrugged their shoulders and moved on to more amenable artists, those ready to attune the Vieux-Colombier to their times, whereas Copeau sought to fine-tune his instrument for all times, future and present alike.

Even Jouvet hesitated to spend another ten years in a theater struggling to make ends meet in a tiny house that, when filled to capacity every night, would still have an annual deficit. Besides, outsiders were already using Copeau's ideas in the commercial theater while the master isolated himself with experiments on the Left Bank. Jouvet could not bear to see others exploit the successful results of Copeau's and his own years of trial and error. But his arguments were to no avail. *Le patron* could understand nothing but the heartbreaking disappointment of finding his most devoted, most cherished co-worker won over to commerce. Copeau could barely bring himself to speak. Both men sat side by side in their dressing room, elbows touching, and felt the wrenching pain of a great love no longer shared. Jouvet decided to leave, even though Copeau begged him to reconsider, saying that this would be the first voluntary departure of an original Vieux-Colombier artist. Jouvet's only reply was: "I am not leaving the Vieux-Colombier. The Vieux-Colombier has left me."[8] As soon as Jacques Hébertot leased the Comédie des Champs-Elysées and asked Jouvet to stage productions alternately with Georges Pitoëff, he accepted.

At that same time Jules Romains, so closely associated with the workings of the Vieux-Colombier, took part in the discussion whether to commercialize the theater or remain on the rue du Vieux-Colombier. He was definitely in favor of increasing the material rewards of their labors. He believed that this would give them enough funds to produce plays with less economy and rigidity, and thereby avoid overly abstract mises-en-scène that were arousing much criticism. Copeau listened attentively and understandingly, but decided in favor of remaining small and pure.

Romains was annoyed as well by Copeau's rejecting his comedy *M. Le Trouhadec saisi par la débauche*, written for the Vieux-Colombier, and producing instead an inferior play like *La Fraude* by Fallens. Jouvet promptly accepted *Trouhadec* for the Comédie des Champs-Elysées and Romains followed him there.

This was a wrenching period for Copeau, the more so because it was brought about, ironically enough, by the resounding success of his work. It disappointed and hurt him to see his closest collaborators join forces with those who had mocked him. Now that they courted him to fill their coffers, he warded them off disdainfully. With so many friends leaving him to carry on the good fight without them, he trusted that at least the audience he had built up would continue to show their faith. He anticipated their questions in the very first number (1920) of his pamphlet *Les Cahiers du Vieux-Colombier*, which he called "Les Amis du Vieux-Colombier." Here he told them why he could not agree to inflate his theater to the unnatural proportions required of a good investment.

There were two sides to the Vieux-Colombier: art and business. As things stood, the first was very large and the second very small.[9] The first was part of a tremendous surge that was carrying the art of the theater to extraordinary heights. The second brought insufficient returns that left the Vieux-Colombier with annual deficits at a time when everyone spoke of its prosperity. Such talk angered Copeau, as it had once infuriated Charles Péguy—author, idealist, and influential publisher of *Les Cahiers de la quinzaine*—when subscribers asked him if he were satisfied with the magazine's success. Péguy answered: "Don't say that! A thousand subscribers! I never exceeded one thousand subscribers. And you speak of success!" That subscriber had confused the fame of Péguy's *Les Cahiers* with its financial return, when one had little to do with the other. Likewise, the spectator who heard of the Vieux-Colombier's artistic success confused it with financial success, which it did not have in spite of playing almost every night to full houses and frequently turning people away.

But there remained the inevitable fact that the Vieux-Colombier could not earn enough money to support the vastness of its experimental output. Its 360 seats ranging in price from five to twenty francs did not suffice to make ends meet. And Copeau refused to raise the medium-priced seats, which brought in "the most interesting part of our audience." Some suggested that he reduce his expenditure to equal his income. That, too, was not feasible in a repertory theater. Whereas the commercial theater was satisfied to produce one model for millions, the very nature of the repertory theater demanded that Copeau "throw on the market ten models for twenty thousand customers."[10] The problem was how to reconcile two opposites.

The Vieux-Colombier was not founded to capitalize on a single play's long run, or even on regular annual short runs of the same play. To keep his public alert and fresh, Copeau was obliged to keep his repertory changing constantly. The functioning of this heavy schedule required a large company of actors and a large administrative personnel. Exploitation of the repertory as a whole was possible, but first the Vieux-Colombier needed time and actors to develop a richer one than it had. This in turn meant larger expenses, which could only be met if the Vieux-Colombier as an art was to be sacrificed to the Vieux-Colombier as a successful business. He refused to bow to that alternative: "the Vieux-Colombier would no longer be for me the living work to which I have consecrated my life and that of my family. I'd rather let it go, this very day, under someone else's direction, towards a prosperity which I refuse to share."

The answer to this problem was an obvious one for a business man. Since the Vieux-Colombier's financial troubles came from the small size of its theater, it should profit from its present popularity by moving into a larger one, supported by backers smart enough to invest in what the public had already approved. Copeau admitted that this reasoning was valid and "would make several of my best friends give a sigh of relief." But for all its validity, he argued that such reasoning was basically unacceptable to the artist who had made something out of nothing. The reasoning was essentially false. The larger theater was not going to continue the artist's work, but rather settle it more or less in its present form—a form that did not yet satisfy Copeau. As a result, his work would be squeezed into a tight mold, the character of which was of a different kind from the one developed by its creator.

The solution offered by a bigger house was a sensible one and Copeau had to face it. That was why it took him so long to decide to part from Jouvet and his other friends. But as sensible and practical as it was, it was the very denial of what the Vieux-Colombier stood for. Dullin said as much to Jouvet a few years later: "Had anyone told us at the time [1913] that we would one day leave the Vieux-Colombier, which we were founding with Copeau, well, he would perhaps have received a couple of wallops. We were all really 'pure.' Which accounts for the vast consequences of that tiny undertaking."[11]

Copeau believed in the long-term success of his ideas against commercialization. These ideas were "momentarily in contradiction with my personal interests, and, to a certain point, with the interests of my friends who are supporting me." But only "momentarily," for the Vieux-Colombier promised to become a prosperous theater without changing its character and on its own standards and momentum, thanks to the rejuvenating power of the school and the additional companies to be sent on the road.

His associates argued that "you must live before philosophizing." Copeau's answer to them was plain and unequivocal:

> What I call living is for a man to assert himself according to his nature, to follow his spiritual destiny. Away from this course, I find death. It is to a real death that you send us if you call us to an artificial life, if you do not respect our thought above all, if you can see only a material power in that which the spirit has alone created, if you wish *to exploit the idea of the Vieux-Colombier* before it has reached maturity, before the *fact* of the Vieux-Colombier has been achieved.

The clearer his art became to him, the stronger his resistance. He could not see himself enlisting it in the service of anyone. On the contrary, whenever possible, he had enlisted for it the services of others. For almost ten years he had actively sheltered his work from all. Now, more than ever, when it was beginning to have a certain influence, he refused to deposit the Vieux-Colombier into the hands of a profit-making corporation. It would create for him the kind of obligations he could never face. "I do not wish to assure my future at the price of my liberty," he protested, the liberty he had grown to cherish from the days when the *Nouvelle Revue Française* was founded to bring together some of the freest writers ever to unite in the service of art. "I would rather live from day to day begging."

The only answer to this solitary cry of an artist was its hollow echo, returning to him from an indifferent Paris. As for Jouvet, Romains, Duhamel, and all the others, they had gone out of the Street of the Old Dove-Cote and walked hurriedly over the Pont des Arts to the Right Bank—which was now ready to receive them.

They had no sooner left when the critics began to protest almost violently against the systematizing of Copeau's repertory. Also, this being Paris, austerity and severity in mise-en-scène were looked upon as so much affectation. One wise-cracking critic rolled out the epithet "Folies-Calvin" to describe the Vieux-Colombier.

When similar doubts about his work began to take hold of the pub-

lic, Copeau sought desperately to justify his actions. He explained to
Parisians—and more particularly to the Vieux-Colombier's audiences—
that his theater had a future, but one that still required preparation and
support, that the day was now visible when that vague future would
evolve into a bright present, proclaiming its arrival and calling out for
its friends to hurry and help celebrate its coming of age: "A theater which
has a mission, which obeys its duties, which considers itself responsible
for public culture, will always need help. . . . And we will continue to
ask for it directly from the community, the public, the elite first and perhaps one day from the masses."

But critics and public refused to hear him. For the 1922–1923 season,
75 percent of Les Amis du Vieux-Colombier failed to renew their subscriptions. People were saying that Copeau was on the wrong road. Even
friendly critics accused him of making his theater "a restricted chapel"
(une étroite chapelle) instead of what he had set out to create: "the meet-
ing-place of a whole people in artistic communion."[12] He was urged to
acquiesce more to the popular taste of his public, since his work had
proven so successful that the Vieux-Colombier was attracting a much
wider audience than the one it had originally set out to please in 1913.

Copeau did not flinch. He answered the critics by telling them that such
pleas from them were the real cause for the decadence of theatrical art.
And just before the opening of Vildrac's *Michel Auclair*, he called a meeting of Les Amis du Vieux-Colombier to justify his work. He again told
them that he had gladly sacrificed everything to the Vieux-Colombier, his
profession as critic, author, and editor, his solitude and his leisure, material security and the moral pleasures of a family man. One thing he would
never sacrifice: his conscience as an artist. He expressed once more his
need for their support and understanding. He told them that he could
bear their hostility, but he could not endure their polite withdrawal. Such
indifference on their part drained the Vieux-Colombier of its courage and
its strength. The meeting resulted in the group's reorganization.

The ravages of these two years of success and worldwide recognition
had been devastating. Jouvet's departure left a huge void. When Romains
relinquished the post of director of the school, it was a great moral loss.
The distrust of close friends left Copeau despondent. The lack of support
from a large number of subscribers left him bewildered and hurt. The
Vieux-Colombier had indeed to pay a heavy price for its success, but at
least it could still take pride in its "ignominious independence."[13]

8

The Last Season
(1923–1924)

WHEN THE 1923–1924 SEASON BEGAN on October 31, there was nothing to indicate that it would end with the Vieux-Colombier's final curtain. On the contrary, Copeau published a tenth-anniversary message in the program on his theater's growing maturity. He wished to make of the Vieux-Colombier:

> a place of artistic conviction, of study and formation. For ten years I tried especially to find myself; then I tried to reestablish for those willing to follow me, working conditions and essential principles of an art whose methods had decayed and, in a manner of speaking, been shorn of ambition. That is what some call my spirit of didacticism. It is easy to distort someone or something with a word. But I should like to ask some of those who throw this reproach at us from whom they learned what they know if not from us.

Copeau faced the critics proudly, aggressively. He admitted that he always preferred collaborators who had goals and visions similar to his own. But this did not make of the Vieux-Colombier a closed corporation. "Even if I remain faithful to old friendships," countered *le patron*, "I have never been their prisoner." (In his office were unproduced scripts by Jules Romains, Jean Schlumberger, André Gide, Henri Ghéon, and others.) He then went on to identify three groups of writers who had met Vieux-Colombier standards. First, there were the neorealists: Charles Vildrac (*Le Paquebot Tenacity* and *Michel Auclair*) and Emile Mazaud (*La Folle Journée*). Then came a much older group of men (with the exception of Romains), who were writers of tragedy and on whom the Vieux-Colombier had no influence whatsoever: Paul Claudel (*L'Echange*),

André Gide (*Saül*), Jean Schlumberger (*La Mort de Sparte*), Henri Ghéon (*Le Pauvre sous l'escalier*), and Jules Romains (*Cromedeyre-le-Vieil*). And finally, the youngest, most numerous and most consistent group were those authors influenced by the Vieux-Colombier's penchant for Molièresque comedy and farce: Roger Martin du Gard (*Le Testament du Père Leleu*), Georges Duhamel (*L'Oeuvre des athlètes*), Emile Mazaud (*Dardamelle ou le Cocu*), Jules Romains (*M. Le Trouhadec saisi par la débauche*, unproduced), René Benjamin (*Les Plaisirs du hasard*), and Régis and de Veynes (*Bastos le hardi*).

In view of all this, Copeau concluded:

> How much longer will one spread the legend of a sad Vieux-Colombier? Certainly, we shall never leave off the search for that modern tragedy. . . . But, for the moment, our obvious inclination is unquestionably towards a fresh comedy, direct, well constructed, of completely Latin and French tradition, inspired by the spirit of the times, its traits, foibles, social life, political customs. A comedy more and more freed from literature and from sentimentality. And a comedy of that kind is the measuring-rod of civilization for an era.

To those who reproached him for using the classics as models, he replied: "Almost all young people today clamor loudly for liberty. Liberty for what? To break their medium and have their talent misused." He urged them to understand his motives. The rejuvenation of old plays—thanks to his mise-en-scène—may not have produced a dramatist of any real influence, but it did inspire new writers to recognize that the art of creating for the theater cannot be detached from the art of acting in the theater. Without this golden rule, Copeau asked, could Romains have written his *Trouhadec*, Mazaud his *Dardamelle*, or Régis and de Veynes their *Bastos*?

The 1923–1924 season opened with a four-act comedy, *L'Imbécile* by Pierre Bost, the first play by this twenty-two-year-old writer, in whom Copeau had great confidence. The critics, too, perceived real promise in him, but for the present found that the action moved too slowly for the stage and was "too faithful to the spirit of the analysts in the *Nouvelle Revue Française*."[1] Even a fervent enthusiast of the Vieux-Colombier like François Mauriac saw in it only a "pleasant play . . . shrewd comedy."[2]

The second work of the evening, however, Goldoni's *La Locandiera*, was a favorable contrast. It raced swiftly and merrily along showing the playful side of Copeau's mise-en-scène. Mauriac, an unusual critic who listened for the public's reaction as well as giving his own, reported that people called *La Locandiera* "*Le Carrosse du Saint-Sacrement* in the setting of *La Nuit des rois*." Antoine protested the cuts made in the script, but almost everyone else accepted it as they saw it and had hearty laughs with Valentine Tessier, the provocative mistress of the inn. Indeed, Mauriac found very strange "this reputation of austerity that people attribute to them [Vieux-Colombier actors]."

A week later, *Bastos le hardi* was revived. Two weeks after that, *Le Testament du Père Leleu*, Benjamin's *La Pie borgne*, and Mazaud's *La Folle Journée* were played on the same bill. The Vieux-Colombier was resuming its usual momentum with its discoveries of 1913, 1920, and 1923. All this time, Copeau was rehearsing the company in a daring venture, finally produced on December 18 when the critics were invited to come and sit in judgment on a new play, his own: *La Maison natale*. A few of them rubbed their hands in anticipation, for many of these critic-dramatists had their own private bone to pick with Copeau for having rejected their scripts. But the author had something to say and the critics of Paris had never yet frightened him into silence or retreat.

This was Copeau's first original play. After Dostoevsky's novel had been dramatized, he adapted Heywood's *A Woman Killed With Kindness*. Then, with Suzanne Bing, he translated *The Winter's Tale*. Dramatization and adaptation he considered a valuable form of discipline for the artist, teaching him one of the primary premises of his craft, "the art of sacrifice."[3] He had also written *L'Impromptu du Vieux-Colombier* and a *Prologue improvisé*, but they could hardly be accepted as plays in the real sense of the word, even though Gabriel Boissy, the *Comœdia* drama critic, suggested that with a few more characters and a simple plot, the *Prologue* would be a good comedy on the charlatanism of miracle doctors. (One can only wonder whether Jules Romains could or would have written his ever-popular *Dr. Knock* without the influence of Copeau and the Vieux-Colombier.)

With *La Maison natale* Copeau came into his own as a mature dramatist who was at long last practicing what he had been preaching. Since 1913, he had set down as a fast rule of the house that writers should be actively involved with the inner workings of the theater in order to learn how to take full advantage of its manifold means of expression. He wanted the art of playwriting to become as intimately bound as possible to the art of acting, a desire that explained why he himself had become so indefatigable a member of the acting company, in spite of friendly entreaties to stop. The writer in him was now ready to show what the actor had learned from these experiments.

The play was completed in the summer of 1923 in the quiet of his house in the country. But it had been conceived long before, and after more than twenty years, still retained its original source of inspiration, the symbolist-classic tone of the early *Nouvelle Revue Française* vintage.

The plot was simple and direct. It was in the characters, more than in the action, that the current of emotional strife moved rhythmically forward. Bernard Hersant, a sick man, is a hard, cold person whose wife and children fear him. His two sons, Maxime and Pierre, have run away from home, and he feels that his youngest, André, will soon follow, encouraged by a grandfather's idealistic talk about a happy and free life. He is unable to forestall this final insult to his vanity, so he confronts his wife's father, Félix Daronge, openly accusing the old man of nurturing the youngest son's decision to leave. At the father's death, André refuses to be shackled into managing the family factory. He wants to lead his own life and find the same happiness his two brothers had. At this point, Maxime suddenly returns, begging his mother's forgiveness. André looks upon him as a coward and leaves to find his freedom—with the blessing of his grandfather (the role played by Copeau).

The drama told a twofold story. It gave the author's philosophy in the characters of André and Daronge, and it showed clearly the kind of serious, personal struggle the Vieux-Colombier preferred. From a literary standpoint, Copeau's play was deeply rooted in the symbolist genre: the affirmation of man's superiority over things and the desire to depict vaguely, not analytically, the intimate and remote corners of the soul without betraying the essential mystery of life. This approach to literature, fortified by Henri Bergson's studies on intuition, had a strong influence on Copeau.

Historically, *La Maison natale* dated back to 1901, as the printed program explained. In November 1902 Copeau had published "*Notes d'enfance*" in a small magazine, *L'Ermitage*, depicting the fears of a growing child dominated by his father and restrained by maternal affection, all of which created the grim silence of "*The House into Which We Are Born.*"[4]

In the summer of 1903, he again wrote of "that *maison natale* where dreams rot." It was the same year that Copeau exiled himself from Paris in order to manage a family factory. Not until 1912 did he complete the first act, and, as usual, lost no time in reading it to his friends. Gide noted in his *Journal*, "I came away from it a bit terrified." The author must have revised it after that reading, for in 1914, just before the war, Gide again heard the first act and mentioned it again in his *Journal*, this time without the terror. The following year he read the second act to Roger Martin du Gard and his wife, making them both burst into sobs. Undoubtedly autobiographical, the play contained the confessions of an adolescent, a popular theme with many *Nouvelle Revue Française* writers.

Copeau found himself in the final year of his theater's life before he dared reveal to the public his dreams and love of adventure in the speculations of Daronge and in the decision of André to flee the chains of conventional responsibilities. With few exceptions, critics complained that this was exactly the type of play Copeau would refuse to produce if he were not the author. As proof, they cited as some of his (supposed) growing dislikes: Gide (*Retour de l'enfant prodigue*), Ibsen (*The Wild Duck*),

Dostoevsky, the realists, the naturalists—as if he did not admire the Frenchman, worship the Norwegian, emulate the Russian, and continue to produce plays by Becque, Courteline, and Renard. They did not think to compare him to Claudel or Romains. Yet those were the writers whose modern tragedies he had preferred and produced, whose works bore a resemblance to his own, and who delved far beneath the surface to reach the authentic bedrock of natural emotion and truthful action.

The critics' reviews showed how little they understood what Copeau had been striving for all those years. Even after the great and continuing popular success of a work like *Le Paquebot Tenacity*, they were still wary of accepting the plays Copeau was most kindly disposed toward: "works of bare outline, of strict economy, of a clear-cut genre, works without shadows, as Jacques Rivière used to say. . . . And I admit that my most heartfelt and even profound admiration is caught by works whose charm and power assert themselves without our being able to explain it, without our being always sure of understanding them."[5]

Even those who praised *La Maison natale* had not understood the author's goals. They called him a greater dramatist than actor. His friends once more urged him to refrain from acting, just as Boileau had once suggested that Molière stop acting and devote his time to writing. Neither then nor now did people understand that it was while acting that the writer's art became ever clearer to him.

Copeau's play answered the grudges of rejected writers who complained that it was useless to bring him their scripts. True, he disdained what was new, curious, amusing, temporary, different, and scandalous when the eternal quality of the authentically beautiful, simple, and sober was absent. True, he admitted, dramatists like Crommelynck, Jean Sarment, J. J. Bernard, and others whose plays he had rejected had ideas and dramatic virtuosity. But he complained that "they don't take the time to recognize their subjects, they don't care to explore and clarify their conceptions, to enlarge them . . . to make them habitable for life. They ignore that reflection, that gradual knowledge, slowness and patience, that obstinate courage, that self-denial which alone leads to mastery."[6]

A flair for drama was not enough to justify production at the Vieux-Colombier. The author had to show respect and great care for detail. Copeau called upon him to acquire the knowledge to meet head-on the possibilities of his medium. He wanted the author to give the work the time it needed to grow naturally and become accustomed to its surroundings, to give it freedom to expand before reducing it to its essential proportions. Without all this, the result, in Copeau's eyes, was incomplete and partial, and its authenticity became mere wishful thinking.

He protested against the custom of his fellow dramatists in France of pulling a character out of his normal life and throwing him into some struggle, there to watch him squirm until he was saved or betrayed. He preferred the style of the Russians with their intimate, Chekhovian glimpses into the everyday doings of their characters. This brings us back to the role of the symbolists, who had been so warmly received by the Russians—and by the Vieux-Colombier. Both accepted the haunting verses of Emile Verhaeren to guide them at the crossroads:

> Penser, chercher et découvrir sont les exploits.
> Il emplit jusqu'au bord son existence brève;
> Il n'enfle aucun espoir, il ne fausse aucun rêve.

"The feat is to think, to seek, and to discover . . ." Yet when Copeau sought to explain, those submitting scripts accused him of trying to change their style and went off in a huff to have their plays produced elsewhere.

Copeau believed in developing clearly the inner conflicts of his characters. He never once let them step out of their "house." When the curtain went up on the first act of *La Maison natale*, old Daronge was busy working with his miniature marionette stage in his attic bedroom. The two remaining acts took place in the dining room of the house. The psychological conflicts in the characters were not sudden; they had existed for years and could very likely continue for as long again. The play's physical structure also supported the characters. In true classic fashion, Copeau maintained unity of time, place, and action. In fact, a play by André Fernet, *La Maison divisée*, dealing with a similar clash between father and son, was produced in the spring of 1913, and Copeau's criticism published in *Nouvelle Revue Française* (May 1) was: "I believe that the conflict would have gained remarkably in condensation and intensity by remaining enclosed in the house." When he completed his own play in the summer of 1923, he made certain that the action never left the house.

The more Copeau tried to put his ideas and theatrical experience into *La Maison natale*, the more the critics (like Lucien Dubech in *Revue universelle*, January 15, 1924) found the drama "dreadful, not so much because all the characters are sad, as because not one of them opposes destiny with a soul capable of surmounting it." Copeau's choice not to make this modern tragedy a more consoling picture of moral beauty caused them to criticize the play for its "frightful dryness." The only justification for doing the play at all, according to Dubech, an admirer of the Vieux-Colombier, was Copeau's need to satisfy a few sentimental notions that he had been nurturing for twenty-odd years. With the exception of Claude Berton (*Les Marges*), Gabriel Marcel (*Europe nouvelle*), and one or two others, the critics refused to accept Copeau's human, simple treatment of a serious theme. Simplicity they interpreted as affectation, and sadness as ugliness. (Copeau never forgave the critics. Some years later, when an indiscreet interviewer asked him whether he intended to revive the play, he is reported to have answered: "Shh! Why do you constantly speak of what hurts me?")

Even though some writers scorned Copeau's manner of envisaging his craft, others were more than willing to let themselves be shown how to attain the maximum return from their subjects and their style. These authors did not accuse him of wishing to change all plays to suit his own taste. They went to him with confidence, feeling that they had much to learn from his experience. René Benjamin, for example, gave a vivid description of the writing of *Il faut que chacun soit à sa place*, the last new play produced at the Vieux-Colombier in 1924. For three days he worked with Copeau in a small tower in the country near Paris, going over the play line by line, *le patron* pointing out blunders and oversights, showing Benjamin where he was chatting instead of speaking: "You forget that you have to construct before you speak." Benjamin called these three days "unforgettable" and recorded them in the postscript of the published play:

> It seemed to me that I was entering into convalescence. I breathed, I became free. For the first time, a doctor soothed me with a gentleness that his sensitivity hid beneath a moody exterior. I found—oh novelty in my literary life!—in this exciting but slippery métier called the theater, a real man who, with all his heart, tried to make me profit from his experience and his knowledge. I had a *master*. . . . When I left him, almost nothing remained of a play over which I'd been yawning for a year. But I went off with the essential, the joyful wish to write a new one, with the same characters, to whom he had given back their real selves by ordering me to make them keep quiet first and to live in silence before giving them a single word. I was happy.

Lucien Dubech (*Revue universelle*) was practically alone in giving the play a favorable review when it was produced on February 14. His fellow critics thought the work of small consequence. But the public enjoyed the fantastic and original ideas in Benjamin's three-act lark, so closely allied to the mocking spirit of Molière's *L'Ecole des maris* and *L'Ecole des femmes*.

However, the failure of *La Maison natale* and the critics' disapproval of so delightful a comedy as *Il faut que chacun soit à sa place* began to unnerve Copeau. It almost appeared as if it were expected of them to deride and belittle his theater. All the old arguments were aired and reprinted. The Vieux-Colombier was again dubbed a curious avant-garde theater, a rendezvous for snobs, Copeau's subtle manner of seeking the directorship of one of the national theaters. He was reproached for devoting most of his repertory to the classics and not introducing enough new authors, especially since he had first choice with such moderns as Jean Sarment (*Pêcheur d'ombres*), Amiel and Obey (*La Souriante Madame Beudet*), J. J. Bernard (*Martine*), Romains, Duhamel, Pirandello, and so on. With these writers being produced by Lugné-Poe, Baty and Dullin, Jouvet and Pitoëff, the public that Copeau wanted most began to divide their interest among the different theaters.

Some critics and a few close friends accused the Vieux-Colombier of sacrificing dramatic art to reforms in mise-en-scène. Others found Copeau's staging stifling and overbearing. Many continued to voice their anger because he had dared to order the doors of his theater locked as soon as the curtain went up. They persisted in their refusal to consider that the noisy, shaky seats annoyed both audience and actors, not to speak of the nuisance caused by ushers running up and down the aisles. (Antoine's Dream Theater contained an automatic device closing all doors into the house at the rise of the curtain. And in order to avoid disturbing spectators, Goethe, and later the Moscow Art Theater, even forbade applause either during or after acts.)

The antagonism of critics would not have affected Copeau very much—it had not in the past—if his overall program had had even the slightest prospect of moving forward at a normal pace. For this he needed the help of devoted associates, needed to be understood. "He could never work in hostility," remarked Jouvet.[7] But the passing years made his comrades wary of his ideals, and particularly of his most important one: the Vieux-Colombier School. The company resented taking second place in Copeau's mind, feeling that they had established the reputation of the Vieux-Colombier and had a right to all his attention. But try as he would, he could not tear himself away from the idealistic goal ahead, from the belief that in the school lay the theater's only hope for remaking the theater.[8] The newness of this experiment thrilled him to the point that he saw in it the one exciting, and dangerous, part of future drama—dangerous because he could not explain to his fellow-artists the reasons for his belief. It was all too strange, too vague to explain, or even to justify. All he could do was move impatiently toward the goal that he discerned in the distance. He trusted that his colleagues would give him the understanding he needed and show confidence in his vision. Some did. But many lost faith and left, convinced that he was no longer true to the spirit of 1913. And he himself soon began to feel what old Daronge in *La Maison natale* bitterly expressed: "It is useless to be certain when others have stopped believing."

The day was now approaching when a clear-cut choice would have to be made between the theater and the school. As that day drew closer and people began to perceive what Copeau was about to do, they shrugged their shoulders as if he were a madman, a coward, or an ungrateful dreamer. His friends began to worry and wonder what he had in mind, why he was so set upon destroying his theater. Charles Vildrac asked: "Would a musical movement be called forth by multiplying instrumentalists' schools or by perfecting the manufacture of flutes and violins?"[9]

At about this time, Copeau wrote to one of his students: "I really believe that I am reaching the moment when I shall finally achieve what I have been going toward for ten years. But must I keep repeating: wait, be patient? Believe me, you will see that I shall end up no longer listening to anything and no longer saying anything."[10]

More and more he felt that he could not work under the prevailing conditions. In June 1924 he appealed, in an article for *Demain*, for the chance to "begin all over again while there is still time, with as much fervor and with added knowledge." His theater, however idealistic in spirit, was nonetheless a place where plays had to be put on regularly for audiences that expected much of it. Copeau suffered to see his experiments nipped in the bud because there was no time for additional rehearsals, because it was impossible to postpone an opening night indefinitely, because his theater, small and pure as it was, still had to pay bills and salaries and therefore had to rush for public appearance many a production that had little or no time to become settled, not to say definitive.

This state of things convinced Copeau that in eleven years of life, from 1913 to 1924, his theater had gone through seven and a half of exploitation. Under the circumstances it could not have been otherwise, since exploitation and dramatic creation had for two hundred years been inextricably linked, to the point that the first now almost obliterated the second. He had attempted to separate them and to a certain extent, he had. But that was not enough. He was faced with the necessity of going all the way as a business man or remaining an artist. That was the real choice he had to make.

In 1924 things came to a head with the proposal that he move into the Cinéma Récamier on the Left Bank (Copeau adamantly refused to cross the Seine), located just around the corner from the Vieux-Colombier. The purchase price was around 500,000 francs. The deal, which was eventually dropped, was as close as Copeau came to commercializing his ideas.

He refused to belong to the art-plus-business hybrid and thus subject himself to the conflicting demands of two masters. For eleven years, he maintained, he had tried to be an artist in spite of the chains that grew heavier with time. He had set the foundations in place and future plans looked promising. Now suddenly, almost in unison, his co-workers tore themselves loose. It was as if a storm had shaken up an apple tree, and although much of the fruit remained, some of the best had fallen away and a few of the branches had cracked from the strain. Copeau knew then that his theater was close to a spiritual breakdown. But he continued working, and the 1922 cleavage widened for two years more. By 1924, "something heavy like a mountain weighed down my development," he later revealed. "I would have broken many other things to find myself again."[11]

With his friends no longer at his side, he became even more violently attached to his ideals. Those who at first found him incomprehensible now called his ideas fantastic, if not ridiculous. They began to take less interest in him and he despaired of accomplishing anything worthwhile in such hostile surroundings. He became irritable and angry at their lack of understanding, isolated himself, shut himself away from critic and counselor, and felt that all about him were seeking to obscure the clear path ahead. He began to fear that they might even succeed in transporting him onto that other path, the one he had already rejected so many times. Before they could prevail, he did what he had threatened to do in 1919: "I did not enter the theater at thirty-five years of age to make myself the servitor of routine low standards. I shall do what I came for, or else I shall leave as I entered."[12]

His fatigue during those crucial days of 1924 was on the verge of becoming an illness. Right after his New York experience, he had told Les Amis du Vieux-Colombier, "My strength is limited. I need to be helped. I need to be followed."[13] When Jouvet left, Michel Saint-Denis and one or two others took his post. But Jouvet was not easily replaced, so that a good deal of the burden fell on Copeau. Jules Romains was no longer director of the school; when he left, Suzanne Bing and Georges Chennevière had taken on the responsible functions of organization and administration. With Copeau's desire to give his students the maximum of attention, he had that much less energy for the theater, which in turn required more and more as the repertory increased, not to speak of the second company traveling all over the continent. Scripts had to be read on the average of one per day. The ateliers were constantly at work and needed the day's output approved. The theater's every repair was supervised by Copeau himself. A new play, frequently a modern one, was always in rehearsal. This meant conferences with the author, with the painter designing sets and costumes, and sometimes with a composer preparing the score. His manifold activities overflowed into the hours when he ought normally to have rested. The evening and matinée performances generally found him in the cast. And as a new opening night approached, the tasks increased tenfold, and in the midst of every discussion and at the making of every decision was—*le patron*.

Even under the best conditions the exploitation of art can be morally discouraging. And so it was to Copeau. He felt that artistically he was running dry and beginning to repeat himself, when what he wanted most was to work freely, always to advance on a constructive, well-defined path. He did not wish to let himself be caught in the snare of success on box-office terms: "It's such a stupid thing!" he complained.[14] That is what he would have had to do, on an ever-increasing scale, to keep his theater alive during those difficult, confusing times. (For example, even a 2,700 franc average out of a maximum 3,000 per performance for the whole 1923–1924 season left a large annual deficit.) The immediate postwar wave of popularity in 1920 had brought a moment of hope that perhaps art and business could be successfully linked, but this was only a temporary surge and soon disappeared. Copeau then appealed to his elite audience of artists and intellectuals, but found a great void left by the social upheaval of the war. They helped but were inadequate to the larger task ahead, particularly since Dullin, Jouvet, Pitoëff, and Baty were appealing to the same audiences. And when Copeau approached his faithful benefactors he heard talk of inflation and devaluation.

Under the strain of inner and outer difficulties, Copeau was gradually led to make one of the most far-reaching decisions in the history of the contemporary French theater: the closing of the Vieux-Colombier. Copeau's tenth anniversary message carried no hint of this (though in retrospect it does have the qualities of a valedictory address) but spoke of the future with anticipation and confidence: "I believe I can add that, *as of next year,* we shall acquire a stability and at the same time a fullness which will reward our collaborators for their patience, our public for their confidence and their friendship, and will permit people to measure better the scope of our work which, until now, we have only been preparing."

As late as April 25, 1924, in a mimeographed letter to Les Amis du Vieux-Colombier, Copeau gave no hint of an impending departure. He confessed to fatigue and looked forward to a long summer's rest "in order to be able to give my attention fully next year to the very appreciable number of new works that have been brought to me."

The theater program-cards for April 27 to May 7 still spoke of its "annual closing" on May 15, but from May 1 on, the newspapers began to publish "reports" that the Vieux-Colombier would not reopen next season. Antoine lost no time in calling France to Copeau's rescue (*Le Journal,* May 2, 1924):

The Demise of the Vieux-Colombier

Disquieting rumors have been circulating the last few days about the Vieux-Colombier, which I have naturally avoided spreading. Now that one of my colleagues has just spoken of it openly, we can, if it is true, draw attention to an event of considerable importance.

We well suspected that Jacques Copeau, accomplishing such a task with limited resources, was not steering his ship without difficulties; but, by dint of labor, unselfishness and talent, it seemed to have won a certain security as well as the warmest esteem of the literary world. . . . Now we learn that he has just given his excellent actors their freedom, anticipating the possibility of not re-opening next season.

There must be something we can do.

Antoine suggested that the government or theater societies go to the rescue, "to help that noble stage which gave the signal for the beautiful movement of renovation that we are witnessing."

The next day, May 3, Copeau released the following statement to the press:

A few days ago I called together my actors to inform them that at the end of ten years of very hard work, my state of health, on one hand, and on the other, certain personal work and the launching of new projects forced me to envisage a truce and the necessity of rest.

It is true that, not being able at this moment to give my comrades an exact date for the resumption of work, I believe it my duty, on principle, to give them their freedom for the 1924–1925 season.

But it is not true that the Vieux-Colombier will remain closed next year. It will certainly reopen its doors either late under my direction, or in October, under a temporary management of my selection, and with which I shall remain in close touch.

On May 16, I leave on a road tour with my whole company to visit eastern France, Switzerland, Belgium and Holland. Until further notice, all Vieux-Colombier activities operate normally.

Nowise is there question of the demise of a house which has struggled ten years for its existence, whose inner life is stronger than ever and which has won so much friendship and devotion. It is only a question of a necessary rest in preparation of a more decisive phase of activity in more favorable material conditions.

Antoine published in *Le Journal* (May 8) Copeau's answer to his May 2 article:

My dear friend,

I have read your theater column on May 2; at no time have you ever failed to give me the words of good sense and kindness that one always expects of you. And this is not the first time that your friendship extends its hand to me. I thank you. You, my dear Antoine, know what the struggle is. I have struggled a great deal and you are willing to recognize that my efforts were the signal for a certain renovation. I gave myself without thought and without any other ambition than to perform my métier properly. That has been going on for ten years. I haven't a *sou* and I am tired. If what I have done is worth something, it is nothing in my eyes compared to what I should like to do, to what I shall do if I am permitted to regain my strength and some security. But I no longer want to beg all my life, from day to day. Nor do I wish to lend myself to questionable factions, to undertakings or to men in whom I have no confidence.

Well? What do I ask for? First, the *means* to rest for a year and to prepare myself for a new, fresh, fiery, fruitful campaign; next, *the means* to undertake this campaign with vision and security. The question is to know whether I deserve that people have confidence in me.

I am, my dear Antoine, very affectionately yours,

Jacques Copeau

To this letter Antoine added a postscript: "Now we know! Copeau is not at all abandoning the struggle; he is simply putting his foot on the brake at a dangerous curve. I went through that four or five times in my life and I didn't die from it. In seeking to help my comrade, I am only paying back the debt contracted toward those who formerly helped me."

Fatigue, the distrust of friends, the public's confusion, the growing likelihood of out-and-out commercialization, these were a few of the reasons why Copeau decided to close the Vieux-Colombier. But there were others, positive ones. By devoting himself completely to his school he would be doing what he had wanted to do from the very start. Right after his return from New York he wanted to leave the theater "in order to serve it better," as he confided later in his *Souvenirs*:

> Mad ambition! They made me swallow it. The public was wait-
> ing for us, calling us. They appealed to my good sense, my reason,
> my duty, and what not. Then I repeated in Paris, more brilliant but
> not much more fruitful, the New York experiment. I undertook it
> with less strength and on a terrain that my dreams had long since
> left. I kept it up for five years without any real hope. I don't say it
> was useless. Far from that. But its spirit came out only in flashes. . . .
>   What could I do? Disappointment had the upper hand. Each year
> at the beginning of the season, I brought a new will to create. . . . It
> was promptly deadened, squandered, exhausted by the horrible ma-
> chine of putting on plays. I took one step forward and was thrown
> back ten. I practiced my métier. I tried to practice it well. I no longer
> found anything new [to say]. I was about to bury myself in virtuos-
> ity. I was clearly conscious of having done two or three things in my
> life, not more, and that the rest was but padding. . . . How could I
> not recoil with horror at the thought that a whole life, still living,
> would henceforth be filled only with padding? In vain did I give
> pieces of myself.

By closing his theater he felt he would preserve his honor and so be able to rebuild his art truly from the bottom. After all, the success of his staging methods had been proven and he was no longer interested in them as he had been during the early days in the heat of learning and experi-menting. Besides, there were now in Paris four metteurs-en-scène with whom scenic art had the imaginative values Copeau had established. Dullin was working away feverishly in his Théâtre de l'Atelier in Montmartre, "the Latin Quarter of the Right Bank." Jouvet and Pitoëff were at the Comédie des Champs-Elysées; Jouvet had just made a popular success of Jules Romains's *Dr. Knock*. And in the background were being formed the colorful concoctions of Gaston Baty, whose Théâtre de la Chimère had lately been forced to close its doors.

Faced with a fait accompli of his own making, Copeau was nonetheless filled with the nostalgia one often experiences upon leaving behind a period of one's life. But he was inspired by what he saw ahead, as he wrote in the monthly *Demain* in June 1924:

> I am going to say adieu to my little theater which I set up with so much love, where I worked, lived and suffered with so much joy and ardor. I am going to separate myself with infinite sadness from my very dear comrades whose pardon I ask for causing them this pain. I am going to leave Paris to work with a small number of collaborators and students. To work in depth, leisurely, to meditate over past experience and develop new plans. . . . If I have not been mistaken, if I am capable of new achievements, we shall know about it in a little more than a year.

One Sunday night in May, after the Vieux-Colombier's final performance, Copeau sat in his dressing-room. He had played Alceste in *Le Misanthrope* during the matinée and had just acted Daronge in *La Maison natale*. This was Copeau's subtle farewell to Paris: like Alceste he had been disliked for his sincerity and, like the idealist Daronge, in his dream world, Copeau, the author-director, had outlived his usefulness in a blasé capital. As he sat there, back of the empty theater, he looked into the mirror. Standing beside him was one of his students, to whom he spoke: "Voilà! We must go away. Far from this theatrical restlessness, from this vain tumult. Back to the country. To begin everything again from the beginning, with a group of very young people."[15]

On the surface, it appeared like an act of madness for Copeau to abandon his work when it was still filling his theater every night. But he left as he had entered, head high, in complete possession of a future that he felt he could not fulfill in Paris. With the departure of Jouvet and the others, he felt that the atmosphere of the Right Bank had penetrated the "shelter" on the Left, forcing him to return where the air was fresh and clear, "back to the country." The critics called it his "flight to Burgundy." It was his flight to freedom.

9

Ideals Multiplied
(1924–1949)

Under the constant pressure of material necessities and without a single
moment of real rest I evolved a stage, organized a theater, formed a
company, brought together a public, discovered writers, founded a
school, developed working principles and methods, recovered a scenic style, revived the interpretation of the old classics, and finally
inaugurated a movement whose imprint . . . [is recognized] in various new enterprises and even in the State theaters. I believe I did
everything I could possibly do in the place, under the conditions and
with the working elements I had at my disposal.

THESE WORDS OF COPEAU'S APPEARED in June 1924 (in *Demain*) as he
prepared to take leave of the capital, to try and find again his old self in
the Burgundian countryside. But before he could do so with a clear conscience, there were many personal and professional knots to be untied.
In addition, his mother living in nearby Versailles had become critically ill,
another reason for remaining in Paris. (She died on September 17, 1924.)

After almost a month of pourparlers between Copeau, Jouvet, and
Hébertot, who was Jouvet's business superior, an accord was reached
authorizing Jouvet to use the Vieux-Colombier actors and repertory at
the Comédie des Champs-Elysées. This agreement was made public on
August 7, 1924, and set in motion a series of rumors that Copeau brought
to a halt in a letter to *Comœdia* on September 17: all changes taking place
at the Vieux-Colombier had his approval. He also expressed full confidence in Jouvet and Dullin: "I am happy that others can continue what
I began. And I don't even have the feeling of abandoning the struggle since

I leave behind me, to lead it worthily, two men who are my friends, two good workers who both came out of the Vieux-Colombier."

One week later he sent Jouvet a very moving letter, published in *Comœdia* on October 4, 1924, repeating his "moral transfer" of personnel and plays. He recalled their first encounters, the birth of the Vieux-Colombier, its early struggles and triumphs, and the forging of a "living spirit" that he hoped Jouvet would keep alive. And in conclusion he sent his best wishes and his friendship: "*Puisses-tu, au moment de tenter ta fortune, en te sentant tout à fait libre, ne pas te sentir tout à fait seul. Il y a toujours un vieil ami auquel tu ne feras jamais appel en vain. Jacques Copeau.*"

A few days later, an old Ford took Copeau and his family to Morteuil in Burgundy, followed by students and teachers. It was a rainy fall day, yet their hearts overflowed with anticipation. Copeau, "the Pied Piper of Paris," began to tremble for the first time while looking into so many expectant faces. He began to wonder whether he was not too old to begin again. He was tired and needed rest; the young folk were enthusiastic and anxious to get on with their work. If only the money that friends had promised him for the next year had arrived, things would have been less difficult. But it did not come and again he had to think of commercializing half-formed ideas with inexperienced actors if the new school were to be started at all. The group played in the villages and at the wine festivals, in barns and public squares to earn some of the money with which to live and study this first year.

Copeau had selected Burgundy after much forethought. He liked the warm-hearted Burgundians, their generosity, their love of gatherings, and their lively wit. The school started functioning in the Château de Morteuil, not far from Dijon, with twenty-odd students all under thirty years of age. It was a cold, isolated old house in which these young Parisians were by no means comfortable. Work began on a strict schedule at seven in the morning—boys and girls in the open doing gymnastics and running in single file on all the roads and paths. It was not surprising that "the peasants regarded them with a bit of ironical astonishment," according to Michel Saint-Denis.[1]

One day, Copeau's student and secretary Léon Chancerel quite accidentally came upon a perfect jewel of a village, Pernand-Vergelesses, not far from Beaune. It had a house available for occupancy, and in December of 1925 they all moved there and settled down into one of the most unusual art communities ever conceived. At the top of the hill was the small village church, its spire reaching high into the sky like a crusader's sword. A few feet away and just below stood the medium-sized house occupied by *le patron* and his family. A bit lower was Suzanne Bing's house, where she lived with her son Bernard, and farther down still lived Alexandre Janvier, the Vieux-Colombier's mechanic-electrician who had followed Copeau out of Paris, bringing his wife and children with him.

The students lived at the bottom of the hill, at the inn, next door to their "classroom," which was a large *cuverie* where wine-makers stored their surplus supplies. Here, even more than on the rue du Vieux-Colombier, there was no division between stage and auditorium. It was all one vast space divided according to the use to which it had to be put. As in Paris, a coat of cement covered the whole floor, and on it were drawn all sorts of geometric designs that were required to guide their movements and groupings. Physical education was once more stressed to make the actor's body as responsive as possible to mind and action. Suzanne Bing resumed her mission to help mold the students into practical theater artists; Georges Chennevière kept them culturally abreast of their objectives in dramatic art; Albert Savry came occasionally to supervise the making of masks, costumes, and sets; Janvier built props; Villard wrote the music; Auguste Boverio was a frequent visiting helper. It was a closely knit family unit, functioning in much the same orderly fashion as in Paris, except this time they were all far removed from the artificial theatricality of the capital, living as well as working together.

Most of the first two years in Burgundy, *le patron* did not give the school the full leadership it looked for and had a right to expect. His state of fatigue and moral depression could explain this in part, but the truer explanation must have been his own change of heart and mind. In leaving Paris, he was for a time leaving a world that he could not understand, and therefore rejected. This was the change that has been generally called Copeau's religious conversion.

Although born into a Catholic family, he had the intellectual's scorn for religious orthodoxy. His admiration and friendship for such ardent converts as Claudel, Péguy, and Ghéon (after World War I) did not affect his own religious thinking. Some of his co-workers at the Vieux-Colombier began to notice a change in him around 1922; he seemed to be going steadily toward another form of great drama to which Shakespeare and Molière were no longer sufficient. Only God, it seemed, could give him what he wanted from life and art. And in 1925, Jacques Rivière's last words—"I am miraculously saved!"—were brought to him by Rivière's widow, Isabelle, the sister of Alain Fournier, herself a fervent Catholic. So profoundly was he affected that he had her and the children live in his own house for a time.

This all-absorbing devotion enveloped him completely and made him almost unapproachable to his students. Days would go by without anyone seeing him. His assistants were competent, to be sure, but the budding artists had left Paris only for Copeau, for his leadership and guidance. When they dared to go and question him on his prolonged absences, they would find him in his study submerged in one or another of the holy scriptures. And it was only when the school was close to the point of crumbling from lack of support and lack of inspiration that Copeau shook himself sufficiently free to resume active leadership. On September 12, 1926, he wrote Valentine Tessier: "Life is starting anew. I needed a long time to have faith in it. I had really worked too hard, suffered too much."

By then the number of students had dwindled from thirty to ten, four of them his own family: daughter Marie-Hélène (Maiène), nephew Michel Saint-Denis, niece Suzanne Maistre, and son-in-law Jean Dasté. All worked with vigor and enthusiasm and soon became a familiar part of the Burgundian landscape. From time to time their heavy schedule of study was put aside for a few days and they set out to perform in and around Dijon and Beaune, at a fair or some traditional celebration. The countryside greeted with knowing smiles the singing "Copiaux," as they were called, striding four abreast into some village inn, their master in their midst. They would set up their "theater" in a large canvas shed filled with garden chairs; up in front on a platform under the projectors would be placed a square, bare trestle-stage that dominated the length of the room; a curtain painted by Bonnard was hung; the actors were ready. Outside, a large, lighted orange lantern would be swinging between two trees. On one side could be read: Les Copiaux; on the other, Le Vieux-Colombier. This was the Fair Theater, flying the familiar standard of the two doves.

At Nuits-St. Georges near Beaune, for example, they would give four performances in three days to three thousand spectators. Once it rained for three days in a row and storms would cut the electricity in the midst of the play; but they had their full quota of audiences nonetheless. From the four corners of the *département* the wine-growers hurried to be on hand to welcome *Jean Bourguignon* in the person of Michel Saint-Denis or one of the other "children." The onlookers waited gleefully for the well-known interruption by old man Noah who would step forward to tell them why to drink wine and lots of it:

> Yesterday I drank—today I drink—tomorrow I shall drink! Did I hear someone say no? Drink consoles you every time. You have worries in your business? Drink a glass of white wine. Your wife deceives you? Drink a glass of red. She does it again? Have another glass! Wine cures all things. You have a toothache? Drink *Romanée*. You have rheumatism? Drink *Nuits-Saint-Georges*. Men like to see women drink *Bordeaux*--so languorous! Women like to see men drink *Burgundy*—so heroic! *Burgundy* cured Louis XIV and gave counsel to Napoleon. We ought to make the Republic drink the wine of Burgundy![2]

So they joked and taunted, blithely and good-naturedly. And when their half-prepared, half-improvised playlet was over, they mingled with the townsfolk in the streets, they were recognized by everyone, questioned and sheltered, fêted and fed, adopted by the whole community and loved by all of Burgundy. Copeau felt he was serving Molière *chez lui* during those precious moments of complete communion between actor and public.

This did not, however, bring in enough funds to support the school. Copeau had to go to Paris to give dramatic readings, a recourse that earned him a large following. His talent in this field was supreme. As early as 1909, he had set up one-man shows on Ibsen, Claudel, and Shakespeare in the Galerie Druet on the rue Royale. When the school was in Paris he had performed about ten readings a year for students and public. His voice was warm, full, and sonorous, and he controlled it with the power of a virtuoso. He became a feature of the Paris season of concerts, recitals, and lectures. Those who had reproached the small Vieux-Colombier its empty stage—where there were actors and sets—now rushed to fill the big, box-like Salle Pleyel where there were only walls and more walls. Intellectual snobbishness played its part in making these readings fashionable, and the crowd's curiosity to see the phenomenon of a martyr to his art also held a certain attraction. Be that as it may, Copeau became a strange new star on the Paris horizon and shed new light on the classics—alone.

After the public's enthusiastic reception of a Copeau reading of Shakespeare's *The Tempest*, Antoine, writing in *Information* (February 22, 1926), proposed his name to head France's second national theater, the Odéon. With its administrator, Firmin Gémier, involved in numerous theatrical activities outside, Antoine asked: "if the task interested Copeau, would it not be to everyone's greatest advantage?" *Comœdia*, always on the lookout for the best in theatrical art, supported this suggestion, while at the same time doubting whether even Copeau's efforts would be of help in a poorly subsidized house.

In a letter sent to *Comœdia* on February 23, 1926, Copeau declined to consider such an appointment, remembering the hopeless difficulties that Antoine and Gémier had had in that house. He deplored that every distinguished man of the theater should be marked to travel "that fateful road, 'Avant-garde-Odéon-Père-Lachaise' [the Montmartre cemetery where many French artists are buried]. . . . It is true," he added, "that not very long ago I almost died of fatigue, sorrow and disgust. But my heart held out, and here I am resuscitated—which is by no means synonymous with 'candidacy for the Odéon'." He concluded by suggesting that people offer him what he asked for and not what he did not ask for. In a separate letter to Antoine on March 1 (published in *Information*), he repeated this: "What they should do is help me in what I am doing with love and joy, to form a tiny troupe as perfect as possible and attempt to do real, new things with it."

A few days later, Copeau was back at Pernand working on his three-act adaptation of Rojas's *La Célestina*, which Les Copiaux were to give on their first major tour the following fall. He developed the role of a youth in search of truth and beauty and with a more important part to play than La Célestina, the old hag of a go-between. This new French version was called *L'Illusion*, and became a success. The critic Jean Gondal (*Comœdia*, October 25, 1926) called it "the comedy of adolescence, just as André Gide's *The Counterfeiters* is the novel of adolescence."

Besides *L'Illusion* they played two Molière comedies, *L'Ecole des maris* and *Le Médecin malgré lui*, in Italy, Belgium, and Holland. In Switzerland, Adolphe Appia came regularly to see them. A few years later after Appia's death in 1928, one of Les Copiaux recalled these spirited meetings:

> I can see him still as he strode backstage, his eyes shining happily, joyfully. With what profound respect we listened to his comments on our performance! With what eagerness he explained and illustrated his reasoning, finding always the right word, the exact image, the illuminating paradox.
>
> He was proud of his 'dear children' as he called us when he talked of us to Copeau. He believed in our future, he understood perfectly that it would be a hard fight to convince others of our sincerity and the ardor we put into our work. But he never doubted that we would reach the goal we had set ourselves.[3]

The summer of the *Illusion* tour, Maurice Wertheim, a member of the Board of Managers of the Theater Guild in New York, was going to France and was delegated to ask Copeau to stage *The Brothers Karamazov* in an English version prepared by Rosalind Ivan. Those were the Guild's experimental years, when it was building up its unique company of actors in preparation for a repertory theater to begin that 1926–1927 season. The Board wanted its players to have the best training and so Copeau became part of that program. He was a universally respected metteur-en-scène, and besides, this particular play, his own dramatization, had left a deep impression on America when produced at the old Garrick Theater, where the Guild had made its own début in 1919 following the Vieux-Colombier's return to Paris. Also, Alfred Lunt saw in *The Brothers Karamazov* an artistic challenge to test the mettle of the new acting unit; and Theresa Helburn, the soul of Guild goings-on, recalled so vividly the twisting staircase in the third act with Smerdiakov slinking along it, that the choice of director-author met with her enthusiastic approval.

Copeau called on Maurice Wertheim at the Hôtel de Wagram and expressed interest in coming to the United States. Two things, however, made him hesitate: his bad health and his poor spoken English. But royalties and directorial fees were attractive, and the school, as usual, needed money.

In the staging of his play, Copeau had one of the most cooperative and homogeneous casts America could offer: Alfred Lunt as Dmitri, Lynn Fontanne as Grouchenka, Clare Eames as Katherina, Dudley Digges as old Feodor, Edward G. Robinson as Smerdiakov, Morris Carnovsky as Alyosha, and Henry Travers as Ivan. Travers impressed Copeau with his ability to remain quiet and at the same time keep the play's action moving. Copeau admired the Lunts and helped polish the fine points of their acting together. In one of their scenes, while they were speaking quickly to each other, there was an infinitesimal pause. Copeau felt that it broke up the scene, which should proceed as directly and as uninterruptedly as a straight line. In the future, the Lunts eliminated such pauses in fast-moving scenes; this became a high point of their art.

All strove to please their French director: Lunt practiced for hours his difficult Russian dances in the fourth act; Fontanne worked hard, and during the rehearsal period wrote Valentine Tessier, "I *cannot* make him say I am as good as you were as 'Grouchenka'. I send you my love just the same." A young Morris Carnovsky said over supper at Sardi's that Copeau was "a great teacher who gave unstintingly of himself." Digges tried to extirpate his old Abbey Theater accent from the heavy Muscovite mood of the play. This veteran actor of twenty-five years' experience was so impressed by Copeau's devotion to art that he was inspired to work harder than ever before. And the Lunts called him "the greatest director with whom we have ever had the privilege of working."[4] The company loved him and had complete confidence in his direction, for he did not seek to impose French manners or methods but sought to have them give an objective interpretation. New York received *The Brothers Karamazov* with flattering reviews. It played the winter of 1927 and was an artistic success—it did not, however, fill the coffers of the Guild.

When Copeau was ready to return to France, after giving a series of lectures and readings at the Laboratory Theater, the company paid him the unusual honor of signing a petition requesting him to remain with the Guild and stage other productions. But he had his job—in Burgundy— and rushed back to the school with his American dollars. Money problems temporarily out of the way, teachers and students set themselves to work with renewed enthusiasm and discipline. And as once again he looked out of his study window, his glance floated dreamily across the rich vineyards unfolding at the bottom of the hill, and he said to one of his students, "Down there, in that prairie, I shall construct the theater." This was one of his fondest visions.

Now that Les Copiaux had acquired a reputation in the art world, *le patron* divided their year into eight months of study and training, and four months of public performances. In 1928 they went to England under the auspices of the Alliance Française, a trip that caused an international incident in the world of culture. Oxford refused to have Molière played there unless the two texts in question, *Le Médecin malgré lui* and *L'Ecole des maris*, were expurgated. The French press became incensed and all approved Copeau's prompt decision to drop Oxford from the tour. Cambridge was more indulgent, but the last word was spoken by Granval, an actor of the Comédie-Française, who summed up English prudishness with the thrust: "Pouah! People who play Shakespeare in tuxedo!" The year 1929 brought with it a major decision. In April and May, six weeks apart, Copeau had two important visitors at Pernand. They were influential in the theater world and came to tell him that the Comédie-Française was in the midst of another of its periodic crises. They asked whether he would accept to become its head if the Fine Arts minister offered him the post. He was impressed by their arguments and answered that he would accept under certain conditions, which he would make known at the proper time. On October 18 and 19 respectively, *Comœdia* and *Les Nouvelles littéraires* launched *la candidature Copeau* in the form of an impressive petition to the Fine Arts minister. Almost all the great names in the arts and politics and in the intellectual life of France signed it.

A week later, on October 26, *Les Nouvelles littéraires* published an article by Copeau on the Comédie-Française. He set forth the facts plainly: "The Comédie-Française is an abandoned treasure." What it needed most, he said, was not a master but an inspiring leader who would be guided by the original agreement of January 5, 1681, between the Hôtel de Guénégaud and the Hôtel de Bourgogne to "nourish peace and union." Copeau refused to consider France's national treasure as a museum. "The art of the theater is a living art, or it is not. Its matter is movement and life. The living actor speaks to the living spectator. Only those dramatic works continue to be admirable, touching, exciting, or simply tolerable on the stage which maintain this principle of life. It is not opposed to the principle of tradition. It is its soul. Tradition is continuity and change."

While opinions rumbled in every actor's dressing room and in several ministers' private offices, les Copiaux were on tour again, this time playing *L'Illusion* in France, at Lyons. André Obey, the playwright, sat enthralled before the unusual spontaneity of their acting and expressed his admiration to the troupe. He then sent his script of *Noé* (Noah) to Copeau, who went directly to him in Touraine and told him to write for La Compagnie des Quinze, the name taken by Les Copiaux when they moved to Paris to play as a regular company. For in July of 1929, when the "*Copeau à la Comédie*" petition was gaining momentum, *le patron* wanted to be free of his moral obligations to the school; accordingly, Les Copiaux dissolved and left Pernand, taking an oath to be together again "soon."[5]

But Copeau's chances at the Comédie were diminishing as the weeks passed. Its actors became panicky at the mere thought of having a director whose individuality and independence would inevitably infringe upon some of their sacred rights. They had never had a metteur-en-scène to tell them that the whole production was more important than their one role, and therefore interpreted the petition as a direct attack against their traditions. Hurriedly one or two actresses spoke to close ministerial friends, and the petition was rejected. Still, the Comédie saw which way the wind was blowing: in 1930 it produced Mérimée's *Le Carrosse du Saint-Sacrement* (last presented at the Vieux-Colombier) and Vildrac's new play, *La Brouille*.

By this time (September 1930), Pernand had been regrouped in Paris—that is, all except *le patron*, who wished Les Quinze to be completely on their own. The company consisted of ten members (Suzanne Bing, Marguerite Cavadaski, Marie-Hélène Dasté, Marie-Madeleine Gautier, Auguste Boverio, Jean Dasté, Pierre Fresnay, Aman Maistre, Michel Saint-Denis, and Jean Villard) and five students (Marthe Herlin, Suzanne Maistre, Pierre Alder, Pierre Assy, and Jean Saran). Its director was the Vieux-Colombier's former general manager and the school's most assertive personality, Michel Saint-Denis. André Barsacq was in charge of sets and other stage technicalities; the devoted Alexandre Janvier took his old post as chief machinist-electrician; and Marie-Hélène Dasté, Copeau's daughter, designed the costumes just as her father had predicted she would, in a letter to Jouvet (August 19, 1915) some fifteen years before: "I have plans for *cette petite*. As soon as she's fifteen or sixteen I shall have her apprenticed to study engraving and the whole métier of manual art. Besides that I shall have her specialize in cutting and dressmaking, everything concerning cloth, dyes and other materials having to do with costumes and ornaments. And in eight or ten years we shall have with us someone who will be *capable*." She did not disappoint her father, for she became one of the most talented, original costume designers on the French stage, as well as a fine actress.

Les Quinze made their début in Paris at the Vieux-Colombier after rehearsing for several months in their studio-school outside Paris at Ville d'Avray. The scheduled opening of André Obey's *Noé* had to be postponed from January 7 to January 17, 1931, because of the illness of Pierre Fresnay, an established boulevard star who had always wanted to work with Copeau. A few critics commented on Fresnay's presence in the company, claiming that he stuck out like a sore thumb in a group whose training and experience had been so vastly different. But he justified his presence by writing in the *Noé* program:

> [I wished] to share with them the treasures of freshness, sincerity and enthusiasm which they accumulated in five years of work in their *cuverie* in Burgundy.
>
> Discovering new techniques, new means of expression, new points of contact between public and actors—amongst actors themselves—a new acting discipline imposed by a new stage concept—that is really something to be tempted by at a time when so many actors are rushing into sound films.

André Obey was company poet, and his first play for them, *Noé*, was their opening bill. He followed this with *Le Viol de Lucrèce* (later translated by Thornton Wilder as *The Rape of Lucretia* and acted on Broadway by Katharine Cornell), *La Bataille de la Marne*, *Loire*, and others. The style of his dramas was presentational, unconventional, highly suited to and indeed created for Les Quinze. "I think I can say," wrote Copeau in the program notes for *Noé*, "that he is linked to the work of the Vieux-Colombier, or more exactly to that of the School of the Vieux-Colombier." Copeau considered him "the only French dramatist of his day who has wished, who has been able to adopt our methods, profit by our experience." Obey, in turn, observed that without Copeau and Les Quinze, he could not have found himself. Copeau was his master, the troupe his instrument and inspiration.

Obey, who became one of the most provocative writers for the French stage, traced Copeau's influence upon him to a night in 1923. He had written a play and submitted it to Copeau, who sent for him. About midnight the young author called on him in his dressing room. Copeau liked Obey's "*qualité sauvage*," his original, poetic approach. He asked the young poet whether he was attracted to the theater, and received a flat "No" in reply. After taking off the last bit of make-up, he casually asked Obey whether he'd like to see the stage. The visitor answered a polite "Yes" and Copeau drew aside the curtain. He walked back and forth across the stage for several minutes without speaking. Obey watched from the first row of the orchestra as he continued moving up and down the stairs of *La Maison natale*. After a long silence, Copeau began to speak, half to himself, half to Obey, revealing his innermost thoughts on what is theater. Tragedy. Comedy. Characters. The phenomenal power of the human presence on a bare stage, ready to transport to all lands and to all ideas hundreds, thousands of spectators. At that precise moment, Obey understood for the first time the real meaning of theater.

When they stepped out into the cold night air, they walked each other home several times, discussing Shakespeare and Molière. He who had not been attracted to the theater was won over. As he described it in conversation: "I never attended a performance at the Vieux-Colombier. I considered the theater a very secondary art. And yet, I am probably the only writer who owes completely to Copeau his conversion to the theater. For it is truly a conversion, as much as was the conversion of St. Augustine."[6]

In March 1946, André Obey's *Maria* was produced in Paris: the principal character, *le patron*, looks at the empty, dark stage from which he is speaking and then addresses the audience directly: "The secret of the theater! . . . It is there, someplace. It's here. . . . It is only asking to come out."

Les Quinze, under Michel Saint-Denis, played Obey, Salacrou, and Giono and tried to bring a new force into the theater. "We believe," said its director, "that a dramatic work, if it is above all the work of an author, of a poet, finds its complete expression only through the close collaboration of all artists in the production. . . . We wish to avoid becoming a machine to be exploited."[7] Their studio was to be their workshop for study and research during seven and a half months of the year, while the rest of the time would be devoted to performing in public. The old Copiaux schedule was intact—except for Copeau.

Le patron had limited his participation in this new venture of his "children" to a moving introduction in the form of two lectures of "memories" on the Vieux-Colombier, delivered from the stage of the Vieux-Colombier. Gide was amazed to hear him say that now, just past fifty and at the height of his maturity, he was ready to start the fight anew. The novelist interpreted this as a useless struggle against fantasy. He had hoped that Copeau would thenceforth devote his energies to a more lasting kind of work—to writing. Copeau had in fact confided this to Gide at Pernand, and Gide in his Journal (January 15, 1931) attributed the change of heart and this contemplated return to Paris to Copeau's refusal "to admit to himself how much his new religious convictions bother him in the production of that work [religious plays] which resists going in the direction of his prayers; just as he shuns admitting to himself that between Catholicism and dramatic art there could be no alliance, unless it be to the detriment of one or the other, and only through an awkward compromise."

Copeau returned to fight at a difficult moment in the life of Paris art theaters. Although Les Quinze had been well received, the capital had not been swept off its feet and they, like Dullin's Théâtre de l'Atelier and others, felt the full brunt of a new crise de théâtre. Les Quinze moved to the Atelier, the two troupes playing alternately during the 1932–1933 season. After a second successful tour of England, where they were acclaimed, Les Quinze were forced to disband. It was at this point that Copeau decided to accept the offer of Les Nouvelles littéraires to become its drama critic. For the first time in almost twenty years, he was once again writing in behalf of an art for whose defense his name had become an international bastion. Two decades of practical experience gave his words the unquestionable authority that in his twenties and early thirties had been construed as the courage of the avant-garde.

The isolation of a disheartened artist was now completely broken. "Do not ask me to speak," he told people, "let me now act." In 1933 the Italian government commissioned him to direct a Florentine Festival production, Santa Uliva, in the Santa Croce Cloister. In 1934, he staged As You Like It (adapted by Jules Delacre) at Dullin's Théâtre de l'Atelier, with the latter's troupe. It was the same Copeau once again at the top of the Paris season with a Shakespearean fantasy. Exactly ten years after leaving Paris, he came back to work under the same roof with Dullin, as a sign of confidence in those serving dramatic art.

From the Atelier he went to the Opéra, where he helped stage Ida Rubinstein's ballet *Perséphone*. "Florence and Santa Croce," he wrote in *Comœdia* (September 25, 1933), "have given me the taste for space." In 1935, assisted by André Barsacq, he was the "hit" of the Florence May Festival with the staging of Nino Alessi's *Savonarola*, in which "the diversity of crowd movements . . . [gave it] a magnificent rhythm," according to Darius Milhaud, writing in *Jour* on June 1. He directed and acted in André Obey's *Don Juan* and Paul Raynal's *Napoléon unique* (in which he was Fouché) at the Porte Saint-Martin. Lectures and dramatic readings filled in the rest of his time, along with a professorship in diction at the Brussels Conservatory, which made drama critic Gabriel Boissy ask ironically in *Comœdia* (14 October 1932): "Is it an honor for France that Belgium should appreciate Jacques Copeau?" *Le patron* took pleasure everywhere in "this role of sculptor and discoverer of new talents," calling himself "an artist in human substance." (One hundred years earlier, the poet-dramatist Alfred de Musset had said, "Art has no frontiers.")

This latest teaching assignment, however, was short-lived for it took time from the stage, where Copeau wanted most to be. He felt the moment was particularly ripe for him to open his own theater, a larger one than the Vieux-Colombier, one that would make ends meet—if, as he wrote in 1932, "there are enough young, new writers with good scripts to warrant the undertaking." But nothing concrete was done until 1935, when again the question came up. He wished to have a repertory acting company, with well-known actors, if this was necessary to guarantee success. He would also maintain a school at Ville d'Avray. To queries on the *crise de théâtre*, he answered, "I have rarely attempted easy things."[8]

Plans were made to rent the Théâtre de l'Ambigu, which contained about a thousand seats. And with his typical refusal to accept mediocre plays, he dusted off his 1915 notes for a February 1936 production of *Macbeth*, with Lucienne Bogaert, a former Vieux-Colombier actress, playing Lady Macbeth. He expected to follow this with a work of Obey. All seemed to be going smoothly when, quite suddenly, a new Fine Arts minister asserted his courage by appointing Edouard Bourdet general administrator for the Comédie-Française and putting all staging under the direction of Copeau, Dullin, Jouvet, and Baty.

Only a few weeks before, an English writer had commented: "It seems unlikely that M. Copeau will ever take part in the organization of the national theater."[9] And in 1933, in a lecture at Lyons on his "memories," Copeau was reported to have announced his intention to regroup all those who were part of the Vieux-Colombier in 1920. "This collaboration," he had declared, "could give an entirely new face to the French theater. If this accord took place, it would permit each one to develop his personality without being oppressed by secondary concerns."[10] What he could not accomplish by himself, it now appeared likely that the government would. All four artists had the same goal—to have spectators live the fuller life of their imagination—even though each had his own path for reaching that goal. Thus working together under the same roof, Jules Romains wrote, the Vieux-Colombier would indeed be "multiplied rather than dispersed."[11]

Charles Dullin

When Charles Dullin left the Vieux-Colombier during its second New York season in 1919, he was asserting his independent will to do and undo as he saw fit. He agreed with Copeau in almost all matters artistic, but he wished to fight his own battle his own way. And so he set out to found the Théâtre de l'Atelier.

The last of twenty-one children, all born in the mountains of Savoy in the French Alps, Dullin was *l'enfant chéri* of the family. His father shared with the lad the mountain-dweller's stock of adventure stories, and his uncle revealed to him the wonders of La Fontaine and Racine. At the age of nine he ran away from school, bored and already thirsty for change. In his early teens he worked in a linen shop in Lyons and was dismissed after one week. He then found a "steady" job in a bailiff's office, from which he was discharged a year later when he intentionally omitted listing an actress's mandolin amongst property to be seized because she tearfully pleaded to retain it for sentimental reasons. That was his first contact with "the theater," soon to be followed by elocution lessons and a short spell at the Conservatory of Lyons. At this time he made the acquaintance of Henri Béraud and Alexandre Arnoux, two ambitious young writers about to seek their fortune in *la capitale*. His parents having died by then, he decided to make a clean break of it. With a head full of ideas and ambition, but with only 27 francs in his pocket, he set out with his new friends.

Then began what he later described as "l'existence terrible." It sent Béraud scurrying back to Lyons within six months; but Dullin persevered, leading a hand-to-mouth existence by reciting Verlaine in courtyards with a friend playing the violin. For a cheese sandwich and a *vin blanc* he would recite poetry in the Montmartre cabarets, following in the footsteps of the great actress Rachel. Lodgings were uncertain, now with one friend, now with another. One time he lived on cod liver oil for eight days. The doctor finally ordered him to the country, for tuberculosis was already setting in. With no money and few clothes he had to leave Paris, worked on a farm for six months, restored his health and finances, and hurried back to the capital.

Only one theater held out any hope to him—the Odéon, under Antoine's direction. He was signed up and made his début as Cinna the poet in Shakespeare's *Julius Caesar*. He remained for two years, but boredom drove him into the open air again: he played in the provinces, founded a Fair Theater at Neuilly, had the courage to audition for melodramas with Baudelaire's poems—and got the parts. When out of work he passed the hat after reciting Villon's *La Ballade des pendus* at Le Lapin Agile, a cabaret in Montmartre. There Robert d'Humières heard him one day and signed him up for the Théâtre des Arts where he played a small role. The following season, 1911, this theater was taken by Jacques Rouché, who asked Durec, Humières's metteur-en-scène, to return. Durec brought Dullin back with him to create the role of Pierrot in *Le Carnaval des enfants* by Saint-Georges de Bouhélier. Copeau's *Les Frères Karamazov* was to be cast next and Dullin was given a bit part. That night in a café, while Dullin bemoaned his fate for not having the rich part he felt himself best suited for, that of Smerdiakov, a messenger rushed in to tell him that Durec and the author wanted to see him immediately: he was assigned to the role he had set his heart on. He worked hard and although he received much encouragement, he was not satisfied: "I felt that I was playing too much from the outside." Not until the very last moment before the opening did he find physical freedom in his character, discovering in it the fundamentals of his craft. "I can say that from that time on, as metteur-en-scène as well as actor," he exclaimed, "I have tried never to let critical sense or intelligence dominate instinct."[12]

Dullin's portrait of Smerdiakov was showered with praise. The boulevard theaters lost no time in approaching him with attractive offers, but they were too late. He had met Copeau. He became a charter member of the Vieux-Colombier in 1913 and Copeau's most valued assistant during those hard, early times. From his first role there as Nicholas in *A Woman Killed With Kindness*, a Dullin scene was always an exciting one, original and personal, in which he showed an extraordinary talent for changing his physiognomy without the aid of make-up.

At the outbreak of war in 1914 he joined the artillery as a private. He went through one great offensive after another until 1917, when he was wounded and sent to the rear. Once out of the trenches he was able to obtain permission to join the Vieux-Colombier in New York, where it was reported that his first move was to borrow a few dollars to buy a red tie and a cowboy hat and thus "become an American." In France, his love of local color had kept a Montmartre kerchief around his neck in place of a tie.

New York acclaimed him for his "powerfully vivid acting" as the miser Harpagon in Molière's *L'Avare*. But he did not wish to limit himself to acting alone. Even before the American tour had come to an end he returned to Paris, impatient to set up his own theater. After a brief collaboration with Gémier, playing in *La Grande Pastorale* (under Gaston Baty's direction) and then following him to La Comédie Montaigne to organize the Gémier school, Dullin dared to undertake what Stanislavsky and Gordon Craig and Copeau had only dreamed of doing, and which no one else had yet done. In 1921, before starting his theater, he organized the New School for Actors, which admitted only those who had never been on the stage. His immediate object was to form actors according to his own rules before permitting them to play. There were improvisations and exercises of all kinds to exhibit the results of courses on diction, rhythmic gymnastics, dancing, and pantomime. Following the precepts of the Vieux-Colombier and with his own added experience in army plays, Dullin was convinced that improvisation was the real art of the theater—the surest, quickest and most logical method for training actors to be pliable, original, and instinctive. It forced their acting to be grounded on genuine emotions and not on words, to find in themselves the right characterization. (This was a far cry from the Conservatory's conventional declamation contests.)

After they had learned some of the fundamentals of their craft and were impregnated with the idea that their first obligation was to the writer, the student-actors were for the first time permitted to step upon a stage—in an empty store. Until then, Dullin's friends followed the school's progress in his small apartment, which was crowded when there were more than three spectators. Here one of the most vital theaters of contemporary France came to life. Following Copeau's example, he had taken his students to a country inn for their first rehearsals of another Mérimée discovery, *L'Occasion*, in which Marguerite Jamois, soon to achieve fame, made her stage début. With the help of friends, Dullin soon found a little theater in the middle of Montmartre on the Place Dancourt. He called it the Théâtre de l'Atelier and wanted it to be what Stanislavsky and Copeau had succeeded in making of their theaters: the artist's workshop, a sacred spot given over to experiment, to making and unmaking, where one seeks and sometimes finds, where one dreams and plans, where one cries with joy and laughs with tears at the smallest discovery. The Atelier was not a place; it was a Spirit, akin to that which had given life and form to the Vieux-Colombier.

Copeau had his symbol in the two doves. Dullin printed his motto on his programs as well: *Rien ne sert de courir*, taken from the Aesop–La Fontaine moral: Slow and steady wins the race. Into the Atelier—and since 1940 into the Théâtre Sarah Bernhardt, where he transplanted his activities—came a long line of some of the most distinguished plays in world literature. His first complete season was a typical selection of his intentions: Calderon's *Life Is a Dream*, Mérimée's *L'Occasion*, plays by Molière, Cervantes, Max Jacob, Alexandre Arnoux, and Pirandello's first Paris production. Classics and moderns, foreign and native, were represented, and continued to be so through the years.

In 1934, after a highly successful production of André Obey's adaptation of Shakespeare's *Richard III* (in which Marie-Hélène Dasté gave a poignant portrayal as Lady Anne), Dullin made a statement in an interview that showed how closely his ideas were linked to Copeau's:

> my program is very clear, very precise. So long as I do not find in the modern theater what one has a right to expect of dramatic art, I shall produce consecrated, authentic masterpieces of the past. I believe that the playing of great works can furnish a happy example to modern authors and actors. It is in reaching for the heights that the theater will pull itself up out of the mediocrity where it has descended. In short, I wish to stage only plays of quality, productions which bring something into the theater.[13]

Such were the goals that endeared him to Copeau, who looked upon his theater as the truest, closest continuation of the Vieux-Colombier and admired Dullin for his faith, enthusiasm, and unselfishness. This respect was mutual, with Dullin saying of his former *patron*: "Copeau's influence has been considerable, because it was wholesome, exempt from bluff, and because it contributed in giving back to the theater a nobility and a distinction which place it very high in the hierarchy of the Arts."[14] From the older metteur-en-scène, Dullin had learned how to apply his critical sense to rediscover the youth and humanness of otherwise distorted classics.

These ideals did not always fill his theater, particularly during the early years. In 1923, for example, articles appeared in the press warning the public of the Atelier's imminent closing. Antoine pleaded for him in the press, trying to shame Paris into helping. Henry Bernstein gave a benefit performance for the Atelier in the Gymnase Theater. It was the irony of fate that made Henri Jeanson, drama critic for *Bonsoir*, call Paris to his rescue on May 21, 1923, four days before Dullin gave a special lecture on "Attempts at Theatrical Renovation" in France's most honored institution of higher learning, the Collège de France. Dullin persevered during those difficult days with a martyr's thirst for sacrifice and an artist's faith in the future. And the opening bill of the very next season saw him rewarded as he never dreamed he could be; the play was Pirandello's *Chacun sa vérité (Right You Are If You Think You Are)*. As is only too often the case, the French Academy waited years; it was not until 1930 that it gave him the Paul Hervieu Prize of 2,500 francs as a reward for his perseverance. Instead of a playwright, a whole theater was for the first time honored in this way.

The form that Dullin wanted his Atelier to have was that of a "fairyland . . . capable of tearing us from our daily life."[15] He tried to transform his studio into "a theater of pure fantasy," in the sense of making it poetic and imaginative. His fairyland had nothing in common with sensational tricks to fill the public with awe. It was not a fairyland décor he wanted, but rather an evocative, spiritual one. To achieve this, he frequently called upon music and the dance. These elements were not employed as ornamental interludes to divert the spectator as in many of Molière's comedies. On the contrary, they became integral parts of Dullin's mise-en-scène, of his "design of dramatic action." Besides, he never called in professional dancers. His own students—or rather, actors—danced the ballet portions of the play, since their school had prepared them for this. Music and ballet, therefore, added much to the inner atmosphere of the action of a play like *Richard III*, in which a war dance had the extraordinary effect of revealing clearly what was then going on in the king's heart. Jean-Louis Barrault was strongly influenced by this type of production, elaborating extensively upon it after studying at Dullin's drama school and acting at the Atelier in 1932.

Dullin sometimes resorted to a linear décor to translate by means of lines, volumes, and colors the play's dramatic values. Cubism then played its part, especially in a work like Jean Cocteau's *Antigone*, for which Picasso designed the set, Mademoiselle Chanel created the costumes, and Arthur Honegger composed the music. But there was nothing exaggerated or incomprehensible about it, and it was far from the abstract concoctions found elsewhere. It was simply that at the Atelier, when a play required such staging, it was given without thought of school or movement.

As at the Vieux-Colombier, costumes had an important role, and were occasionally designed and executed by Copeau's daughter, Maïène Dasté. The link between Atelier and Vieux-Colombier was strong spiritually and artistically. Both were guided by the rule that when the play's outside becomes too important, the theater is no longer doing its part. Like Copeau, Dullin believed, "Everything must be concentrated on the actor who is in the service of the poet's thought"—be the writer Molière, Shakespeare, Pirandello, Musset, or Cocteau. Dullin and Copeau were pensive, wise men who listened more than they spoke and preferred to do their work rather than talk about it. And Dullin's all-absorbing ambition, he told the public in his 1946 program, was to continue "to believe, to love, to construct." Which he did, and did admirably well, until his death at age sixty-four in November 1949, one month after his old *patron*.

Louis Jouvet

Louis Jouvet, born in Brittany on December 24, 1887, shocked his family of doctors by acting even while he was a pharmacy student in Lyons. Before graduating in 1910 with highest honors, he had already played on road tours throughout France. He held roles from the chorus leader in the first provincial performance of *Oedipus Rex* in Saint-Dizier (1908) to three or four parts in *La Tosca*, where he first met Dullin.

After a brief experience as assistant pharmacist to a relative in Paris, he turned definitely to the theater, and to the precarious life of an artist who could not agree with the prevailing standards of his art. "My youth," he wrote in a short *Homage to Antoine* in 1937, "was spent in revolt against his theories and his influence," and the ambitious pioneer was determined to take Antoine's advice to newcomers in the theater: "Be fearless, young men, step all over us!"

This was "a sordid period," Jouvet said, to make one's début in the theater. Having been refused three times by the conservatory (probably because of a bad stammer that he eventually controlled but never conquered psychologically), he played in one melodrama after another in Léon Noël's stock companies, holding forth in such old standbys as *The Courier of Lyons, The Wandering Jew,* and *Monte-Cristo.* Two or three times he managed to slip into a company playing Victor Hugo's *Hernani* and *Ruy Blas,* but there was little in all this to satisfy him until he was engaged by Jacques Rouché to play at the Théâtre des Arts. By then he and Jacques Copeau had already met through their Danish wives; but not until Copeau's dramatization of *The Brothers Karamazov,* in which he played the small part of Father Zossima, did Jouvet become fully familiar with Copeau's ideas. Two years later, after a short stint with his own Théâtre d'Action d'Art, he joined Copeau's Vieux-Colombier to become stage manager and general factotum.

With determination and ambition Jouvet lost no time in becoming as familiar with one branch of theatrical art as another: painter, decorator, carpenter, cabinetmaker, machinist, prop-man, electrician, costumer, architect, and one of the outstanding actors on the continent. To be sure, at the Vieux-Colombier this jack-of-all-trades soon developed into the finest technician on the French stage.

By October 1922, when he began to stage his own productions at the Comédie des Champs-Elysées under Jacques Hébertot's management, Jouvet felt more strongly than ever before the need to work in closer kinship with the general public, the one that he believed had to be pleased if the art of the theater were to be reborn. The elite audience, which he estimated at one to two thousand spectators, was "the most precious for the theater and . . . often, not the richest," he told an interviewer. Like Dullin, he promoted the artistic and technical principles of the Vieux-Colombier, but disapproved Copeau's persistence in remaining impervious to public reaction regarding the manner in which those principles were to be applied. "The theater," he noted, "must never lose sight of what one calls 'lofty subjects', but it must constantly establish a bond of harmony between these lofty subjects and the public of each period, of each season."[16] He sought and needed his audience's approbation in order to justify his work, agreeing with Molière that the real art is "the art of pleasing." Whereas for Copeau, success was no more than a point of departure leading to the next rung on the ladder of perfection, to Jouvet, as in any commercial theater, it was a point of arrival, an artistic success per se, there to bathe in gold and glory until the public became satiated with the creator's achievement and forced him on to something else.

Jouvet, in spite of his willingness to bend to public pleasure, maintained high standards nonetheless. Along with Dullin, he held that forgetting and escaping daily preoccupation was the theater's true objective. "We are thirsty for wonder," he exclaimed, "we want the theater to be a fairyland for us and not a flat picture of everyday life." To answer this requirement, he assigned to the stage director the task of "costuming feelings and ideas, but first he must serve them and not substitute himself for them. His function," Jouvet emphasized, "is to find new and fresh means for reviving old emotions. . . . I recognize only that theater which expresses and presents itself with dignity, without sentimental blackmail in the script, without intellectual blackmail in the sequence of ideas, without vulgar displays in acting."[17]

In 1924 Jules Romains's *Dr. Knock* gave Jouvet his first popular success and he revived it annually for thirty or more performances. It was Jouvet who persuaded the novelist Jean Giraudoux to write for the theater, which he then did for twenty years. Jouvet was Giraudoux's sole producer-director (and actor of course) in France, from *Siegfried* to *Amphitryon 38* and *The Madwoman of Chaillot*. Upon occasion he turned to Molière—by exception, for Jouvet, director of the seven-hundred-seat Right Bank Théâtre de l'Athénée, sought to stay as close as possible to his public by staging modern French works. He left to Copeau and Dullin the task of putting on the classics, both native and foreign.

As for mise-en-scène, he utilized all the successful experiments that he and Copeau had tested on the Left Bank. Two elements in particular he carried across the Seine: the architectural, three-dimensional stage and a subtle, effective use of lighting. In fact, Jouvet was the Frenchman who understood best the power of stage lights, drawing from them ingenious combinations of colors and forms which gave his stage a distinctive, unique atmosphere. His lighting tended toward the clarity of sunlight that eliminated the shadows from every corner of the stage and gave the impression that the actors were in the open, breathing fresh air. This bright, clear-weather effect even slipped into the auditorium and Jouvet's suggestive use of lights became a strong link between actor and audience.

Like Copeau and Dullin, he abhorred the painted set. But he used it from time to time in order to stress the caricatural side of a play's action. For example, the opening scene of *Knock* has a comical, but graceful, backdrop on which mountains and peaks are sketchily outlined. And the bare skeleton of a grotesque-looking Model T Ford sets off all the more the jaunty hills behind it. Some critics saw in this somewhat burlesque tableau a reflection of Jouvet's burlesque acting of the part. Be that as it may, *Knock*'s staging and sets were the essence of simplicity.

In latter years, Jouvet sometimes resorted to tricky mechanical devices.

In Molière's *L'Ecole des femmes*, a white wall runs along the full length of the stage, in front of which much of the play's action takes place. Behind the wall is Agnès's delightful little garden, which one reaches quite miraculously when the wall splits in two before the enchanted eyes of the audience and transports the character into the garden without his taking a single step. So thrilled is everyone by this wall trick that, by comparison, the character study of Arnolphe received relatively little attention from the public. In reply to criticism, Jouvet was reported to have answered: "I tried to stage it in as attractive and picturesque a manner as possible." Some critics reproached him for turning Molière's four acts into two, but he justified this by recalling that Molière's footlights were candles and frequently had to be replaced.

Rarely, if ever, was Jouvet accused of offering his public a displeasing mise-en-scène. He was meticulous and took a great deal of time with his work: *Ondine* took six and a half months of active planning. *The Madwoman of Chaillot*—for which Jean Giraudoux in 1943 had prophetically (he died in 1944) set aside October 17, 1945, as the First Night—opened on December 17. "We are late," Jouvet explained in the program, for he would not rush or take risks with art.

As for acting, he shared the same criteria as his former co-workers: the stage was just so much space to set off the player. But there were not many actors in Paris who could stand on their own merits alone, so that when the Vieux-Colombier closed its doors in 1924 he was glad to take part of its company. It gave him the best troupe in Paris: Valentine Tessier, Romain Bouquet, and Lucienne Bogaert were with him for many years, while from boulevard theaters came Pierre Renoir and Michel Simon. Jouvet was careful to choose good actors, but had little desire to develop his own. True, he expressed his admiration for Copeau's "courage and abnegation . . . to try and find a new formula of dramatic art with young elements."[18] But not until 1934 did he become connected with a drama school, when the Conservatory appointed him one of its professors. Then he even propounded ideas which, as a young actor, he had once personally disliked, such as physical training.[19] He thus became the first official link between the clear, subdued style of acting as practiced at the Vieux-Colombier and the artificial, outmoded, declamatory style so carefully preserved in the Comédie-Française.

Though Jouvet seemed to have moved outside the orbit of the workshop spirit as typified by Copeau and Dullin, he remained nevertheless a son of that same spirit. No actor ever starred in his productions, and he himself often played minor roles. Only one person came first in his productions, the author. In this he was a firm believer. "The art of pleasing in the theater," he held, "is the art of writing plays; then, and far below this summit, there is the art of staging and acting them." As success-minded as he was, rejecting like Baudelaire "the useless dreamer who . . . sought to mingle honesty with things of love," he could still write fifteen years after leaving Copeau, "The theater is a passion more than a profession." And when asked to define a work of art he would answer: "a work of love, of tenderness and of faith." Copeau and the Vieux-Colombier had indeed left their mark on Jouvet, who, until his sudden death in August 1951, spelled clarity and truth in the service of art.[20]

Gaston Baty

Gaston Baty, the fourth metteur-en-scène whom the Ministry of Fine Arts included with the other three to rejuvenate the Comédie-Française, had no Vieux-Colombier to inspire and develop his early years. After conscientiously studying the history of art, in Paris and at the University of Munich, Baty marked time until the age of thirty-five (1919) before he had a chance to work in the theater. That year, Gémier put him in charge of staging *La Grande Pastorale* in the Cirque d'Hiver, after which he branched out on his own and organized La Baraque de la Chimère with a group of authors. He founded his theater in 1921 on "enthusiasm, faith and voluntary poverty," exactly when the Vieux-Colombier was at the height of its popularity; it closed its doors in 1924 for lack of funds when the Vieux-Colombier closed down for lack of heart. And while Copeau and his group worked far from Paris, Baty was flourishing as an important director.

In 1924 Jacques Hébertot called him and his company to play at the Studio des Champs-Elysées, where they gradually acquired so firm a reputation that they had to move four years later to the larger Théâtre de l'Avenue. Baty, however, already had his eye on the more spacious Théâtre Montparnasse on the rue de la Gaîté, but he had to wait until the fall of 1930 before this house of old melodramas, once the home of Antoine's Théâtre Libre, would accommodate his dreams of what the modern theater should strive toward: "We wish to ignore current events," he wrote in the program of the Théâtre du Montparnasse. "On the contrary, we want the spectator, crossing our threshold, to be able to put aside his cares and worries, rid himself of his ideas, and no longer think he is a man of today. We are trying to make him live another life, to lead him towards other countries, other times, other souls."

To achieve this, Baty emphasized the physical side of the stage as much as, and frequently much more than, script and actor. To him there were two groups of actors: those who spoke and were heard, and those who should be made to speak even though they could not be heard: colors, lights, silence. It was the director's duty to regulate the relationship between these two sets of actors and to show no preference for one or the other. The text was one part of the performance, living actors another, sets a third. Each element was given its place as conceived by an impartial coordinator—the metteur-en-scène—and not by the writer's words, the actor's impulse, or any other single factor. Baty saw nothing sacred in the script to justify its domination over everything else, and this led him to the conclusion that "the beauty of a drama is like a bolt of lightning, magnificent and brief."

With a nobleman's love of pageantry, he reproached Racine, most revered of French classic dramatists, for stressing "but one aspect of dramatic art: words, which he forces to express many things that other elements would express as well or better." This theory, revolutionary for France where the theater was primarily a literary genre, was set forth in his book *Le Masque et l'encensoir*. Yet Baty felt he was entirely faithful to "His Majesty the Word" by completing the poet's thoughts instead of just translating them plastically for the stage. The script was, therefore, put in its place alongside other components needed to complete or "prolong his [the writer's] thought and emotion beyond words," such as acting, pantomime, rhythm, forms, lights, colors, voices, noises, dance, music, and—silence. (The latter was stressed to the point of launching a School of Silence.) These had all been used and developed by Copeau, Dullin, and Jouvet, but were, as a rule, no more than working instruments secondary to the text. The three Vieux-Colombier artists sought to evoke in their mise-en-scène the atmosphere of the play. Baty found this insufficient, and so set out to give each element its own atmosphere, its own "voice," which would speak to the spectator as directly as did the playwright or the actor. For the script was but "a small seed . . . [from which] the tree is slowly born."[21] The "tree," of course, was the outgrowth of Baty's imagination, the symbol and seal of his art.

Because of this doctrine, he was reproached for making the theater a series of tableaux that satisfied the eye alone. This did not so much matter when he produced a play like Musset's *Les Caprices de Marianne*, which had a profusion of theatrical values: the décor was evocative, the costumes were picturesque, the actors graceful and natural, the music and dance charming, the dialogue bright and swift, and the diction clear. It was pure Musset: fantastic, light, colorful, and psychological. Baty could neither hide nor change him; and the same could be said of the two Molière comedies he staged, *Le Médecin malgré lui* and *Le Malade imaginaire*, and possibly of Pirandello's *Comme tu me veux (As You Desire Me)*. But on the whole, his other twenty-odd productions were often scenarios, inferior to Molière, Musset, and Pirandello. That was the weak spot in his conception of the art of the theater. In order to capitalize on inferior texts, he drowned them in colors and paints and music until the result resembled the proverbial Miss who was all dressed up and had nowhere to go. This was true of Lucienne Favre's *Prosper* and of Baty's own dramatizations, or rather illustrations—Flaubert's *Madame Bovary* and

Dostoevsky's *Crime and Punishment*. The picturesqueness of it all carried the audience away into "dreams and forgetfulness."

Baty may be compared to a symphony conductor more concerned with his own orchestration and arrangements than with the composer's original score. One would almost believe that he shunned superior modern writers whose works did not yield thankfully to his theories, For example, his distinguished principal actress, Marguerite Jamois, tried for years to persuade him to stage Eugene O'Neill's *Mourning Becomes Electra*, but without success. Baty's baton had to swing supreme or the play was simply not worth working for.[22]

Although Copeau had openly reproached him for his theories ten years earlier, he did have in common with his three colleagues at the Comédie-Française the desire to use all styles to project his ideas. His stage was realistic or synthetic, depending upon the play. He often had recourse to the architectural set, although unlike Copeau, he did not automatically reject the painted set. But regardless of style, his objective was to bring out "the mystery . . . [lurking] beyond appearances and the poetry behind the secret realities." In that he saw eye to eye with Copeau and his followers and agreed with Dullin that "dream and forgetfulness" were the qualities the stage had to create. As Dullin remarked, Baty and he were on their way to the same place, but Baty was traveling on the elevated while he was taking the subway.

As for style of acting, Baty had implicit faith in the methods of Copeau and Dullin. Two of his best male actors, Lucien Nat and Georges Vitray, came from the Vieux-Colombier and were directors of the Ecole du Théâtre du Montparnasse, while Marguerite Jamois was a product of Dullin's School.

In a sense, Baty's conception of theater might be considered closer to the richness and color of Jacques Rouché's days at the Théâtre des Arts, in which case he would be in reaction against the austere bareness of the Vieux-Colombier. Nevertheless, his doctrines were as sharp a break from the conventional, realistic theater as were those of his codirectors at the Comédie. For he wished above all "to create next to the world the illusion of another world, still more beautiful." And this search for fresh illusions led him to develop a marionette theater during the last few years of his life. He died in September 1952, the last of the foursome to pass away (all within three years of one another), leaving behind a much younger generation of artists inspired by their elders.

Returning to Copeau, we find him working in harmony with the Comédie-Française. Although he did not have to concern himself with the productions of Dullin, Jouvet, and Baty—for each had complete direction over his own—he could not have worked in a theater where he was at loggerheads with the ideas of fellow workers. They did not necessarily agree on details, but they did agree on the broad artistic objectives.

Since each of the others had his own theater to manage, Copeau could feel all the more at home in the House of Molière. The thought of dividing the Comédie into equal quarters was completely absent, for to them it was extra work and for Copeau it was all. Not only that, he had staunch friends there; the new *administrateur-général*, Edouard Bourdet, looked upon him as one of the world's great directors and inaugurated his "administration" on December 7, 1936, with Copeau's staging of Molière's *Le Misanthrope*; Jean Croué, acting at the Comédie since 1909, was his close friend and collaborator on the dramatization of *The Brothers Karamazov*; Charles Granval, Denis d'Inès, André Brunot, Julien Bertheau, Aimé Clariond, Jean Debucourt, Berthe Bovy, and Madeleine Renaud were among the popular actors of the House who had confidence in Copeau's ideas; André Bacqué and Jean Legoff, formerly at the Vieux-Colombier, were now in the national company.

Above all, Copeau's ten years away from the stage of the French capital (1924–1934) did for him what a similar absence in the seventeenth century had done for his master, Molière. The provinces gave him time and the opportunity to take inventory: he learned to be less impatient with the doubters and more patient with himself. "Work and believe in what you do," he was quoted as saying in 1933.[23] He realized that what he had taken as a victory over Paris in 1924 had in reality been Paris's victory over him. He thought then that he had escaped the noose and would grow to new heights in the provinces, when actually he was being crushed. In his *Souvenirs du Vieux-Colombier* (1931), he remarked knowingly, "He who has not been broken at least once in his life is not aware of his true resources."[24]

By the time he was called to the Comédie in 1936, he knew his "resources." Little by little, those who had feared and rejected him in 1929, when the *Nouvelles littéraires* petition was making the rounds, began to appreciate in him the man's honesty and the artist's superiority. In 1940, Administrator Bourdet was the victim of a motor accident in which he lost the use of both legs. When this developed into phlebitis, it became too much for him to direct France's national theater from his hospital bed. Telegrams were hastily dispatched across Europe to reach Copeau, who was on a lecture tour. The second telegram from Bourdet caught him in Ankara as he was about to leave for Athens. It read: "Between you and me, this temporary [appointment as administrator] could become definitive." By a decree of May 12, 1940 [the Prime Minister, by law, had to approve major changes at national theaters], Bourdet left his post and the one-time arch-rebel of the French stage and erstwhile bitter adversary of the Comédie-Française was named to succeed him. Jacques Copeau became the incarnation of the best in French theater tradition and a welcome leader of France's First Theater. *Sic itur ad astra.*

His tenure of office lasted a few brief months. He staged Vildrac's *Le Paquebot Tenacity*, with Jean Legoff playing the role he had created at the Vieux-Colombier in 1920; *La Nuit des rois* was produced in the same Lascaris translation; Jean-Louis Barrault was brought into the Comédie to play Rodrigue in *Le Cid*. During the terrifying days of 1940, when panic flooded the streets of the capital as the Nazi army marched in, the Comédie was ordered south along with the other remnants of a still-free land. Transportation, however, was not available, so Copeau kept the Comédie as intact as circumstances would permit, reopening in Paris during August. By February of 1941, Copeau became persona non grata to Vichy and the occupation forces when they learned that his son, Pascal, was playing an important part in the resistance movement. He was presented with an ultimatum: to make his son quit the resistance or himself resign as head of the Comédie-Française. A few days later Copeau fled back to Burgundy, back to Pernand-Vergelesses, back to relative freedom once again.

There he lived the quiet life of enforced silence following the example of Duhamel, Valéry, Giraudoux, and other *esprits libres* living under Nazi *Kultur*. Upon occasion he would write to a close friend, as he did to Valentine Tessier (September 28, 1943) when he learned of a Vieux-Colombier actor's death while on tour with Jouvet in South America: "Yes, *ma chérie*, I too have been cruelly upset by the passing of poor Romain [Bouquet]. Everything which touches our past, our youth, possesses something almost sacred." Once, in 1943, he helped observe the fifth centenary of the Hospice de Beaune by staging a miracle play in that hospital's strikingly beautiful medieval courtyard. Whenever possible he would meet his son secretly to learn how Free France was faring. He took pride in his nephew, Michel Saint-Denis, the Compagnie des Quinze director, who had since 1933 staged important English productions with Laurence Olivier, among others. Using the name Jacques Duchêne, Saint-Denis became for Occupied France one of the most eagerly awaited radio voices, "Ici Londres," broadcasting on the program *A Frenchman Speaks to Frenchmen.*

On May 27, 1944, nine days before Allied troops landed in Normandy, Copeau addressed students and teachers on "Devotion to Dramatic Art," interpolating an appeal in his remarks on the theater: "God knows that our time does not lack tragic subjects and characters. . . . Therefore try to be men. . . . My friends, in the midst of such confusion, the only important thing is to make a pact with your soul and to keep to it faithfully. . . . You have no choice. Each one of you, at heart, must be a hero . . . worthy in every way of the France of tomorrow."

Three months later, American Seventh Army troops liberated Burgundy as Copeau was completing his six-act drama on St. Francis of Assisi, *Le Petit Pauvre*, a work he had been tempted to do twenty years earlier.

This was his final word in the theater. On October 20, 1949, while France was still celebrating his seventieth birthday and his American friends, led by old Theater Guild associates, were establishing a Birthday Fund in his honor, *le patron* died quietly in the Hospice de Beaune where only a few years before he had staged in the courtyard his unforgettable production of the medieval *Miracle du Pain Doré*. He was buried in his tiny village churchyard, making Pernand an international site of pilgrimage for lovers of the theater.

10

Conclusions

THE UPHEAVAL CAUSED BY THE French Revolution opened wide the gates to two centuries of "isms" in art as well as politics. Sturm und Drang manifestos and clashes lost no time stepping into the breach. Victor Hugo's celebrated "Battle of *Hernani*" was one of the first dramas of romanticism to attack head-on the Comédie-Française stronghold of archconservative classicism. The poet-dramatist did not hide his objective when he wrote "Guerra" in angry letters across the title page of his manuscript. The 1830 audience came to fight the rebel and stayed to acclaim his dazzling lyricism and dramatic force.

Paris also discovered Shakespeare then, thanks to a company of English players in the capital. Hector Berlioz fell madly in love with their Ophelia and married her. His passion for opera followed, and romanticism was on its way there, too. But all this love at first sight did not inhibit unsatisfied artists—writers, painters, sculptors—from pursuing other obsessions, such as realism, naturalism, and symbolism. New ideals stimulated stage directors and theorists to experiment: Gordon Craig's übermarionette, Stanislavsky's method, Reinhardt's style, Antoine's fourth wall, Piscator's epic theater, Brecht's alienation, and Gropius's total theater stand out as examples.

As for Copeau, he came on the scene out of frustration and indignation, to change theater per se and its affected way of life, as he observed it. Not that he had premeditated dogmas and doctrines to promote. On the contrary, what he asked of the theater was a new beginning to make a clear break from its cozy, artificial crust of convention. For this, he sought an unheard-of renovation: "a bare stage." Paradoxically, the Vieux-Colombier was a revolutionary theater *because* it had no sensational ideas to launch. The Théâtre du Globe had the romanticists, Scribe led the realists, Antoine the naturalists, Lugné-Poe the symbolists, and the boulevards the "well-made" play of Dumas *fils*. Houses were labeled and scripts made to measure. The same was true for sets and acting. All was stereotyped and categorized when Copeau revolted against this deadening ingrown atmosphere by opening a theater for plays regardless of style or period.

This attempt to unshackle the stage from "special interests" was too novel to be taken seriously, for it had the doubtful attraction of giving away something for nothing. Many expected the Vieux-Colombier would disappear quietly in the face of Parisian skepticism, but that was before *Twelfth Night*, when public enthusiasm gave vent to the kind of faith that Copeau easily rekindled at the end of the First World War, after an absence of almost six years from the capital.

The first postwar season—with its plays by Vildrac, Duhamel, Romains, Mazaud, and Mérimée, each of a different, distinct style, and all under the same roof—showed the heights that a theater could reach when it kept open house. Those works had, however, to achieve the standard of dramatic art established by Copeau, or rather by the best models of the past to which he looked for guidance. As a result, the critics became more and more impatient with the Vieux-Colombier's lack of modern works. True, French and foreign classics combined accounted for more than half the total of 2,315 performances from 1913 to 1914, 1917 to 1919, 1920 to 1924, while seventeen modern authors receiving their first productions at the Vieux-Colombier constituted about 40 percent: Benjamin, Bost, Claudel, Copeau, Duhamel, Fallens, Ghéon, Gide, Roger Martin du Gard, Mazaud, Nigond, Porché, Régis and de Veynes, Romains, Schlumberger, and Vildrac.

These productions represented a paltry number when compared with the 139 plays by ninety-four authors produced by Antoine at the Théâtre Libre. But Copeau's goal was not to give a school of writers their own stage, or even to discover new dramatists. That would have defeated his long-range purpose: a complete renovation of the French stage. This, he had hoped, would of itself evoke more active interest in the theater among talented writers who had until then looked down upon dramatic art as an inferior means of artistic expression. Copeau and his disciples were successful, for they attracted authors who would otherwise have written only novels or poetry or essays. Most of the great names in contemporary French drama wrote expressly for Copeau, Dullin, and Jouvet because their theaters were not the rendezvous of single-type playwrights, self-satisfied stars, or dead-end theories.

Copeau's policy of freedom in art breached his country's traditional wall of insularity by encouraging the production of foreign writers. Lugné-Poe and Antoine had tried to do this, but their efforts had received only a condescending welcome and rarely reached the general public. Not until the great popular appeal of *Twelfth Night* at the Vieux-Colombier did

Goldoni, Gozzi, Calderon, Pirandello, Gogol, Andreyev, Chekhov, Tolstoy, and Shaw win recognition, thus to form part of the French theater, thanks to the success of Copeau and his followers.

The recreative forces set loose by their originality, good taste and common sense, seconded by the development of stage technique, gave writers for the theater the same unique liberty they had formerly had only in poetry, novels, or short stories. Without regard to size, the stage now had the limitless space that even the Greeks did not possess, for the architectural, three-dimensional set with its extraordinary power of modern lighting could create any locale and evoke any mood that the most imaginative writer wished to conceive.

The rich possibilities of such a stage risked making it an element apart from the drama, one with which a virtuoso director might become so infatuated that he would see in it alone the whole art of theater. Reinhardt and Baty, each in his own way, frequently fell victim to visual cadenzas, while Copeau and his fellow artists used stage technique as a means to an end rather than the end itself. The Vieux-Colombier lineage rarely lost command over the instrument they held in their hands. A strong sense of discipline dominated their overall control.

Indeed, discipline and the search for rules of technique are two of the most significant strides forward in twentieth-century theater. Drama schools have more and more become reliable sources for fresh theater material. After Russian and German schools had begun to flourish, there were the French, started by Copeau and followed by Dullin, Baty, and a slowly changing Conservatory. And when Copeau came to New York in 1926 to stage *The Brothers Karamazov*, he found his theater-plus-laboratory idea taking shape at the Theater Guild, which had recently opened a drama school of its own. Once Theresa Helburn complained to him that their students had too many grand illusions of graduating right on to the Guild stage instead of thinking only of their craft. To which Copeau commented: "The trouble with your school is that you hold classes on the top floor. Move to the basement." (Erwin Piscator must have felt this instinctively in 1938 when he organized the Dramatic Workshop at the New School for Social Research and had Stella Adler give her acting course in the Dance Studio, which was literally in the cellar.) Harold Clurman, as well, founded his school alongside the Group Theater, and was directly inspired and influenced by Copeau:

> What Copeau gave us was a sense of the theater as a serious institution, as a place and as an art to which one had to be as deeply devoted as were writers, painters and musicians to their respective work. He made us feel that the theater required real study, practice, through years of training. When he said to us, "After all, there have only been five or six really great actors in the history of the theater," we realize that he was talking in terms of standards far beyond the

scope and interest of Broadway, and it was to those standards that we looked for justification of our efforts.[1]

Throughout the theater world there is today the conviction that the best type of theater calls for trained workers who can carry on, and not repeat, from where their predecessors leave off. With this realization, the teaching of theatrical arts has become a proud part of many English and American universities, and this stresses even more the theater's cultural heritage and responsibility.

The principles of discipline scrupulously followed by the Vieux-Colombier resulted in forming the most homogeneous acting unit since Antoine's theater twenty years before 1913. Even today, so many years after the Vieux-Colombier's closing, there is probably no company in France, or in America or England, that can boast the same qualities of ensemble acting. Dullin was the only real actor at the Atelier, which may explain why he gradually transformed his school from a workshop for actors to one for playwrights. Jouvet, often in spite of himself, outshone all those around him. Baty had two or three good actors but the ensemble was weak. Georges Pitoëff had his wife, Ludmilla, but the rest of the company was far inferior.

The Vieux-Colombier, on the contrary, excelled as a single unit. Copeau was a good actor but he never had to act in order to assure the play its best casting. Even after Dullin and Jouvet left, there was no company in Paris to equal Copeau's, so right was its general tone. They had an easy simplicity that abhorred overemphasis and yet was not what Dullin called *"l'horrible naturel."* They had a touch of mystery and delicate ease that had something fairylike and poetic about it and appealed to the spectator's imagination. For actor, set and script were woven together by Copeau into one tapestry of symbol and evocation, of atmosphere and mood. It was typical of the Vieux-Colombier not to state bluntly what it had to say, and this quality sometimes earned it the reproach of being austere, ascetic, and affected. Yet a Vieux-Colombier production was clear and original, and gradually attracted a surprisingly diverse audience.

In 1913, it will be recalled, Copeau believed that only a critical elite audience could guarantee the theater its artistic progress and growth, as in the seventeenth century. In looking to the elite for support, he chose to ignore momentarily the vast distant audience on the boulevards. He did not object to their coming to the Vieux-Colombier—his theater was not an insular, dilettante affair—but he preferred people who had never gone to the theater or who no longer went, just as he preferred co-workers with a minimum of commercial experience. He wanted to convince people of his theater's worth so that they would attend all productions and not merely those the critics approved.[2]

It took time for the Vieux-Colombier to win its supporters, and as more people came the less it resembled a rendezvous for the literati. When *Twelfth Night* became a success, it brought the Right Bank to the Left, filling the theater with the good bourgeois stock of Paris who needed an all-powerful push to be budged. After the war, the public became more and more general, attracted as much by the sincere simple spirit in the house as by the high quality of the productions. The discreet, informative program, person-to-person reporting, lectures, and readings were the only means of advertisement. This word-of-mouth publicity created an esprit de corps that the French theater had lacked since Molière's time. And when the Vieux-Colombier closed its doors, it could do so with a clear conscience: an audience for art had been found and formed to appreciate the work of Dullin, Jouvet, Baty, Pitoëff, and others.

This multiplication (the word is Jules Romains's) of the Vieux-Colombier explains why Copeau was called the "discoverer of stage directors," not alone in France, but throughout Europe and in the United States. For he was recognized as a great leader in dramatic art whose humanism was part of the general wave that swept across the continent at the turn of the century, carrying along the French as it had the Russians, the Germans, the English, and the Swiss. In 1913, Copeau's first objective when he started to serve the theater was to study all experiments and use whatever he thought would help French drama recover some of its lost dignity as an art. He wanted to place the theater on the same level with music, painting, and sculpture, and that is why his goal had been so enthusiastically welcomed by Debussy, Bonnard, and Rodin.

His work in New York undoubtedly helped promote a more artistic theater in America. Clayton Hamilton credited Copeau with having exercised "an appreciable influence upon the American theater, particularly along the line of *simplification* of stage design and decoration"; and Kenneth Macgowan wrote that "the Vieux-Colombier helped to reinforce the great tendency of the next ten years away from a realistic theater toward a more formal one."[3] To mention a few examples, the bare stage for Thornton Wilder's *Our Town* and Orson Welles's *Julius Caesar*, the presentational staging of Wilder's *The Skin of Our Teeth*, the evocative use of screens and curtains and bareness, all recall vividly the staging of a Copeau, whose name led Wilder to pronounce an enthusiastic "very great."[4]

Ever since Copeau followed Stanislavsky's example by taking his troupe to the country, art became a way of life in the theater. In America, it was Eva Le Gallienne who decided upon the untheatrical method of having her actors, who had not yet played together, work in the country to rehearse *The Three Sisters* for the Civic Repertory. Katharine Cornell did not star in her own productions, believing that stars are helped by fine ensemble acting, and anyway, she insisted in her book *I Wanted to Be an*

Actress, "First and foremost always is the play"—two revolutionary ideas for a star-producer to put into practice. Ethel Barrymore, in a *New York Times Magazine* interview on August 13, 1939, looked toward the little theaters to help the future of the drama. William Saroyan, "the bad boy of Broadway," felt that "We can't have fresh art until at least someone somewhere lives freshly."[5]

These views revealed a few of the criteria with which Copeau governed the Vieux-Colombier. How they reached all these artists, whether they were breathed in from the air of changing times, is of small consequence. Yet, after Stanislavsky, Reinhardt, and others had won a following in America, Harold Clurman's impression was that "Copeau was more fervid and earnest about the theater than any person we had contact with up to that time [1927]. This was a great encouragement to us [the Group Theater, 1931–1941] and a great stimulus."[6]

The Vieux-Colombier was an outstanding example of a company that lived theater as a community experience. When it was threatened by commercialization or by a weakening in the ranks, it lost the will to live. Jules Romains interpreted this as "the refusal of a chapel to become a cathedral," and he compared Copeau to a leader of the opposition who is unwilling to accept his place of power when the time comes for him to lead. He saw in Copeau a reflection of the period between the two world wars, a period of missed opportunities.

André Gide had another explanation. He contended that Copeau's "glorious effort" on behalf of the French stage "remained without any direct relation to his period. It is against it that he struggled, as every good artist must do" (*Journal*, January 15, 1931). Copeau later regretted not having continued the struggle, but added: "I would have needed more strength and genius than I had."[7] On the other hand, had he not closed his theater, it would eventually have led him into the commercial "cathedral." The alternative was a clean, quiet little temple in the country. Copeau's nature dictated his choice. One may venture to predict that he would have been a great force in the commercial theater, judging from Jouvet's work. But the Vieux-Colombier as a clarion call of dramatic renovation would have been forever stilled. With Copeau consistently aloof to the boulevards, he became a symbol of the artist's respect for his work and for himself. He may have missed his great opportunity, but as always, it was of the future and not of the present that he was thinking. He knew instinctively and from bitter experience that when money controls art, art no longer controls itself.

This awareness gradually reached boulevard theaters, torn as they were between the old, realistic ways of Emile Fabre entrenched at the Comédie-Française and the growing popularity of *"le cartel des quatre"* (Dullin, Jouvet, Baty, and Pitoëff). The boulevard no longer knew which way the weathervane of public opinion was pointing. By 1935, however, the Comédie had invited Copeau and his followers to govern it, and the public's preference was no longer in doubt. The new art of the theater had been tested—and approved—before World War I; it was developed for twenty years after that, appreciated and faithfully followed, then as now. All this was a wholesome sign that the stage was winning its right to be considered a truly creative experience. It reflected the courage of theaters everywhere to proclaim with resounding successes and no less resounding failures that dramatic art had at last been freed from the strict confines of one or another literary school, that it was no longer fettered to narrow dictatorial programs. This freedom in art has been long in coming, but like other freedoms, it will not be easily relinquished.

Postscript
(1949–1999)

In the history of French theater, there are two periods: before Copeau and after Copeau.

—Albert Camus

THE DEATH OF JACQUES COPEAU and his two closest fellow-artists, Charles Dullin and Louis Jouvet, coincided at midcentury with the end of World War II. The coming of peace led most people in Europe and Asia, ally and enemy alike, out of the overbearing darkness of fear and hate but not out of the mental and moral trauma of the times. Mourning the death or disappearance of loved ones, civilian and military, gone by untold millions, was heart-rending for both survivors and witnesses. France, like other countries, had been bled dry by the Nazis and the hardships of daily existence took place within a grim context: rationing of necessities—food, clothes, heating—was tight and pathetic; the ugly stains of black markets would not go away; political instability was nerve-wracking for peace-hungry citizens; the bitter freeze and dangers of the Cold War with its nuclear threats hung ominously over both sides of the Iron Curtain.

The shadows, however, were dispelled by a reassuring glimmer. The light of Liberty radiated hope for the future. Personal and national dignity took immense comfort in a single thought: Civilization was saved! The poet Jean Cocteau reminded us that statesmen and politicians make History, but artists, scientists, and scholars make Civilization. Jacques Copeau's heritage had taken root and rose to the occasion by pointing the way towards moral, spiritual, and artistic rejuvenation, and ultimately expansion, both national and international.

Albert Camus, who had never met Copeau nor seen his work, heard the message and took his cue. Unequivocally, in typical straight-from-the-shoulder determination, Camus wrote in the 1950s in an essay entitled "Copeau, Sole Master" that the French theater had two periods: Before

Copeau and After Copeau. He spoke of "periods" as a sportsman—Camus had been an active teenage soccer player in his native Algeria. Team spirit was a spontaneous outlet for solidarity and fraternity, until tuberculosis forced him to relinquish one team for another: an amateur theater that he organized and called *L'Equipe (The Team)*. Instinctively he turned for guidance to the plays and methods of the Vieux-Colombier, long before he left for France.

In the preceding fifty years teamwork and community spirit—that is, sharing professional pride and gatherings in regional playhouses—had become more and more part of the world's cultural experience, as Copeau had said they must. Camus agreed wholeheartedly with this ideal because of his own standards of morality and fairness—in short, of justice. He thrived on the powerful bond of team spirit linking art, technique, and integrity that took shape in his successful play *Caligula*. Crime and cruelty were depicted as gratuitous and absurd, a theme in his novels that had already made him an international figure.

In the 1950s he devoted considerable time to the stage. Just before his death in 1960 he had been about to acquire his own theater in Paris, subsidized with the help of an older friend and literary sponsor, André Malraux, who was De Gaulle's Minister of Culture. Like Copeau, Camus had a visceral need for theater as an open community dialogue and, had he lived, would no doubt have expanded the vision of his "sole master" to include a geocultural dimension far beyond national borders.

Camus said he learned from Copeau that "theme, style and beauty" were essential for a play to "unite, not divide the audience . . . so as to share emotion and laughter." Copeau, he hastened to add, was pitiless towards theater without style, contemptuous towards propaganda that sought only to destroy and alienate. Both rejected the notion of actors being used as the author's mouthpiece: the actor must give of himself, but first he must possess himself. This, Camus concurred, "runs the risk of disturbing actors who believe that emotion can replace technique and training, whereas training is meant precisely to liberate emotion." The Vieux-Colombier spirit and its school program of the 1920s were very much alive in the 1950s. Michel Saint-Denis, Copeau's nephew and assistant in Burgundy, demonstrated this when he set up theater schools in Strasbourg, Montreal, at the Young Vic in London, and at the Juilliard School in New York.

Camus also emphasized that Copeau wanted the metteur-en-scène to be discreet. "Initiate feeling in the actor, don't dictate it," they each insisted. It was clear to Camus that "Copeau hid the director behind the actor and the actor behind the play." *Le patron* had denounced in no uncertain terms both the ham actor and the ham director.

From the start, they considered dramatic art, as Camus put it, *"un fait*

de culture," a cultural event meant to reach out to everyone. "*Un fait*"—
a fact, a truth beyond doubt or discussion, a crossroads where all should
try to agree. This convinced him, as it had Copeau in 1913 at the launching of the Vieux-Colombier, that culture was threatened more in the theater than elsewhere. Money, intrigue, greed, hate, politics, financial, or
ideological interests had to be held at bay to defend the integrity of dramatic art and its public.

Sharing such rigid criteria would eventually oblige these two vision-
aries to separate painfully from intimate associates and friends. Copeau
separated quietly from Dullin and Jouvet after years of daily heart-to-
heart teamwork, from Gide and Roger Martin du Gard, from Georges
Duhamel and Jules Romains, from Jean Schlumberger and the others. He
was profoundly hurt by their lack of understanding and shocked by their
arguments to commercialize ideas-in-the-making. As for Camus, the novelist, essayist, and journalist broke publicly from his nocturnal drinking
companions Jean-Paul Sartre and Simone de Beauvoir. Those two belittled
Camus's approach to people and art, and Camus and Sartre differed radically on the place of man in society.

Sartre's existentialism imposed freedom at any price, even if one had
to resort to cruelty or oppression or tyranny to achieve it. Camus demanded
tolerance and justice and could not abide by Sartre's foreboding philosophy. His sense of the integrity and dignity of mankind could not live in
comfort with Sartre's perception of existentialism—that is, separating the
"good" from the "bad" by eliminating the bad. Nor could Camus agree
with Sartre's politically oriented theater, which he found was devoid of
human emotion and provoked conflict and hatred. Theater for Copeau
and Camus was definitely not the place for ideological dispute. On this
Copeau was adamant, which led people to love him or hate him.

"What interests us," Camus said about Copeau, "is what he did by
virtue of persistence . . . and it is for us to remember and appreciate, always, the severe judgment of the only master who can be accepted at the
same time by writers, actors, and directors."

The day Copeau addressed students and artists in Occupied France by
pleading with them to identify with the tragedy of the time, to create and
produce great works in keeping with the time, his only son Pascal was a
leader in the Resistance, imprisoned and tortured; his nephew Michel
Saint-Denis was with De Gaulle in London broadcasting regularly to the
French on behalf of Free France. Copeau himself had been dismissed by
the Germans in early 1941 from his post as head of the Comédie-Française.

In 1955 Camus spoke similarly in his Athens lecture on *The Future of
Tragedy*: "Great periods of tragic art take place in history, at turning points,
at moments when the future is uncertain and the present dramatic, when
the lives of people are heavy with glory and threats . . . after all, Aeschylus

fought in two wars and Shakespeare was the contemporary of a horrible series of events. Both lived at a crisis in the history of their civilizations."

This deeply shared view of life, to be reflected in dramatic art, existed at moments when Copeau and Camus were each overwhelmed by events. For Camus it was in the resistance against the Nazis, then once again when France was fighting a bitter colonial war in Algeria, where Camus's mother still lived. His pen and person were actively engaged in this turmoil, which tore him apart and forced him to state openly that if he had to choose between freedom for Algeria, which he supported under certain conditions, and his mother's safety, he would not hesitate for a moment to choose his mother. That was the dividing line between Sartre's campaign—combat for freedom at any price—and Camus's visceral attachment to humanity, a conflict that grew ugly after Camus gave his anticommunist Nobel address on the humanistic role of the artist in our society and Sartre refused the same award a few years later with a volley of angry peevish insults.

Camus was 36 when Copeau died at age 70. They were more than a generation apart, yet the meeting of minds and ideals between them offers unique insight into the optimism they projected towards community spirit at all levels, towards people in every activity. Theater was their springboard for communicating independence of thought and emotion. Copeau went so far as to refuse government or private subsidies that might interfere with his independence; Camus, on the other hand, welcomed subsidies since his fame as a writer and journalist gave him the power to assert convictions and not yield to unjustified objections.

The Copeau concept of team spirit subsequently developed into a way of cultural life in dozens of French towns and cities, thanks to Drama Centers that had state-supported permanent companies and theater schools. They dotted the map of France after World War II and gave artists a community base, a spiritual home that Copeau had initiated in the Burgundy countryside when he left Paris in the 1920s to raise a new generation of artists. In the 1960s, Minister of Culture André Malraux gave body to the soul of Copeau's plan for a People's Theater by building "Houses of Culture" in the provinces.

The Copeau-Camus faith in theater as a cultural fact of life helped to make Paris a world theater center under the direction of a former Vieux-Colombier student, A. M. Julien, who had followed his *patron* to Burgundy and married Copeau's niece. From 1954 to 1968 the French government financed an annual two-month summer festival of foreign troupes acting in their native language and called it "Theater of Nations." Thanks to vast media coverage, Bertolt Brecht's East Berlin company excited one country after another with his challenging mix of alienation and propaganda, superb acting, and dynamic direction. Copeau and Camus would never have subscribed to such aggressiveness except in the name of freedom of expression. Whatever his politics, Brecht did have a strong sense of justice.

The festival managed to persuade Communist China to let its extraordinary Peking Opera Company be seen in the West for the first time. Not since Diaghilev revealed the Russian Ballet, Nijinsky, and Stravinsky to Paris and the world fifty years before was there such an outburst of enthusiasm. The creativity of foreign artists filled several Paris theaters, including the Vieux-Colombier. International theater competed successfully for the attention of tourists; never had there been such a popular picnic of participation, such surprise packages of plays, opera, and dance.

The idea behind it all came from the International Theater Institute, a UNESCO-sponsored non-governmental organization that I had the privilege of creating and serving as secretary-general. This program increased the momentum of community and people-to-people festivals everywhere, on all continents. The Vieux-Colombier welcomed numerous foreign productions: The Old Vic from London; Ireland's best; Italy's magnificent Piccolo Teatro from Milan; the Living Theater with Julian Beck from the United States; and many others. During the regular season the Vieux-Colombier presented the first French productions of Thornton Wilder, Arthur Miller, Tennessee Williams, Edward Albee, Murray Schisgall, and T. S. Eliot. In May 1944, a few days before D-Day, Sartre came out of hiding, so to speak, from the Café de Flore to make his debut as a dramatist at the Vieux-Colombier with *Huis-Clos (No Exit)*.

Copeau's "shelter" continued to serve French and foreign talent until the owners of the building refused to renew the lease in order to conclude a real estate deal. Their philistine plans were foiled by street demonstrations and the government declared the Vieux-Colombier a "national monument," thus cutting short any change of status. The Ministry of Culture then purchased and modernized the premises and reopened the theater in 1993 as the second house of the Comédie-Française, exactly eighty years after Copeau announced his intention to renovate dramatic art and made of it, in the words of Jean Cocteau, the stage "where so much glory was born."

Brooks Atkinson's book *Broadway* (1970) gave the reason for this "glory" by extolling Copeau's overall purpose. "Good theater," the dean of American drama critics wrote, "is usually a dictatorship . . . the expression of one dominating person, like Henry Irving, Constantin Stanislavsky, Jacques Copeau, or Max Reinhardt." *Leadership* would be preferable to explain Copeau's control over his team, over the community spirit he wished to build.

Peter Brook calls his theater community in Paris an international research center where creative experiments are conducted with French and foreign artists. Before going on worldwide tours, Brook and his group share the results with large devoted audiences in an unusual dilapidated theater that has become a favorite showcase for the best of the offbeat. Another Paris seeker of freshness has been Ariane Mnouchkine (president of the association Friends of Jacques Copeau), who carries on into the present generation the principles of le patron. She has formed her own special art community of young people at the Théâtre du Soleil, deep in the Bois de Vincennes in Paris. There she excites the imagination by the forceful originality of her productions and the newness of her fantasies.

Newness never meant being different for the sake of novelty. Copeau experimented with newness, the better to capture the imagination of artist and public, and to make of the Vieux-Colombier an umbrella-like shelter to protect and promote experiment against the assault of conventional exploitation of that shelter. Artists and audiences understood and appreciated this priority of innovation, but not always to the point of accepting failure as inevitable in the natural course of progress. In the end, this demoralized Copeau and closed the laboratory of the Vieux-Colombier in 1924. Years later le patron admitted that he would have needed more strength and will to compromise somewhat with his time until compromise, as in the world of politics, could bring in certain rewards and become a step in the right direction: people's trust.

This occurred, it should be emphasized, in 1935 as a long-awaited "revolution" toppled the theatrical pyramid in Paris. A successful dramatist, Edouard Bourdet, was named by the government to run France's national theater, the Comédie-Française. Bourdet accepted on one condition: a new style and new methods of production had to be introduced into the old house through the appointment, as artistic directors, of Jacques Copeau, Charles Dullin, Louis Jouvet, and Gaston Baty. They became a focal point for renewed adventures in the noblest perception of the word. The raison d'être of Copeau's Vieux-Colombier was "officially" recognized. But suddenly the Good Fight had to be suspended to cope with other battles.

The pervasive cruelty of the Second World War showed how essential it was to pursue Copeau's ideals of teamwork and community spirit, of solidarity and fraternity, and how theater could advance audience awareness and sensitivity to help approach this goal.

Jean-Louis Barrault, an ambassador to the world theater community, called Copeau "le grand patron, who seemed to possess the keys to our mysteries: intelligence, sensibility, vision." One magic key was the powerful, evocative poetry of pantomime, in which Barrault excelled in the film Les Enfants du Paradis. He and Marcel Marceau had found the same teacher and master in Etienne Decroux, a Vieux-Colombier Theater School student whom Copeau encouraged to turn from acting to pantomime.

Another devoted artist, Giorgio Strehler, founder and head of Milan's Piccolo Teatro, said in 1997 on its fiftieth anniversary: "Copeau gave theater a certain light."

Copeau's lifework has served as a lighthouse for artists and audiences. Fifty years ago, the British dramatist J. B. Priestley was in step with Copeau and Camus when he declared that "theater can contribute to the new world civilization that is now struggling into existence. . . . [It] at least provide[s] one stout thread for the fabric of a world society."[1]

The struggle continues, as theater flourishes in what Camus called "an inspired disorder." This recalls the profession of faith of the great seventeenth-century English divine Richard Baxter, that "it is better to go to heaven in disorder than to hell in order."

Notes

Bibliography

Index

Notes

1. The Birth of a Theater

1. Most art theaters could afford a house at irregular intervals only, and for no more than a few performances.

2. Jacques Copeau, *Souvenirs du Vieux-Colombier*, 22.

3. Principal source of details about Copeau's life is his *Journal*.

4. Copeau, "André Baine," *Europe* 23 (June 15, 1930), 212.

5. André Gide, *Oeuvres Complètes*, 4:532–33. The entry is dated July 10, 1905.

6. Gide, *Oeuvres Complètes*, 4:508.

7. Copeau, *L'Ermitage*, Mar. 1904, 146.

8. Copeau, *Critiques d'un autre temps*, 227.

9. H. Béranger, *La Revue* 34, 1901; Jules Guillemot, *L'Evolution de l'idée dramatique*, 295; Rolland quoted by Y. M. Gobelet, *La Revue*, Sept. 1, 1910; Bordeaux, *Revue hebdomadaire*, April 1911.

10. These plays have been chosen at random from the 1912–1913 season.

11. Gide, "L'Evolution du théâtre," in *Oeuvres Complètes*, 4:209, 214.

12. Quoted in L. Morino, *Nouvelle Revue Française*, n.d., 85.

13. Quoted in Henri Morin, *Grande Revue*, Dec. 1928, 248.

14. Copeau wrote regularly on theater for the *Nouvelle Revue Française* from 1910 to 1913.

15. Constantin Stanislavsky, *My Life in Art*, 143.

16. Copeau, "Un Essai de rénovation dramatique," *Nouvelle Revue Française*, Sept. 1, 1913, 338.

17. Copeau, "Le Théâtre," *Nouvelles littéraires*, Nov. 18, 1933.

18. Quoted in Pierre Ducrocq, "Interview with Jane Lory," *L'Epoque*, Sept. 12, 1937.

19. Copeau, "Le Pain, d'Henri Ghéon," *Le Théâtre*, Dec. 1, 1911.

20. G. Charensol, "Jacques Copeau," *Nouvelles littéraires*, April 29, 1933, 2.

21. Dullin quoted in Yette Jeandet, "Copeau fondait le Vieux-Colombier," *Nouvelles littéraires*, Oct. 29, 1938.

22. André Antoine, "Causerie sur la mise-en-scène," *Revue de Paris*, April 1, 1903, 602.

23. Quoted in "Jacques Copeau Off Today," *New York Times*, Jan. 27, 1927.

24. Waldo Frank, "The Art of the Vieux-Colombier," 39; republished in *Salvos*, 119–67.

25. See Copeau, "Un Essai de rénovation dramatique."

26. Copeau, "Le Théâtre du Vieux-Colombier," *Le Théâtre*, Sept. 11, 1913, 21.

27. In 1913 the U.S. dollar was worth five francs.

28. Dorothy Thompson, "The Theater," *Tomorrow*, May 1942, 12.

2. The First Season's Struggle (1913–1914)

1. Copeau, "Le Théâtre," *Nouvelles littéraires*, June 16, 1934.

2. "The French Repertory Movement," *The Times* (London), Nov. 24, 1913, 7.

3. Copeau, *Souvenirs*, 29–31.

4. Paul Claudel, "How My Plays Should Be Acted," *Theater Arts Magazine*, May 1917, 117.

5. André du Fresnois, "L'Echange," *Revue Critique des idées et des livres*, Feb. 10, 1914.

6. An invited audience of drama critics and guests comparable to a First Night. American opening-night seats are, however, on sale to the public, whereas *générales* (*répétitions générales*—that is, dress rehearsals) are not.

7. "French Plays in London," *The Times* (London), Mar. 30, 1914, 12:2.

8. Sheldon Cheney, "The New Movement in the Theater," *Forum*, Nov. 1914, 763.

9. Copeau, "Le Pain, d'Henry Ghéon."

10. Copeau, *Souvenirs*, 28.

11. Jean Schlumberger, "L'Eau-de-vie, d'Henri Ghéon," *Nouvelle Revue Française*, July 1, 1914.

12. Valdo Barbey, "Les Peintres modernes et le théâtre," *Art et décoration* 37 (1920): 155.

13. Copeau, *Souvenirs*, 37.

14. Ibid., 35.

15. René Doumic, "Nuit des rois," *Revue des deux mondes*, June 15, 1914, 933.

16. Henry Bordeaux, "La Vie au théâtre," *Revue hebdomadaire*, June 1914, 218.

17. Gabriel Trarieux, "Le Mouvement dramatique," *La Revue* 48 (1904): 511.

18. Copeau, "Shakespeare à l'Odéon," *Nouvelles littéraires*, March 31, 1934.

19. Claude Cézan, *Louis Jouvet et le Théâtre d'Aujourd'hui*, 100.

20. Letter to Copeau, Nov. 24, 1916, in *A New French Theater in America*, 1917.

21. Introduction, *Les Tragédies de Shakespeare*, 1:xix.

22. Ibid., 1:xi.

23. A. Villeroy, "Le théâtre du Vieux-Colombier," *Nouvelle Revue*, Aug. 1, 1914.

3. Three Years of Silent Life (1914–1917)

1. Charles Dullin, "Les Essais de rénovation dramatique," *Revue hebdomadaire*, June 1923, 299.

2. Copeau, *Souvenirs*, 73.

3. Gide, *Oeuvres Complètes*, 4:103, 106.

4. Excerpts from Copeau's letters to Jouvet are taken from unpublished correspondence in the Jouvet Papers, Département des Arts du Spectacle, Bibliothèque Nationale de France, Paris.

5. Copeau, "Le Théâtre du Vieux-Colombier," *Nouvelle Revue Française*, Sept. 1, 1913.

6. Obey, *Théâtre*.

7. Copeau, *Souvenirs*, 92.

8. Gordon Craig, *The Theatre Advancing*, xxv.

9. Ibid.

10. Gordon Craig, *On the Art of the Theatre*, 103.

11. Jean Mercier, "Adolphe Appia," *Theater Arts Monthly* 16 (Aug. 1932), 622.

12. Craig, *On the Art of the Theatre*, 61.

13. Harley Granville-Barker, *The Exemplary Theatre*, 102.

14. Copeau, *Souvenirs*, 93; Stark Young, "Acting," *Theater Arts Monthly* 6 (Oct. 1922), 288; Constantin Stanislavsky, *An Actor Prepares*, 67; and "An Aesthetic of Acting," *Theater Arts Monthly* 15 (Sept. 1931), 736.

15. Copeau, *Oeuvres de Molière*, 1:64–65; Willis Steell, "Jacques Copeau," *The Theatre*, Nov. 1917.

16. Copeau, "Réflexions d'un comédien sur le Paradoxe de Diderot," *Revue universelle* 33 (June 15, 1928), 647–48.

17. Ibid., 649.

18. Copeau, "An Address Before the Drama League of America," Mar. 27, 1918, 12–13.

19. Q. K., "After the Play," *New Republic* 13 (Dec. 15, 1917), 187; Pitts Sanborn, "M. Copeau Reformer," *New York Daily Tribune*, July 8, 1917.

20. Copeau, "La Française, de Brieux," *Le Théâtre*, June 1907.

21. Copeau, "True Spirit of the Art of the Stage," *Vanity Fair*, Apr. 1917, 49.

22. Quoted in Willis Steell, "Jacques Copeau," *The Theatre*, May 1917.

23. Otto H. Kahn, "Art and America," *Drama League*, Feb. 5, 1924, 17.

24. Clayton Hamilton, *Studies in Stagecraft*, 262; Montrose J. Moses, "Craze for Little Theatres," *Bellman*, Mar. 17, 1917.

25. Clayton Hamilton, "Le Théâtre du Vieux-Colombier," *Bookman*, Jan. 1918; Minnie Maddern Fiske, "Actors and Repertory," *The Nation* 104 (Jan. 11, 1917): 39; Sheldon Cheney, "The Most Important Thing in Theater," *Theater Arts Magazine* 1 (Aug. 1917): 167; Clayton Hamilton, *Problems of the Playwright*, 261.

26. Granville-Barker and Winthrop Ames attempted to popularize theatrical art in New York City (that whole New Theater venture) and met with complete failure. Arthur Hopkins's productions and the sets of Robert Edmond Jones were only now getting under way.

4. New York (1917–1919)

1. "The Coming of Copeau," *New York Times*, May 20, 1917, section 3, 6:1.

2. Ibid.

3. See Robert A. M. Stern, *New York 1930* (New York: Rizzoli, 1987), 231–34.

4. Copeau, "Mlle Van Doren," *Le Théâtre*, Sept. 1911.

5. Quoted in Léon Chancerel, *Revue des jeunes*, Mar. 15, 1935, 371.

6. Louis De Foe, "French Theater Begins with Queer Ceremonies," *New York World*, Nov. 28, 1917; Arthur Hornblow, *Theater Magazine*, Jan. 1918, 21.

7. Geraldine Bonner, "M. Copeau's Players," *New York Times*, Mar. 17, 1918, section 4, 13.

8. "The Rise of the Little Theater," *American Review of Reviews*, Jan. 1918, 107.

9. Louis V. Defoe, *New York World*, Mar. 20, 1918.

10. Jules Janin, *Rachel et la Tragédie*, 1859, 511.

11. Waldo Frank, "Art of the Vieux-Colombier," 58.

12. Copeau, *Souvenirs*, 79.

5. Reaching the Parisian Heights (1919–1921)

1. Personal interview.

2. Copeau, *Critiques d'un autre temps*, 234. Copeau's ears must have been filled by the caustic comments accompanying the rise and fall of the New Theater in New York a few years before his arrival.

3. Copeau, "Les Amis du Vieux-Colombier," *Nouvelle Revue Française*, Nov. 1, 1920, 14–15.

4. Albert Feuillerat, *Revue anglo-américaine* 2 (Apr. 1925): 339.

5. André Antoine, *Semaine théâtrale*, Apr. 5, 1920.

6. "Les Théâtres," *Revue du Mois*, July 10, 1920. It may interest the reader to note that during its initial 1913–1914 season, the Vieux-Colombier put on a total of 128 Molière performances, while for a ten-year period (1890–1900) the state-supported House of Molière, the Comédie-Française, averaged 92 performances per year.

7. Romains's *L'Armée dans la ville* had been given a single matinée performance by Antoine in 1911. The Vieux-Colombier gave him his first full-fledged production.

8. Fernand Vandérem, *Le Miroir des Lettres*.

9. Marc Henry, "Vieux-Colombier," *Europe nouvelle* 3 (June 6, 1920): 761.

10. Quoted in Lucien Dubech, "Une Saison au Vieux-Colombier," *Revue universelle*, Aug. 1920.

11. Copeau, "Le Théâtre," *Nouvelles littéraires*, Jan. 6, 1934.

12. Ibid.

13. Jules Romains, "Sur les conditions actuelles du théâtre," *Mercure de France*, Dec. 1, 1918.

14. Cornelia Otis Skinner attended the school at the insistence of her famous father.

15. Quoted in Copeau, *Souvenirs*, 100.

16. Copeau, "Les Amis du Vieux-Colombier," 18.

17. Pierre Scize, "Interview," *Rive Gauche*, Sept. 7, 1920.

18. André Lang, "Voyage en Zigs-Zags dans la république des lettres, Paris," *Renaissance du Livre*, 1922.

6. The Ways and Means of Copeau's Art

1. Charles Vildrac, "La Mise-en-scène au Vieux-Colombier," *Art et décoration* 44 (1923): 114.

2. Edouard Bourdet, "Playwrighting a Profession," *Theater Arts Monthly* 15 (Apr. 1931), 295.

3. Copeau, *Souvenirs*, 73.

4. Antonin Raymond, "Le Théâtre du Vieux-Colombier in New York," *American Institute of Architects Journal*, Aug. 1917.

5. For details on lighting, see Florence Gilliam, "The Vieux-Colombier," *Freeman* 8 (Oct. 10, 1923), 112.

6. Adolphe Appia, "Comment réformer notre mise-en-scène," *La Revue* 50 (1904), 349.

7. Copeau, *Oeuvres de Molière*, 2:3.

8. This is one of many points about Copeau's staging that I learned from talks with Dudley Digges (Feodor), Morris Carnovsky (Alyosha), and Alfred Lunt (Dmitri), all in the same Theater Guild production of *The Brothers Karamazov* in 1927, under Copeau's direction.

9. Quoted in P. A., "Jacques Copeau: On a Possible Renaissance in the Theater," *Christian Science Monitor*, Nov. 12, 1924.

10. Robert Edmond Jones, personal interview.

11. Xavier de Courville, *Revue Critique des idées*, May 25, 1920, 485.

12. Vildrac, "La Mise-en-scène au Vieux Colombier," 117.

13. Copeau, *Revue générale*, Apr. 15, 1926.

14. Charles Dullin, "Dialogues avec Jouvet," *Nouvelles littéraires*, July 20, 1929.

15. Jacques Rivière, *Nouvelle Revue Française*, February 1, 1924. Rivière was one of Copeau's closest friends and his successor as editor of the *N.R.F.*

7. Bitter Fruits of Fame (1921–1923)

1. André Bellessort, "Le Théâtre," *Revue de la Semaine*, Nov. 1921, 102; Xavier de Courville, "Le Vieux-Colombier," *Revue critique des idées*, Nov. 1921, 234; Pierre Guitet-Vauquelin, "Le Vieux-Colombier," *Revue de France*, Nov. 15, 1921, 442; François Mauriac, *Revue hebdomadaire*, Nov. 1921.

2. Jean Sarment, *Revue hebdomadaire*, Dec. 1922, 329.

3. Valentine Tessier, personal interview, January 1946.

4. Copeau, "Constantin Stanislavsky," *Nouvelles littéraires*, Jan. 21, 1933.

5. Ibid.

6. Louis Jouvet, "Les Problèmes du théâtre contemporain," *Revue hebdomadaire*, May 1935, 8, 26.

7. Stanislavsky, *My Life in Art*, 380.

8. Jouvet, personal interview, Dec. 1945.

9. The discussion on art and business is based on Copeau's views as expressed in "Les Amis du Vieux-Colombier."

10. Quotes from Copeau on art and business here and following are from his booklet, "Les Amis du Vieux Colombier."

11. Charles Dullin, "Dialogues avec Jouvet," *Nouvelles littéraires*, July 20, 1929.

12. Xavier de Courville, "Une Chimère: le théâtre populaire," *Revue critique des idées*, Nov. 1922, 641.

13. That is the resentful reproach thrown at an honest shoelace vendor by a crooked speculator in Jean Giraudoux's play *The Madwoman of Chaillot*.

8. The Last Season (1923–1924)

1. Lucien Dubech, "L'Oeuvre et la crise du Vieux-Colombier," *Revue hebdomadaire*, Mar. 1926, 167.

2. François Mauriac, *Revue hebdomadaire*, Nov. 1923: 244–45; "Revue de la quinzaine," *Mercure de France*, Dec. 15, 1927, 712.

3. Copeau, "Marquisita," *Grande Revue*, Mar. 1, 1909, 173.

4. Staged off-Broadway in 1927 by Lee Strasberg.

5. Copeau, "Le Théâtre," *Nouvelles littéraires*, Jan. 27, 1934; May 12, 1934.

6. Ibid.

7. Charles Dullin, "Dialogues avec Jouvet," *Nouvelles littéraires*, July 20, 1929.

8. Copeau, *Souvenirs*, 82–83.

9. In Jouvet's program for Gogol's *Le Revisor* (The Inspector) at Comédie des Champs-Elysées, 1927.

10. Quoted in Léon Chancerel, *Revue des jeunes*, Apr. 15, 1935.

11. Copeau, *Souvenirs*, 104.

12. Quoted in R. M. du Gard, *Nouvelle Revue Française*, Dec. 1, 1919.

13. Ibid.

14. Quoted in Georges Chaperot, "Copeau à Paris," *Candide*, Oct. 21, 1926.

15. Quoted in Chancerel, *Revue des jeunes*, Apr. 15, 1935.

9. Ideals Multiplied (1924–1949)

1. Michel Saint-Denis, "La Compagnie des Quinze," *Revue française*, Mar. 22, 1951, 269.

2. Copeau, *Souvenirs*, 117.

3. Jean Mercier, "Adolphe Appia," *Theater Arts Monthly*, Aug. 1923.

4. Personal interview, Oct. 30, 1940.

5. Saint-Denis, "La Compagnie des Quinze."

6. Ibid.

7. Ibid.

8. Quoted in Andre Bellessort, *Journal des Débats*, July 1, 1935.

9. Phyllis Aykroyd, *The Dramatic Art of La Compagnie des Quinze*, 24.

10. Copeau, "Souvenirs," *Comœdia*, Jan. 18, 1933.

11. Jules Romains, Preface, *Souvenirs du Vieux-Colombier* by Berthold Mahn, ix.

12. Charles Dullin, "Mon premier rôle," *Le Figaro littéraire*, Apr. 27, 1946.

13. Roger Régent, "Un Entretien avec Ch. Dullin," *L'Intransigeant*, Apr. 6, 1934.

14. Charles Dullin, "Noces d'argent du Vieux-Colombier," *Ordre*, Oct. 29, 1938.

15. Charles Dullin, "Le Mouvement théâtral moderne," *Revue de l'Amérique latine* 6 (Oct. 1923): 178, 183.

16. Louis Jouvet, *La Grive*, July 1933.

17. Ibid.

18. Charles Dullin, "Dialogues avec Jouvet," *Nouvelles littéraires*, July 20, 1929.

19. Jouvet, "L'Art du comédien," *Encyclopédie Française*, 1936. By this time Jouvet was a film star and spoke out eagerly of "theater and its problems," as in the ensuing quotations.

20. Ibid.

21. Program, Théâtre du Montparnasse, 1945–46.

22. Mlle. Jamois finally produced and staged the O'Neill play herself in 1947 and acted the title role.

23. Quoted in Paul Vialar, "Un Soir à l'Atelier," *Les Annales*, Jan. 6, 1933.

24. Copeau, *Souvenirs du Vieux-Colombier*, 106.

10. Conclusions

1. Personal letter, May 1, 1942.

2. This was the case with *Le Paquebot Tenacity*, which the critics found hard to classify yet the public flocked to applaud.

3. Personal letter, May 30, 1941; personal letter, March 11, 1941.

4. Personal letter, undated.

5. William Saroyan, "The Coming Reality," *Theater Arts Monthly*, Dec. 1939.

6. Personal letter; see note 1.

7. Copeau, *Souvenirs du Vieux-Colombier*, 105.

Postscript (1949–1999)

1. J. B. Priestley, address before the inaugural congress of the International Theater Institute, Prague, 1948.

Bibliography

Correspondence of Jacques Copeau

Letters of Copeau and Paul Claudel. *Nouvelle Revue Française*, no. 6. Paris: Gallimard, 1966.

Letters of Copeau and André Gide. *Nouvelle Revue Française*, nos. 12 and 13. Paris: Gallimard, 1987.

Letters of Copeau and Louis Jouvet. 1914–1917. Jouvet Papers. Département des Arts du Spectacle, Bibliothèque Nationale de France, Paris.

Letters of Copeau and Roger Martin du Gard. 2 vols. Paris: Gallimard, 1972.

Letters of Copeau and Jules Romains. *Nouvelle Revue Française*, no. 2. Paris: Flammarion, 1978.

Letters of Copeau and Valentine Tessier. 1916–1943. Copeau Papers. Département des Arts du Spectacle, Bibliothèque Nationale de France, Paris.

Writings of Jacques Copeau

"An Address Before the Drama League of America." March 27, 1918.

"Les Amis du Vieux-Colombier." *Nouvelle Revue Française*, Nov. 1, 1920.

"André Baine." *Europe*, June 15, 1930.

Conte d'Hiver. Adaptation (with Suzanne Bing) of *The Winter's Tale* by William Shakespeare. *Nouvelle Revue Française*, 1924.

Critiques d'un autre temps. *Nouvelle Revue Française*, 1923.

"Un Essai de rénovation dramatique: Le Théâtre du Vieux-Colombier." *Nouvelle Revue Française*, Sept. 1, 1913.

Une Femme tuée par la douceur. Adaptation of *A Woman Killed with Kindness* by Thomas Heywood. *Nouvelle Revue Française*, 1924.

Les Frères Karamazov. Adaptation of *The Brothers Karamazov* by Feodor Dostoevsky. *Nouvelle Revue Française*, 1924.

Impromptu du Vieux-Colombier. *Répertoire du Vieux-Colombier*. Paris: Gallimard, 1917.

Journal (1901–1948). Edited by Claude Sicard. N.p.: Seghers, 1991.

La Maison natale (The house into which we are born). *Nouvelle Revue Française*, 1923.

Le Petit Pauvre (Francis of Assisi). *Nouvelle Revue Française*, 1946.

Preface to *Ma Vie dans l'art*, by Constantin Stanislavsky. Paris: Editions Albert, 1934.

Preface to *Oeuvres de Molière*. Paris: Cité des Livres, 1930.

Prologue improvisé. 1925. Copeau Papers. Département des Arts du Spectacle, Bibliothèque Nationale de France, Paris..

Registres. Edited by Marie-Hélène Dasté. 5 vols. Paris: Gallimard, 1974–1993. Vol. 1: *Appels* (Roll Call of People and Events), 1974. Vol. 2: *Molière*, 1976. Vol. 3: *Founding the Vieux-Colombier*, 1979. Vol. 4: *America* (1917–1919), 1984. Vol. 5: *Le Vieux-Colombier* (1919–1924), 1993.

Souvenirs du Vieux-Colombier. N.p.: Nouvelle Editions Latines, 1931.

"To the American Public: A New French Theater in America" (pamphlet). N.p.: 1917.

Le Théâtre populaire. Paris: Presses Universitaires de France, 1941.

Les Tragédies de Shakespeare. Trans. Jacques Copeau and Suzanne Bing. N.p.: Union latine d'édition, 1939, 1952.

"The Vieux-Colombier Theater." *Drama*, Feb. 1918.

Secondary Sources

Aykroyd, Phyllis. *The Dramatic Art of La Compagnie des Quinze*. London: Eric Partridge, 1935.

Blum, Léon. *Au Théâtre*. N.p.: Ollendorff, 1911.

Borgal, Clément. *Jacques Copeau*. Paris: L'Arche Editeur, n.d.

Camus, Albert. *Théâtre*. Paris: Gallimard (La Pléiade), 1962.

Cézan, Claude. *Louis Jouvet et le Théâtre d'Aujourd'hui*. Paris: Editions Emile-Paul Frères, 1938.

Christout, Marie-Françoise, Noëlle Guibert, and Danièle Pauly. *Théâtre du Vieux-Colombier*. N.p.: Editions Norma, Institut Français d'Architecture, n.d.

Claudel, Paul. "How My Plays Should Be Acted." *Theater Arts Magazine*, May 1917.

Cornell, Katharine. *I Wanted to Be an Actress*. New York: Random House, 1938.

Craig, Gordon. *On the Art of the Theatre*. London: Heinemann, 1911.
———. *The Theatre Advancing*. London: Constable, 1921.

Croce, Benedetto. "Commedia dell' Arte." *Theater Arts Monthly*, Dec. 1933.

Debussy, Claude. *A New French Theater in America*. N.p.: 1917.

Dickinson, Thomas H. *The Theater in a Changing Europe*. New York: Henry Holt, 1937.

Exhibition Catalogue on Jacques Copeau. Département des Arts du Spectacle, Bibliothèque Nationale de France, Paris, 1963.

Frank, Waldo. "The Art of the Vieux-Colombier." *Nouvelle Revue Française*, 1917; republished in *Salvos*. London: Boni & Liveright, 1924, pp. 119–167.

———. "Copeau Begins Again." *Theater Arts Monthly*, Sept. 1925.

Gide, André. *Oeuvres Complètes*. Vol. 4: Journal, 1889–1939; Journal, 1939–1949. Bibliothèque de la Pleiade. Paris: *Nouvelle Revue Française*, n.d.

Granville-Barker, Harley. *The Exemplary Theater*. Boston: Little, Brown, 1922.

Guillemot, Jules. *L'Evolution de l'idée dramatique*. Paris: Perrin, 1910.

Hamilton, Clayton. *Problems of the Playwright*. New York: Henry Holt, 1917.

———. *Studies in Stagecraft*. New York: Henry Holt, 1914.

Janin, Jules. *Rachel et La Tragédie*. Paris, 1859.

Kurtz, Maurice. *Jacques Copeau: Biographie d'un Théâtre*. Letter-Preface by Jacques Copeau. Paris: Les Editions Nagel, 1950.

Kuster-Leigh, Barbara. "Jacques Copeau's School for Actors." *Mime Journal* (Allendale, Mich.: Grand Valley State College), 1979.

Lerminier, Georges. *Jacques Copeau*. Paris: Les Presses Littéraires de France, n.d.

Macgowan, Kenneth. "The Next Theater." *Theater Arts Magazine*, Oct. 1921.

Macgowan, Kenneth, and Robert Edmond Jones. *Continental Stagecraft*. New York: Harcourt Brace, 1922.

Mason, Hamilton. *The French Theater in New York*. New York: Columbia University Press, 1940.

Mignon, Paul-Louis. *Charles Dullin*. Lyon: La Manufacture, n.d.

———. *Jacques Copeau*. Paris: Juillard, n.d..

Moses, Montrose J. "Craze for Little Theatres." *Bellman*, Mar. 17, 1917.

Nathan, George Jean. *The Popular Theatre*. New York: Alfred A. Knopf, 1918.

Obey, André. *Théâtre*. Paris: Gallimard, 1948.

Palmer, John. *The Future of the Theatre*. London: G. Bell and Sons, 1913.

Peters, Rollo. "To Jacques Copeau." *Theater Arts Magazine*, Feb. 1918.

Phelps, William Lyon. *The Twentieth Century Theater*. New York: Macmillan, 1918.

Raymond, Antonin. "Théâtre du Vieux-Colombier in New York." *American Institute of Architects Journal*, Aug. 1917.

Saint-Denis, Michel. *Training for the Theater*. New York: Theater Arts Books, n.d.

Saroyan, William. "The Coming Reality." *Theater Arts Monthly*, Dec. 1939.

Simonson, Lee. "Faith and Works." *Theater Arts Monthly*, Dec. 1939.

———. *Stage Is Set*. New York: Harcourt Brace, 1932.

Spiers, A. G. H. "The Opening of the Vieux-Colombier." *The Nation*, Dec. 6, 1917.

Stanislavsky, Constantin. *An Actor Prepares*. New York: Theater Arts, 1936.

———. "An Aesthetic of Acting." *Theater Arts Monthly*, Sept. 1931.

———. *My Life in Art*. Boston: Little, Brown, 1938.

Stern, Robert A. M. *New York 1930*. New York: Rizzoli, 1987.

Thompson, Dorothy. "The Theater." *Tomorrow*, May 1942.

Valéry, Paul. "Caractères de l'Esprit Européen." *Revue universelle*, July 15, 1924.

Waxman, Samuel. *Antoine and the Théâtre Libre*. Cambridge: Harvard University Press, 1926.

Young, Stark. "Acting." *Theater Arts Magazine*, Oct. 1922.

Index

Achard, Marcel, 64
Adler, Stella, xii, 149
Aeschylus, 72, 85, 156
Albane, Blanche (Mme. Georges Du-
     hamel), xv, 2, 11, 25, 29, 51
Albee, Edward, 158
Alessi, Nino: *Savonarola*, 132
Amis du Vieux-Colombier, Les, 64, 69,
     75, 101, 103, 106, 116–17. *See also*
     Friends of the Vieux-Colombier
Anderson, Sherwood, 62
Antoine, André, xi–xiii, 8, 11–12, 14,
     26–28, 49, 65–66, 68–69, 80, 84,
     86, 100, 108, 114, 117–19, 125,
     133, 137, 138, 141, 147–48
Appia, Adolphe, 35, 37, 42, 58, 75, 82,
     84–86, 126
Aristophanes, 53, 72
Arnoux, Alexandre, 133, 135
Atkinson, Brooks: *Broadway*, 158

Bacqué, André, 67, 72–73, 144
Baker, George Pierce, 45
Baraque de la Chimère, 99, 141
Barbieri, Gina, 11, 23, 87, 100
Barrault, Jean-Louis, xiii, 86, 137, 145,
     159
Barrymore, Ethel, 152
Barsacq, André, 129, 132
Baty, Gaston, 80, 86, 99, 113, 117,
     120, 132, 134, 141–43, 149–52
Baudelaire, 134, 141
Baxter, Richard, 160
Beaumarchais, 6, 53, 96; *Le Mariage
     de Figaro*, 60, 97

Beauvoir, Simone de, 156
Beck, Julian, 158
Becque, Henri, 24, 27, 111; *La Navette*,
     23, 54, 96
Belasco, David, xi, 59
Belmont, Mrs. August, 52
Benjamin, René, 96–97, 148; *Il faut
     que chacun soit à sa place*, 95, 113;
     La Pie borgne, 109; *Les Plaisirs du
     hasard*, 79, 96, 108
Béraud, Henri, 97, 99, 133
Bergson, Henri, 27, 45, 110
Berlioz, Hector, 147
Bernard, J. J., 111; *Martine*, 113
Bernhardt, Sarah, 11, 27, 29
Bernstein, Henry, 136; *Le Secret*, 59–60
Besnard, Albert, 6
Bidou, Henri, 75, 97–98
Bing, Suzanne, xv, 2, 12, 25, 28, 38, 51,
     53, 60, 62, 70, 72–74, 83, 97, 109,
     116, 122–23, 129
Blum, Léon, xiii, 6, 68
Bogaert, Lucienne, 52, 132, 140
Boileau, 10, 111
Boissard, Maurice, 23–24, 102
Boissy, Gabriel, 109, 132
Bonnard, 124, 151
Bordeaux, Henry, 7, 24, 29, 67–68
Bost, Pierre, 148; *L'Imbécile*, 108
Bouquet, Romain, 25, 28–29, 51–52,
     72, 140, 145
Bourdet, Edouard, 79, 132, 144, 159
Boverio, Auguste, 97, 123, 129
Brecht, Bertolt, 147, 157
Brochard, Louis, 72–73

Brook, Peter, 86, 158–59
Butler, Nicholas Murray, 50–52

Cahiers de la Quinzaine, Les, 103
Cahiers du Vieux-Colombier, Les, 64, 103
Calderon, 149; Life Is a Dream, 135
Camus, Albert, 154–157, 160; Caligula, 155
Carnovsky, Morris, xv, 127
Carr, Philip, 26
Cercle des Amis de la France, 52
Chambers, C. Haddon: Tyranny of Tears, 26
Champmeslé. See La Fontaine
Chancerel, Léon, 122
Chanel, "Coco," 137
Chekhov, 112, 149; The Three Sisters, 151
Cheney, Sheldon, 26, 45, 48
Chennevière, Georges, 67, 72–74, 116, 123
Chéreau, Patrice, 86
Christian Science Monitor, 85
Civic Repertory (New York), 151
Claudel, Paul, 25–27, 29, 51, 54, 68, 94, 111, 123, 125, 148; L'Echange, 21–23, 26, 30, 107
Clemenceau, Georges: Le Voile du bonheur, 59
Cleveland Playhouse, 70
Clurman, Harold, xv, 85, 89–90, 149, 152
Cocteau, Jean, 154, 158; Antigone, 137
Comédie des Champs-Elysées, 7, 101, 103, 119, 121, 138
Comédie-Française, xv, 7–8, 17, 25, 31, 53, 67, 75, 80, 86, 99, 128–29, 138, 140–41, 143–45, 147, 152–53, 156, 158–59
Commedia dell' arte, 39, 42, 53
Conservatory of Brussels, 132
Conservatory of Lyons, 133
Conservatory of Paris, 11, 37, 74, 135, 138, 140, 149
Copeau, Jacques: as actor, 9–10, 27, 29–30, 35, 60, 91, 94, 132; as critic, 11–12, 14, 132; as director, 3–4, 8–9,

13, 15, 21, 23, 27, 37, 54, 65–66, 93, 98–99, 126–27, 132, 151
Copeau, Marie-Hélène. See Dasté, Marie-Hélène "Maïène"
Copeau, Pascal, 53, 60, 145, 156
Copiaux, Les, 124–26, 127–28, 131
Corbin, John, 53, 55, 90
Cornell, Katharine, 130, 151
Courteline, Georges, 27, 68–69, 96, 111; La Peur des coups, 21
Craig, Edward Gordon, 14, 35–38, 40, 42, 58, 64, 82–83, 85–86, 99, 101–2, 134–35, 147
Cravath, Paul, 51
Crémieux, Benjamin, 74
Croce, Benedetto, 39
Croué, Jean, 8, 11, 99, 144
Curel, François de: La Nouvelle Idole, 56

Dalcroze, Jacques, 37–38, 42, 74
Dasté, Jean (Maïène's husband), 123–24, 129
Dasté, Marie-Hélène "Maïène" (Copeau's daughter), xv, 73, 124, 129, 136–37
Debussy, Claude, 27, 30, 45, 51, 151
Decroux, Etienne, 159
Delacre, Jules, 33, 99, 131
de Veynes, François. See Régis, Léon, and François de Veynes
Dhurtal, Henri, 52
Diaghilev, 8, 47, 158
Digges, Dudley, xv, 126–27
Dostoevsky, 74, 109, 111; Crime and Punishment, 143; The Brothers Karamazov (Les Frères Karamazov), xv, 8, 11–12, 24, 27, 56–57, 84–85, 87, 89, 92, 96, 99, 109, 126–27, 134, 138, 144, 149
Drama League of America, 58
Drinkwater, John, 25
Duchêne, Jacques. See Saint-Denis, Michel
Duhamel, Georges, xv, 3, 25, 51, 66–68, 76, 101–2, 105, 113, 145, 148, 156; Le Combat, 11; L'Oeuvre des athlètes, 67, 108
Dullin, Charles, xii, 2, 11–12, 21–24, 32, 34, 42, 51, 57–58, 62, 80, 86,

93, 98, 104, 113, 117, 119, 121, 131–41, 143, 148, 150–52, 156, 159
Dumas, Alexandre, 4, 59, 148; *La Femme de Claude*, 60
Duse, Eleanora, 16, 37, 40, 99–100

Eames, Clare, 126
Eliot, T. S., 158
Erler, 14, 86
Euripides, 72
Evreinov, 86

Fabre, Emile, 17, 152
Fallens, Louis, 148; *La Fraude*, 95, 103
Fargue, Léon-Paul, 3
Fauconnet, 65
Favre, Lucienne: *Prosper*, 142
Fehling, 86
Fernet, André: *La Maison divisée*, 112
Feuillerat, Albert, 65
Fiske, Mrs. (Minnie Maddern), 48
Flaubert, 4, 8; *Madame Bovary*, 142
Flers, Robert de, 98
Fontanne, Lynn, 126–27
Forbes-Robertson, 40
Forestier, Hélène (Mme. Roger Martin du Gard), 3, 93
Fournier, Alain, 123
Frank, Waldo, xii, 13, 63, 85
Fratellini Brothers, 72, 73
Free France, 145, 156
Fresnay, Pierre, 129
Freud, 74
Friends of Jacques Copeau, 159
Friends of the Vieux-Colombier, 60
Fuchs, 14, 86

Gallimard, Gaston, xv, 10, 31, 33, 52, 83
Garrick Theater (New York), 51, 81, 126; renamed Théâtre du Vieux-Colombier de New York, 51
Gaumont Films, 44
Gémier, Firmin, 86, 99, 125, 134, 141
Ghéon, Henri, 5–6, 8, 11, 23, 27, 63, 68, 74, 96, 107, 123, 148; *L'Eau-de-vie*, 26–27; *Le Pain*, 11, 26; *Le Pauvre sous l'escalier*, 76, 108
Gide, André, 5–8, 10, 13, 31, 33, 36,

42, 45, 74, 94, 101, 107–8, 131, 148, 152, 156; *Retour de l'enfant prodigue*, 110; *Le Roi Candaule*, 96; *Saül*, 96–97, 109
Giono, 130
Giraudoux, Jean, 69, 145; *Amphitryon 38*, 139; *The Madwoman of Chaillot*, 139–40; *Ondine*, 140; *Siegfried*, 139
Goelet, Robert, 51
Goethe, 9, 18, 34, 114
Gogol, 96, 149
Goldoni, 149; *La Locandiera*, 108
Goldoni Arena, 36
Gozzi, 149
Grande Revue, 6, 8, 59
Grant, Duncan, 28
Granval, Charles, 99, 128, 144
Granville-Barker, Harley, 14, 29, 38, 55, 75, 86
Gropius, 147
Group Theater (New York), 149, 152
Guilbert, Yvette, 52
Guitry, Lucien, 88, 96
Guitry, Sacha, 88
Guthrie, Tyrone, xiii, 86

Halévy. See Meilhac and Halévy
Hamilton, Clayton, 48, 81, 151
Hébertot, Jacques, 103, 121, 138, 141
Helburn, Theresa, xv, 126, 149
Hervieu, Paul, 5, 59
Hervieu Prize, 136
Heywood, Thomas, 2–3, 22, 27, 30; *A Woman Killed with Kindness*, 1, 19, 81, 109, 134
Hilar, 99
His Majesty's Theatre (London), 25
Honegger, Arthur, 97, 137
Hornblow, Arthur, 54–55, 60, 90
Hospice de Beaune, 145–46
Hugo, Victor, 147
Hume, Sam, 99

Ibsen, 4, 9, 47, 125; *Rosmersholm*, 60; *The Wild Duck*, 11, 110
International Theater Institute, xiii, 158
Irving, Sir Henry, 38, 40, 90, 158

Jacob, Max, 135
Jaloux, Edmond, 74
Jamois, Marguerite, 135, 143
Janvier, Alexandre, 122–23, 129
Jeanson, Henri, 136
Jessner, 86
Jones, Robert Edmond, 90
Jordaan, Catherine, 66
Jourdain, Francis, 2, 10
Jouvet, Louis, xii, 2–3, 11, 25, 28–29, 32–34, 36, 41–44, 51–54, 62, 64, 67, 72, 80, 82–83, 86–88, 90, 99–101, 103–6, 113, 116–17, 119–22, 129, 132, 137–42, 145, 148, 150–52, 154, 156, 159
"Jouvets" (lighting), 83
Juilliard School, 155
Julien, A. M. *See* Maistre, Aman
Jusserand, Jules, 51

Kahn, Otto H., 47–49, 51, 56, 59
Karl, Roger, 2, 11, 87

La Fontaine, 10, 133; *La Coupe enchantée* (adapt. by Champmeslé) 60, 68
Lascaris, Théodore, 29, 65, 145
Le Gallienne, Eva, 151
Legoff, Jean, 66, 74, 144–45
Le Limon, 8, 13, 26, 33, 59
Lemaître, Frédérick, 4
Lensvelt, Fritz, 99
L'Ermitage, 6, 110
Lessing Theater (Berlin), 24
Lewis, David, 25
Little Everyman's Theatre (London), 99
Little Theater, 26, 46
Littman, 14
Living Theater, 158
Lory, Jane, 11, 25, 28, 51
Lugné-Poe, 4, 9, 11, 17, 23–25, 47, 96, 113, 148
Lunt, Alfred, xv, 126–27
Lydig, Mrs. Philip, 52, 70

Macgowan, Kenneth, 78, 81, 90, 151
Mackaye, Percy: *Washington*, 59

Maeterlinck, Maurice, xiii; *Pelléas et Mélisande*, 60
Maistre, Aman (A. M. Julien), 129, 157
Maistre, Suzanne, 72, 124, 129
Mallarmé, 2, 4, 21
Malraux, André, 155, 157
Marceau, Marcel, 159
Marcel, Gabriel, 112
Marivaux, 36
Marque, Albert, 53, 72–73
Martin du Gard, Roger, 3, 25, 27, 41, 43, 92, 96–97, 110, 148, 156; *Le Testament du Père Leleu*, 23–24, 91, 94, 96, 108–9
Matisse, 47
Mauriac, François, 76, 108–9
Mazaud, Emile, 76, 102, 148; *Dardamelle ou le Cocu*, 108; *La Folle Journée*, 68, 107, 109
Meilhac and Halévy: *La Petite Marquise*, 57
Mercure de France, 23, 48, 97, 102
Mérimée, 68, 102, 148; *Le Carrosse du Saint-Sacrement*, 54–55, 65, 67, 79, 88, 91–92, 94, 108, 129; *L'Occasion*, 135
Meyerhold, 14, 86
Milhaud, Darius, xii, 132
Miller, Arthur, 158
Mirbeau, Octave: *Les Affaires sont les affaires*, 57; *Les Mauvais Bergers*, 57
Mnouchkine, Ariane, 159
Molière, xi, 1–3, 9, 12, 17, 27, 39, 41, 43, 52–56, 67–69, 79, 82–83, 92, 111, 123, 125–27, 130, 138, 139–40, 144, 151; *L'Amour médecin*, 39, *L'Avare*, 21, 57–58, 96, 134; *L'Ecole des femmes*, 113, 140; *L'Ecole des maris*, 113, 126–27; *Les Fourberies de Scapin*, 53, 56, 67, 84, 99; *La Jalousie du barbouillé*, 25, 54; *Le Malade imaginaire*, 142; *Le Médecin malgré lui*, 60, 126–27, 142; *Le Misanthrope*, 60, 96, 120, 144
Monteux, Pierre, 52
Morand, Paul, 69
Moscow Art Theater, 12, 16, 39, 100, 114

Musset, Alfred de, 27, 68, 132, 137; *Barberine*, 20–22, 25, 30, 54–56, 94; *Les Caprices de Marianne*, 142

Nat, Lucien, 143
Nathan, George Jean, 27
Naumburg, Margaret, 70
New School for Social Research, xii, 149
Nijinsky, 47, 158
Nouvelle Revue Française (N.R.F.), 8, 10–11, 13, 31, 52, 69, 80, 105, 108–10, 112
Nouvelles Littéraires, 22, 128, 131, 144

Obey, André, xv, 113, 135; *La Bataille de la Marne*, 130; *Don Juan*, 132; *Loire*, 130; *Maria*, 130; *Noé*, 128–30; *La Souriante Madame Beudet*, 113; *Le Viol de Lucrèce*, 130
Occupied France, 145, 156
Oettly, Paul, 24, 29, 42
Olivier, Laurence, 145
O'Neill, Eugene: *Mourning Becomes Electra*, 143

Péguy, Charles, 10, 63, 103, 123
Peking Opera Company, 158
Pernand-Vergelesses, 122, 125, 128–29, 131, 145–46
Peters, Rollo, 56, 59
Picasso, 137
Piccolo Teatro (Milan), 158, 160
Pirandello, 113, 135, 137, 149; *Chacun sa vérité*, 136; *Comme tu me veux (As You Desire Me)*, 142
Pirchau, Emile, 99
Piscator, Erwin, xii, xiii, 86, 147, 149
Pitoëff, Georges, 86, 103, 113, 117, 119, 150–52
Porché, François, 148; *La Dauphine*, 76
Portmanteau Theater, 45
Porto-Riche, Georges de, 6
Priestley, J. B., xiii, 160
Proust, Marcel, 69, 74
Provincetown Playhouse, 45

Quinze, Les (La Compagnie des Quinze), 128–31, 145

Racine, 9–10, 76, 133, 142
Rau, Valentine, 2
Raymond, Antonin, 51
Raynal, Paul: *Napoléon unique*, 132
Régis, Léon, and François de Veynes: *Bastos le hardi*, 98, 108–9, 148
Reinhardt, Max, 14, 37, 48, 86, 91, 147, 149, 152, 158
Renard, Jules, 27, 67, 69, 111; *Le Pain de ménage*, 21, 25
Renaud, Madeleine, 99, 144
Renoir, Pierre, 140
Revue blanche, 7, 9
Rimbaud, 4
Rivière, Jacques, 5, 45, 74, 111, 123
Robinson, Edward G., 127
Rodin, 27, 45, 90, 151
Rojas: *La Celestina (L'Illusion)*, 125–26, 128
Rolland, Romain, xii, 7
Romains, Jules, xiii, xv, 68, 72, 74, 76, 93, 101–2, 105–7, 109, 111, 113, 116, 133, 148, 151–52, 156; *Cromedeyre-le-Vieil*, 67, 71, 77, 96, 108; *Dr. Knock*, 109, 119, 139; *M. Le Trouhadec saisi par la débauche*, 96, 103, 108
Rondel, Auguste, 69, 98
Roosevelt, Theodore, Jr., 51
Rostand, Edmond, 11, 59
Rouché, Jacques, 6–9, 11, 24, 26, 35, 134, 138, 143
Rubinstein, Ida: *Perséphone*, 131–32

Saint-Denis, Michel, xv, 69, 95, 116, 122–24, 129–30, 145, 155–56
Salacrou, Armand, 130
Sanborn, Pitts, 50
Sarcey, Francisque, 4
Sardou, Victorien: *La Patrie*, 21
Sarment, Jean, 51, 60, 96, 111; *Pêcheur d'ombres*, 113
Saroyan, William, 152
Sartre, Jean-Paul, 156–57; *Huis-clos (No Exit)*, 158

Savoir, Alfred, 65, 88–89

Schisgall, Murray, 158

Schlumberger, Jean, xv, 5–6, 8, 10, 22, 24, 27, 96, 107, 148, 156; *Les Fils Louverné*, 20; *La Mort de Sparte*, 76, 108

Scribe, Eugène, 147

Shakespeare, xi, 3, 9, 25, 29–30, 41–42, 53, 55, 58, 65, 68, 82, 87, 90, 123, 128, 130, 137, 147; *As You Like It*, 33, 131; *Julius Caesar*, 133; *Macbeth*, 33, 42, 132; *Richard III*, 136; *The Tempest*, 125; *Twelfth Night (La Nuit des rois)*, 28, 31–33, 43, 47, 54–57, 62, 64, 76, 79, 81, 87, 90, 94, 96, 108, 145, 148, 151; *The Winter's Tale*, 33, 42, 63–64, 83, 90, 94, 109

Shaw, G. B., 149

Sheridan: *School for Scandal*, 26

Simon, Michel, 140

Simonson, Lee, xv, 80, 86

Sophocles, 72

Souday, Paul, 8, 67

Spiers, A. G. H., 54

Stanislavsky, Constantin, xi, xviii, 9, 12, 14, 16, 37, 39, 58, 79, 84–86, 100–101, 134–35, 147, 151–52, 158

Stendhal, 12

Stravinsky, Igor, 51, 158

Strehler, Giorgio, 160

Suarès, André, 3, 10, 65

Tairoff, 86

Tarbell, Ida, 52

Terry, Ellen, 35, 38, 85

Tessier, Valentine, xii, xv, 22, 25, 33, 42, 51, 87–88, 100, 109, 124, 127, 140, 145

Theater Arts Magazine (Theater Arts Monthly), 45, 50, 54–56, 60, 78, 80–81, 85, 90

Theater Guild (New York), xv, 99, 126–27, 146, 149

Theater of Nations, 157

Théâtre Antoine, 4

Théâtre des Arts, 8, 11, 25–26, 35, 134, 138, 143

Théâtre de l'Atelier, 119, 131, 133, 135–37, 139

Théâtre de l'Athénée St.-Germain, 1, 10, 51, 80

Théâtre de la Chimère, 120

Théâtre Français des Etats-Unis, 51

Théâtre du Globe, 147

Théâtre Libre, xi, xiii, 9, 11, 14, 17, 20, 69, 86, 141, 148

Théâtre du Marais (Brussels), 99

Théâtre du Montparnasse, 141

Théâtre de l'Odéon, 7, 9, 11, 24, 27–28, 68, 99, 125, 133

Théâtre de l'Oeuvre, 4, 9, 24

Théâtre Réjane, 7

Théâtre Sarah Bernhardt, 135

Théâtre du Soleil, 159

Théâtre du Vieux-Colombier: administration, 12–16, 31, 34; audience, 15, 20–21, 23, 75, 77, 97, 151; costumes, 12, 28, 54, 92–94; improvisation, 39–40, 84, 87, 93; lighting, 33, 92–93, 139, 149; mise-en-scène, 14, 57, 79–94; of New York, 51; organization, 69, 84, 104; players, 11–13, 28, 35, 35, 38; playhouse, 1–2, 15, 69, 81; press reviews, 19, 24–27, 29, 31, 54, 66, 68–69, 93, 98, 105, 112, 114; stage, 20–21, 29, 44, 65, 81–85, 91–92, 98, 149; tours, 24, 31, 44, 126, 128, 131; in the U.S., 50–61. *See also* Vieux-Colombier Theater School

Thibaud, Jacques, 52

Thompson, Dorothy, 15

Thomsen, Agnes (Mme. Copeau), 5

Travers, Henry, 127

Tree, Sir Herbert Beerbohm, 25

UNESCO, xiii, 158

Valéry, Paul, 46, 69, 74, 80, 145

Vanderbilt, Cornelius, 51

Van Rysselberghe, Théodore, 82

Verhaeren, Emile, 27, 51, 112

Verlaine, 4, 21, 133

Viélé-Griffin: *Phocas le jardinier*, 68

Vieux-Colombier Theater. *See* Théâtre
  du Vieux-Colombier
Vieux-Colombier Theater School, 34,
  37–39, 41–42, 46, 63, 70–76, 87,
  114, 116, 124, 129
Vilar, Jean, 86
Vildrac, Charles, 52, 65–68, 77, 79, 92,
  102, 114, 149; *La Brouille*, 129;
  Michel Auclair, 98, 100, 106–7; *Le
  Paquebot Tenacity*, 65–67, 76, 79,
  95, 97–99, 107, 111, 145
Villeroy: *La Traverse*, 57
Vitray, 66, 72–73, 84, 143
Voltaire, 17

Walker, Stuart, 45
Washington Square Players, 45
Waxman, Samuel, xiii, 86
Weber, Lucien, 3, 29, 57
Welles, Orson: *Julius Caesar*, 151
Wertheim, Maurice, xv, 126
Wilder, Thornton, 151, 158; *Our Town*,
  151; *The Rape of Lucretia (Le Viol
  de Lucrèce)*, 130; *The Skin of Our
  Teeth*, 151
Williams, Tennessee, xii, 158
Woollcott, Alexander, 47–48, 69

MAURICE KURTZ holds graduate degrees from the Sorbonne and from Columbia University. He studied at the Dramatic Workshop in the New School for Social Research and became Erwin Piscator's assistant and dramaturge in his off-Broadway Studio Theater. He proposed and helped to launch the theater program at UNESCO and served as the secretary-general of the International Theater Institute. His plays and adaptations have been produced in the United States and Europe, and his play *Jeanette* was selected as the best new work at the Dublin Theater Festival. His theater articles have been featured in the *New York Times*, the *New Statesman*, *Le Monde*, and *Figaro*, and he was formerly on the staff of *Arts*, a Paris weekly.